Managing Chronicity in Unequal States

EMBODYING INEQUALITIES: PERSPECTIVES FROM MEDICAL
ANTHROPOLOGY

Series Editors
Sahra Gibbon, UCL Anthropology
Jennie Gamlin, UCL Institute for Global Health

This series charts diverse anthropological engagements with the changing dynamics of health and wellbeing in local and global contexts. It includes ethnographic and theoretical works that explore the different ways in which inequalities pervade our bodies. The series offers novel contributions often neglected by classical and contemporary publications that draw on public, applied, activist, cross-disciplinary and engaged anthropological methods, as well as in-depth writings from the field. It specifically seeks to showcase new and emerging health issues that are the products of unequal global development.

Managing Chronicity in Unequal States

Ethnographic perspectives on caring

Edited by
Laura Montesi and Melania Calestani

First published in 2021 by
UCL Press
University College London
Gower Street
London WC1E 6BT
Available to download free: www.uclpress.co.uk

Montesi, L. and Calestani, M. (eds). 2021. *Managing Chronicity in Unequal States: Ethnographic perspectives on caring*. London: UCL Press. https://doi.org/10.14324/111.9781800080287

ISBN: 978-1-80008-030-0 (Hbk.)
ISBN: 978-1-80008-029-4 (Pbk.)
ISBN: 978-1-80008-028-7 (PDF)
ISBN: 978-1-80008-031-7 (epub)
ISBN: 978-1-80008-032-4 (mobi)
DOI: https://doi.org/10.14324/111.9781800080287

Contents

List of contributors

Editors

Laura Montesi is a CONACyT (National Council of Science and Technology) researcher and lecturer at the Centre for Research and Advanced Studies in Social Anthropology (CIESAS) in the city of Oaxaca, Mexico. Her work focuses on the lived experiences and social representations of diabetes and other chronic conditions in Mexico. She has carried out field research in rural Indigenous Mexico and, more recently, in urban health centres with mutual-aid groups for chronic patients. She combines experience-near accounts of what it means to live with chronic conditions with larger, political economy analysis; she has explored the intersections of diabetes and gendered violence, syndemics of alcohol abuse and diabetes, and diabetes and healthy eating. She is involved in civil society organisations working on gender equality, environmental sustainability, and food and energy sovereignty.

Melania Calestani is a senior lecturer at Kingston University and St George's, University of London, UK. She has mainly carried out field-work in Andean Bolivia and in the UK. In Bolivia, she focused on individual and collective definitions of 'the good life', exploring religious and medical pluralism among Aymara people. In the UK, she carried out research on processes of decision making and patient-centred care in the NHS, from the perspectives of both patients and health-care professionals. Most recently, she has conducted critical ethnographic research in hospitals, examining how practices of prayer can be transgressive, affecting power relations and experiences of inclusion/exclusion. Her research interests also include critical understandings of race and ethnicity, health inequalities and perspectives from critical medical anthropology.

Contributors

César Abadía-Barrero, DMD, DMSc, associate professor of anthropology and human rights at the University of Connecticut, USA, is a medical anthropologist whose research has demonstrated how for-profit interests transform access, continuity and quality of health care. He has conducted action-oriented ethnographic and mixed-method research on health-care policies and programmes, human rights judicialisation and advocacy, and social movements in health in Brazil and Colombia. Currently, Dr Abadía-Barrero is examining the environmental, cultural, economic and political aspects of an intercultural proposal to replace environmental degradation with 'buen vivir' (good living) in post-peace accord Colombia. In another project in the US, he is studying the role of capitalism in dysregulating children's bodies and harming their health and development. He is the author of *I Have AIDS but I am Happy: Children's subjectivities, AIDS, and social responses in Brazil* (2011) and *Health in Ruins: The capitalist destruction of medical care* (forthcoming).

Nelson Arruda completed his master's degree in anthropology at the Université de Montréal, Canada. His research interests are situated at the intersections of addictions, cultures of drug use, opioid crises, care practices, biomedical interventions, public health polices and structural inequalities. He has extensive ethnographic fieldwork experience with persons who use drugs in Downtown Montreal. He has also been working in multidisciplinary research teams constituted of physicians, epidemiologists, health providers and stakeholders, in academic and governmental institutions. Currently, Nelson Arruda is a research agent at the Public Health Department of Montreal (CIUSSS du Centre-Sud-de-l'Île-de-Montréal – Direction régionale de santé publique), where his overall role is to bring a critical perspective in the analysis of practices of drug use among persons who live in vulnerable conditions, as well as in the development of harm reduction policies.

Lisa Ballesteros studied modern languages as an undergraduate, after which she spent eight years travelling the world. She returned to the UK and completed a master's degree in the anthropology of development before conducting anthropological fieldwork with migrants in London for her doctorate in social anthropology. Her research interests include the third sector, care, wellbeing, austerity, post-colonialism and migration. She is based in the UK.

Chiara Bresciani is external lecturer in global studies and a PhD candidate in anthropology at the University of Aarhus, Denmark. Since 2010, she has conducted research in the Huave (Ikojts) region of the Isthmus of Tehuantepec, Oaxaca, Mexico, where she studied the patterns and cultural determinants of alcohol consumption, and the strategies in place to recover from alcohol abuse, particularly religious conversions. Her current research explores the role of conflict, heritage, moral economies and temporalities in the study of social change. Working on different layers of time and competing historical narratives, she tries to bridge classic ethnography and the challenges posed to Ikojts by their unequal inclusion in the globalised world. She has also published on the politics of envy, and conducted ethnographic work on renewable energy projects.

Giorgio Brocco completed his doctoral research at the Free University of Berlin Institute of Social and Cultural Anthropology, Germany. His doctoral research examined the life situations, everyday experiences and subjectivities of people with albinism in Tanzania. Giorgio Brocco has taken part in international conferences and workshops, and has published peer-reviewed articles, book chapters, blog posts and magazine articles on the topic of his doctoral research.

Devin Flaherty is a medical and psychological anthropologist. She received her PhD in anthropology from the University of California, Los Angeles, USA in 2018 for her work studying ageing, care and end of life in St Croix, US Virgin Islands. Since 2019, she has been an assistant professor in the Department of Anthropology at the University of Texas at San Antonio, USA. Her current research in St Croix examines ageing and end of life in the context of long-term disaster recovery following Hurricanes Irma and Maria (2017). Her work has been published in several places, including the journals *Medical Anthropology*, *Death Studies* and *The Cambridge Journal of Anthropology*.

Marcos Freire de Andrade Neves is research associate at the Institute of Social and Cultural Anthropology, Free University of Berlin, Germany, where he is a member of the research area Medical Anthropology. His most recent research project, 'Lawful life: Itineraries of care and life in a landscape of assisted suicide', explored the mobility of people, documents and technologies in the context of transnational assisted suicide, particularly in Switzerland, Germany and the United Kingdom. He is the author of the book *Por Onde Vivem os Mortos* (*Where the Dead Live*, UFRGS

University Press, 2017), and he is a member of the Scottish Parliament Cross-Party Group on End of Life Choices.

Lilian Kennedy earned her PhD in anthropology from the University of Edinburgh, UK for her thesis '"Still There": Mediating personhood, temporality, and care in London Alzheimer's Society support groups'. She helped coordinate the Dementia Buddies project, which brought together people living with dementia, their carers and biomedical university researchers for experiential lab tours and knowledge-exchange sessions. This project was featured on BBC Scotland and published in the journal *Dementia*. She is currently a social researcher for the Scottish government and a teaching fellow in the University of Edinburgh Medical School.

Ciara Kierans is professor of social anthropology at the University of Liverpool, UK. She works at the intersections of health, environment and labour, with an interest in political economy and a commitment to transdisciplinary working. Her current research focuses on the entangled social-environmental conditions of chronic kidney disease of unknown origin in Mexico, with ethnographic focus on the Lake Chapala region, west-central Mexico. In relation to this topic, she has focused on state–market–health relations in Mexico, documenting how those suffering from kidney failure without adequate social protections navigate entwined public/private regimes of care (*Chronic Failures: Kidneys, regimes of care and the state in Mexico*, Rutgers University Press, 2019).

Sudarshan R. Kottai is assistant professor in the Department of Psychology, Christ (deemed-to-be) University, Bengaluru, India. He is a clinical psychologist by training, and his doctoral work, carried out at the Department of Liberal Arts, Indian Institute of Technology Hyderabad, revolves around everyday narratives and practices of mental health care and chronicity that are constructed by official discourses of state and biomedicine. His research has been published in peer-reviewed journals such as *Medical Anthropology: Cross-cultural studies on health and illness*, the *Indian Journal of Medical Ethics* and *Economic and Political Weekly*. Informed by the politics, history and philosophy of psy disciplines, his broad interests lie in mental health interventions with minority/ marginalised populations, mental health in the context of gender, disabilities and sexualities, and intersections in mental health, all taking an interdisciplinary perspective.

Maria D. LaRusso, EdD is an assistant professor in the Department of Human Development and Family Science at the University of Connecticut, USA. Dr LaRusso is a developmental psychologist, and former child and family therapist, who studies clinical and school-based interventions to support social and emotional development and wellbeing of children and adolescents. She earned her doctorate in human development and psychology at the Harvard Graduate School of Education, completed post-doctoral fellowships awarded by the American Psychological Association and the Institute of Education Sciences, and by the American Association of University Women, and received a Fulbright Award for research in Colombia. Her current research focuses on school and medical professional responses to increasing emotional and behavioural issues among youth, the role of childhood epidemics and environmental stressors, and how the inadequate social protections in wealthy countries such as the United States are violating children's rights to healthy development.

Rossio Motta-Ochoa completed her doctorate in cultural anthropology at the University of California, Davis, USA. Her fields of specialisation are science and technology studies, medical anthropology and anthropology of addictions. Her research focuses on how technologies are conceived and used by experts and lay people to provide care for populations defined as vulnerable in Canada and Peru. The technologies at the centre of her studies have ranged from psychiatric technologies, to assistive technologies, to artificial intelligence. Currently, Dr Motta-Ochoa is a research associate at the Biosignal Interaction and Personhood Technology Lab (BIAPT) at McGill University, Montreal, Canada. Dr Motta-Ochoa conducts ethnographic fieldwork about the impact of assistive technologies on the lives of those who can potentially benefit from them, such as individuals with dementia and their caregivers, and provides their viewpoints that inform the decisions around the design of these technologies.

Shubha Ranganathan is associate professor in the Department of Liberal Arts, Indian Institute of Technology Hyderabad. Her work is broadly located at the interface of culture, gender and psychology, particularly with reference to issues of women's health and illness. Her research is interdisciplinary, drawing on the fields of medical anthropology, gender studies and alternative paradigms within psychology, such as critical psychology. She has been engaged in explorations of local practices of healing among marginalised groups, carrying out ethnographic studies of phenomena such as spirit possession, trance and Indigenous healing. In the area of mental health and psychosocial disabilities, her research is framed by critical perspectives, and focuses on lived experiences and narratives of people presumed to be 'abnormal' or 'different'. Her work also engages with issues surrounding the politics of mental health and healing, and contemporary debates around the legitimacy and credibility of Indigenous healing practices.

Erika Takahashi is associate professor at the Graduate School of Humanities, Chiba University, Japan. She has conducted her fieldwork in the Archipelago area of Finland since 2001. She received her PhD in cultural anthropology from the University of Tokyo in 2011. Her research interests include the eldercare system, its privatisation, kin care and ageing.

Emily Yates-Doerr is associate professor of anthropology at Oregon State University, USA and the University of Amsterdam, the Netherlands. She is principal investigator on a European Research Council grant titled Global Future Health, which examines the temporalities and practices of care in maternal health projects. She is writing a book that documents the intersection of development and health in nutrition science. Her first book, *The Weight of Obesity: Hunger and global health in postwar Guatemala*, was published in 2015 by University of California Press.

Foreword

Emily Yates-Doerr

> We aim to explore how chronic conditions reorganise family as well as citizen–state relations within the arena of care, while also discussing how care can lead to, shape, alleviate or complicate chronicity. (This volume, p. 8)

Hurricane Eta has been pounding Guatemala for days, and much of the country is underwater. The news is full of nightmares, including one story of a mountain in the highlands that suddenly liquified, burying houses and the people in them 30 feet deep (Alonzo 2020; Menchu 2020). Already, 2020 has been the most active hurricane season in the Atlantic on record, with two months still to go. Five years of intense drought have added to the crisis. Crops everywhere in the country are failing – too little rain, too much rain – as people starve. 'This is a crisis on top of a crisis on top of a crisis', says the regional director of the World Food Programme when asked about the floods (Cuffe 2020).

The other news making international headlines out of Guatemala is about borders. Investigative journalist Jeff Abbott (2020) reports that the US has deported at least 1,400 unaccompanied minors to Guatemala so far in 2020 – three times more than in all of 2019. It does not seem legal, and by international laws it is not, but the Trump administration is citing the threat of coronavirus, making use of a loophole provided by an obscure 1944 public health law that grants executive power to block asylum claims and initiate deportations under conditions of communicable disease (Abbott 2020). That Trump has named COVID-19 as the reason for closing borders is obviously disingenuous, since Guatemala's first COVID cases came from US deportations (Dickerson and Semple 2020); the point was never to stop COVID, but to spread cruelty and fear.

Meanwhile, the US government has classified many of the deported children as 'unaccompanied', but people inside and outside of Guatemala do not trust this classification. Immigration and Customs Enforcement officials have violently separated thousands of children from their parents at the border in recent years. Hundreds of children have yet to be reunited with their parents; several children have died from common illnesses in detention, making reunion impossible (Yates-Doerr 2019). Everyone leaving Guatemala for the US knows the journey is dangerous, but people are running out of food, aid programmes have disappeared, Indigenous healers have been murdered, and many of the few health clinics that do exist have been overwhelmed by the intersections of infectious and metabolic disease.

This is the terrain of complex chronicity documented by *Managing Chronicity in Unequal States*, where the past and present loop together, creating sudden crises that manifest out of deep, enduring structures of violence. Whether focused on the forces of climate migration, medical diagnoses, viral plagues or the surge in long-present white supremacy, the book makes an excellent companion for thinking through conditions of 'chronic disaster' (Galvez et al. 2020; see also Moran-Thomas 2019; Manderson and Wahlberg 2020; and 'Chronic living: Quality, vitality and health in the 21st century, an international conference': https://eventsignup.ku.dk/chronic-living). It adds nuanced 'ethnographic perspectives on caring' (the book's subtitle) to conversations about the emergence of illness and the temporalities of this emergence. Its focus on the chronicity of emergency sheds light on how acute and enduring crises co-constitute risk and poor health outcomes.

A strength of the book is how it shows 'chronicity' to be an interactive, negotiated space, which enfolds within it numerous temporalities, rather than a linear movement from one point of time to another. The authors give visibility to the often slow and contested emergence of whatever becomes recognised as an emergency. For example, the death certificates of Guatemalan children who have died in detention may list the common cold as the cause of death, but the book would point us toward colonial dispossession, the legacies of genocide, and the environmental racism that makes certain kinds of lives disposable. Montesi and Calestani (this volume, p. 2) write: 'social inequalities are the greatest determinants of ill health'; not only do they become embodied, they also produce stigma that 'By strengthening racism, classism, sexism and many other "isms" ... further exacerbates the social inequalities that determined stigmatised biologies in the first place' (see also Horton and Barker 2010).

The book's ten chapters together help readers understand how health-care delivery – be it competent, compassionate, neglectful or negligent – is deeply informed by social histories, and shaped by a dynamic interaction between the state, public health systems and kin or other social networks. In this foreword, I use some of the book's core arguments to unpack analytical dilemmas I have encountered in my own fieldwork, taking up the authors' call to draw sociopolitical histories of care into the landscape of illness and how we write about it.

> The concept of care is permeated by moral and political tensions. (This volume, p. 10)

In 2009, at the conclusion of a large medical anthropology conference, I walked through downtown New York City with one of the keynote speakers, Annemarie Mol, who had recently published a slim book describing diabetes management, titled *The Logic of Care: Health and the problem of patient choice* (2008). In her lecture, she had shown the audience a photograph of a wooden gate with a soft cord that could be looped around the fence – this simplest of technologies would loosely enclose pastureland in the Dutch countryside to keep animals safe. In a capitalist landscape that pushes ever-more elaborate and expensive technologies, good care, she suggested, could be as mundane as a well-tied knot.

I had just returned from fieldwork in Guatemala, where I had followed how the diagnosis of obesity circulated between communities of scientists, nutritionists and patients as they shopped and cooked and nourished their families. 'Stop talking about our bodies' was a message I had heard frequently from people who were tired of the calorie counting, body mass indices, and neoliberal mandates from doctors to 'take care of yourself' that we also read about in Montesi and Calestani's introduction.

People spoke to me instead about how traffic in their cities kept them from returning home for mealtimes, how the pollution caused by this traffic choked their lungs, the loss of city parks which were transformed into strip malls, and frequent kidnappings and street violence related, in no small part, to how US weapons dealers pushed guns south (Yates-Doerr 2015; see also Yablon 2019). No one spoke about US drug trade and trafficking, but I suspect this was only because the topic was too dangerous to safely broach (Menchu 2019). The effect of it all was that people stayed fearfully inside far more than they wanted to. For many, the ability to safely enjoy Guatemala's verdant mountain pasturelands was entirely out of reach.

I had the three heavy deadbolt locks on the door of the home I shared with a Guatemalan family in mind when Mol showed her photograph of the knot. In this home, a rope enclosure would not be care but careless, facilitating an opening for violence. As we walked and talked about this problem of context – how technologies might travel or not, how theories might travel or not – we came to stand under a large billboard advertising Citibank. 'We CARE', it read, the bright bold printing of the advertisement transforming 'care' into the promise of capital accumulation.

'Don't become too attached to the term,' Mol cautioned me, her point clear: if one word becomes corrupted, look for another (see also Law and Mol 2020). This lesson is evident in Montesi and Calestani's text, which charts networks of care from central London (Ballesteros, Chapter 1, and Kennedy, Chapter 4), rural Mexico (Bresciani, Chapter 6) and humanitarian projects in Tanzania (Brocco, Chapter 5) to show how technologies and the conceptual vocabularies that surround them do not remain stable from place to place, or from one moment to the next. For example, in Kottai and Ranganathan's chapter on the psychiatric treatment for the unhoused community in India, 'care' is not a feel-good path toward healing, but a violent means of policing. The care work in and of the book's ethnography entails attending to how care happens, holds or falls apart. Since care is a temporary achievement, the trick of the text is to treat care as an always empirical issue.

'Understanding how chronic conditions are lived through, experienced and cared for is crucial,' Montesi and Calestani write (p. 8), pointing to how paying attention to situated configurations of care is especially vital, given how care has frequently 'given in to the lure of the market'. LaRusso and Abadía-Barrero (Chapter 9) discuss how health-care providers and patients who are invested in the care of paediatric acute-onset neuropsychiatric syndrome (PANS) negotiate diagnostic uncertainties in the context of 'market-based health-care systems' (p. 213). Brocco's chapter on albinism illustrates how the designation of a condition as chronic paves the path for intervention – yet many ongoing conditions should not be associated with disease and are not in need of treatment. Overall, rather than advance a master narrative about what care is, the chapters illustrate when, where, for whom and how care comes to matter.

> Deservingness often goes hand in hand with extraordinariness: people are increasingly compelled to demonstrate extraordinary merits or needs to be considered worthy of care. (p. 14)

Coming to matter is a central theme in the book, which develops the analytic of 'deservingness' to point out how some lives come to be afforded better care and more chronicity than others. The book situates deservingness as an outcome of pathways of inequity, which inform both official state policies and unofficial practices of care. At times in the collection, the state emerges as a shadow figure, as in the 'penumbral periphery' of the unincorporated US territory of St Croix, where people fight for citizenship (Flaherty, Chapter 2). At other times, the state is a commanding presence, as in Nordic welfare states (Takahashi, Chapter 3), or in Leeds, England (Andrade Neves, Chapter 10), where caregivers and their patients must fight bureaucracy for recognition. All chapters are connected by the authors' attention to how people must perform themselves as worthy of state-based care, whether this care takes the form of citizenship protections or municipal support.

Montesi and Calestani suggest that an implicit 'social contract' between people and the state makes the claim to deservingness a constant negotiation. Underlying the social contract is the idea that citizens will give up individual freedoms in return for state protection. A novel claim in the text is that deservingness of health care in the contemporary neoliberal era is determined by political-economic factors that give rise to capability assessments, affordability, citizenship rights and access to services. In other words, people are not treated as deserving of care by virtue of their very existence, but must uphold contractual obligations to the state to be worthy of care – even if they never signed on to this contract. Treating the value of life as negotiable allows the state to assume the position of a gatekeeper that can distribute its protections and services differently to different groups and individuals, with those people who fit the ideals of the state (white, male, able-bodied and so on) granted more protections and services than others. Montesi and Calestani (this volume, p. 13) write:

> We use the concept 'distributed intensities of worth' to address how care policies and practices can sustain or deepen inequalities and shape (un)deserving subjectivities, while simultaneously normalising this stratification. In neoliberal capitalism, these distributed intensities of worth materialise through the politics of deservingness.

The book documents the authority of the state in distributing care, but it also recognises how people at the margins of the state have created alternative assemblages of support. In Chapter 8, Motta-Ochoa and Arruda analyse the informal care networks that emerge among people who use drugs in Downtown Montreal. Participants in their research, who were struggling through city-sponsored gentrification, had to 'create their own ways to provide care for themselves', which included combining street and prescription drugs, and building an informal network for drug sharing (p. 183). In Chapter 6, Bresciani shows how Pentecostal churches in Indigenous Mexico have become a primary site for the treatment of alcoholisation, occupying the spaces where state-based medical treatment is lacking, or is racist and culturally insensitive.

A lesson of the book is that the state's absence must be understood through a broader historical context of stratified violence that benefits a select, politically powerful contingent. In Guatemala, many people have necessarily stopped waiting for the state to deem them to be deserving. Investigative journalist Sandra Cuffe (2020) writes about mutual aid networks emerging in the highland Ixil region following Hurricane Eta's heavy rains. Despite the devastation, the presidential administration sent no real emergency or protective services. Instead, families with trucks drove those without transportation to dry land, families with homes offered shelter to those who had been displaced, families with food fed those whose crops had been destroyed, and mothers, grandmothers and aunts prepared herbal teas to help Eta's victims with both obvious sickness and the trauma of the storm. As the destruction of the ever-more unpredictable climate combines with the destruction of the coronavirus pandemic across the region, neighbours are turning to each other – not to the government.

The move away from state services comes as no surprise when considering the social history of the Ixil region. This region was at the heart of Guatemala's genocide, with tens of thousands of mostly Indigenous people murdered or disappeared by military or paramilitary forces. What is often framed as state abandonment or benign neglect might be better understood as an extension of centuries of wilful violence, where the country's political elite actively sought to keep the largely Indigenous plantation class of the country sick and subservient (Olson 2018; Manz 2005). Here, 'neglect' of health and social services was a means of maintaining political power. In other words, neglect is not a shortcoming, but a strategy of the state's 'regimes of care' (Montesi and Calestani, this volume, p. 14).

> Through caregiving/receiving practices, however, individuals and group formations have carved room for resistance, deviation, co-optation or simply adjustment. (p. 15)

I phone a friend in Guatemala to check in on her and her children. She tells me that her city, for now, has been spared from the damage of the rains. The sun has come out and the streets are beginning to dry. The internet connection that facilitates our call crackles but holds. My friend speaks to me not of terror but about needing to get to the market to buy groceries later in the day, and being uncertain about what she will find. She is worried about the farmers in the countryside, and everyone's future, but even in emergencies there are mundane chores, the kind that never make the news, that require care. In fact, we end up speaking not of the storm, but of the persistent cough that her teenage daughter has developed. It's probably nothing, she says hopefully, although the spectre of COVID surrounds us all.

Managing Chronicity in Unequal States works to hold space for how quotidian practices intersect with deeply harmful structures of inequality. While the uneven struggles of the everyday are a product of state violence, these struggles can also work to remake the operations of the state. Defining politics as 'the struggle for resources and control', as the authors do (following Sampson 2014), allows politics to become the domain of the kitchen, as well as of the theatres of the state (see p. 11). Part of the call is to make the underappreciated activities of cooking, feeding and cleaning visible, so that readers can better understand the vital role that they play in health governance.

Yet the authors also do not take their eyes off the often-abusive forces of the state. It is telling that several of the cases of 'care from below' described in the book may provide crucial resources and community, but like a Band-Aid over a deep wound, do little to address the deep harm of gentrification, poverty and mental health stigma. Motta-Ochoa and Arruda, for example, show how networks of mutual support provide drug users with some comfort, but ultimately these networks are not enough. More than half of the 50 individuals they followed had died, far too young, within a few years of their research. In Bresciani's chapter, the care offered by the evangelical church to those who have been alcoholised provides individuals with support and solidarity. Yet it also leaves Indigenous families deeply enmeshed in Christian religious orders, which comes with its own costs. In highland Guatemala, the mutual aid networks that have arisen in the shadow of the state provide a vital form of care, but whether it is enough to withstand the brutality of ongoing forces of genocide that leave people sick and suffering remains to be seen.

The tension between the violence and the healing power of the state, or between health work that merely trades one form of suffering for another and health work that undertakes radical structural repair, lies at the heart of the care work encouraged by the book. The authors ask that we approach problems of health not from the outside, but through ongoing – chronic, we might say – engagement with people on the front lines of illness and its alternatives. They ask that we build this ongoing-ness into our analysis, taking stock not only of what works in a moment, but whether and how it endures or transforms over time. This temporal commitment is especially critical given the *longue durée* over which chronic illnesses take hold of people's lives. In Guatemala, so many of the nutrition technologies that claimed to make things better – the diet foods, the weight-loss pharmaceuticals, the nutrition supplements, the green-revolution agrochemicals – eventually made people sick. These treatments for obesity and malnutrition consolidated profit and exacerbated inequality, people told me, and I saw myself.

My friend is able to head to the market in Guatemala, and it is likely that today she will find food. Presumably this is the case for most of us reading this book, who are, by virtue of being in a position to read about the chronicity of unequal states, not in acute crisis ourselves. Although we may well be – whether we are aware of it or not. After all, one of the book's enduring lessons is that crisis builds up over time – the boundaries around when it begins and when it ends are loose and contingent. *Now* has histories; the future is a composite of the various chronicities of now. Vital relief may come in the passing of the rains or a negative diagnosis. But an effect of analysing care, chronicity and deservingness as 'an entangled whole' (this volume, p. 14), as Montesi and Calestani do, is that we must place this relief within a broader temporal context. A deadbolt offers little protection against an avalanche of mud, and at the time of writing, another storm is making landfall in COVID-stricken Guatemala.

References

Abbott, Jeff. 2020. 'US accused of using Covid as excuse to deny children their right to asylum', *The Guardian*, 10 November. Accessed 15 May 2021. https://www.theguardian.com/world/2020/nov/10/us-child-deportations-guatemala-pandemic.

Alonzo, Yeimi. 2020. 'Aquí nada es firme. Triste crónica de una visita a Quejá', *Plaza Publica*, 9 November. Accessed 15 May 2021. https://www.plazapublica.com.gt/content/aqui-nada-es-firme-cronica-de-una-visita-queja.

Cuffe, Sandra. 2020. '"The Ixil helping the Ixil": Indigenous people in Guatemala lead their own Hurricane Eta response', *The New Humanitarian*, 10 November. Accessed 15 May 2021. https://www.thenewhumanitarian.org/news-feature/2020/11/10/guatemala-hurricane-eta-indigenous-response.

Dickerson, Caitlin and Kirk Semple. 2020. 'US deported thousands amid Covid-19 outbreak. Some proved to be sick', *New York Times*, 18 April. Accessed 15 May 2021. https://www.nytimes.com/2020/04/18/us/deportations-coronavirus-guatemala.html.

Galvez, Alyshia, Megan Carney and Emily Yates-Doerr. 2020. 'Chronic disaster: Reimagining non-communicable disease', *American Anthropologist* 122 (3): 639–40. https://doi.org/10.1111/aman.13437.

Horton, Sarah and Judith C. Barker. 2010. 'Stigmatized biologies: Examining the cumulative effects of oral health disparities for Mexican American farmworker children', *Medical Anthropology Quarterly* 24 (2): 199–219. https://doi.org/10.1111/j.1548-1387.2010.01097.x.

Law, John and Annemarie Mol. 2020. 'Words to think with: An introduction', *The Sociological Review* 68 (2): 263–82. https://doi.org/10.1177/0038026120905452.

Manderson, Lenore and Ayo Wahlberg. 2020. 'Chronic living in a communicable world', *Medical Anthropology* 39 (5): 428–39. https://doi.org/10.1080/01459740.2020.1761352.

Manz, Beatriz. 2005. *Paradise in Ashes: A Guatemalan journey of courage, terror, and hope.* Berkeley: University of California Press.

Menchu, Sofia. 2019. 'Deep in Guatemala's jungle, drugs and murder are new neighbors to palm oil', *Thomas Reuters Foundation News*, 9 October. Accessed 15 May 2021. https://news.trust.org/item/20191009073334-ls6zj/.

Menchu, Sofia. 2020. 'Woman loses 22 relatives after landslide hits storm-hit Guatemalan village', *Reuters*, 7 November. Accessed 24 May 2021. https://www.reuters.com/article/us-storm-eta-guatemala/woman-loses-22-relatives-after-landslide-hits-storm-hit-guatemalan-village-idUSKBN27N0SO.

Mol, Annemarie. 2008. *The Logic of Care: Health and the problem of patient choice.* London: Routledge.

Moran-Thomas, Amy. 2019. *Traveling with Sugar: Chronicles of a global epidemic.* Oakland: University of California Press.

Olson, Krisjon. 2018. 'Waging peace: A new generation of Ixiles confronts the debts of war in Guatemala'. In *Guatemala, the Question of Genocide*, edited by Elizabeth Oglesby and Diane M. Nelson, 207–25. London: Routledge.

Sampson, Steven. 2014. 'Politics and Morality'. PhD course, Department of Anthropology, Stockholm University. Accessed 24 May 2021. https://www.socant.su.se/english/education/phd-studies/resa/politics-and-morality/politics-and-morality-1.202136.

Yablon, Alex. 2019. 'US gun makers send weapons south as migrants flee north', *The Trace*, 8 March. Accessed 15 May 2021. https://www.thetrace.org/2019/03/american-gun-exports-violence-latin-america-colt/.

Yates-Doerr, Emily. 2015. *The Weight of Obesity: Hunger and global health in postwar Guatemala.* Oakland: University of California Press.

Yates-Doerr, Emily. 2019. 'SICK: The deadly logic of the limited good', *Medicine Anthropology Theory* 6 (1): 132–50. https://doi.org/10.17157/mat.6.1.700.

Acknowledgements

This book is the result of a four-year conversation, which began at an interdisciplinary workshop in Mexico on critical medical anthropology organised by UCL and the Centre for Research and Advanced Studies in Social Anthropology (CIESAS). Some of the book's authors met for the first time on that occasion, and discussed the commonalities and specificities of care practices across different places and times.

The conversation continued a year later in Brazil, at the 18th IUAES World Congress, where we invited scholars to explore chronicity and care through the multiple epistemological and praxiological lenses provided by Global North and South experiences. All the participants were instrumental in helping us to deepen, expand or contrast our understandings of care practices within lives conditioned by chronic health issues.

Taking this ongoing, plural and transnational conversation to another level, we decided to turn it into a book – and found a suitable environment for this project in the recently created UCL Embodying Inequalities series, edited by Sahra Gibbon and Jennie Gamlin. We are deeply grateful to Sahra and Jennie for their constant support, insightful comments and belief in this book. We would like to thank Chris Penfold, UCL Press editor, for his professional guidance throughout the process, as well as the whole editing team. The book has also been greatly improved thanks to the anonymous reviewers' thoughtful suggestions and constructive feedback.

We would like to say thank you to Christine Streit Guerrini, our proofreader, for her attention to detail, and to Diego Martínez García, for his artistic rendering of care practices on our book cover.

We appreciate the patience and perseverance of all the book's contributors, especially during 2020 and 2021, years that have changed our lives dramatically. Some of us have been ill with COVID-19, others have had friends and family members pass away or face new or exacerbated health issues. The book has acquired even more relevance in this challenging context; we sincerely hope it will shed light on the transcendence of care for our communities and on the often undervalued work of carers, further enhancing understanding of why care should be central to politics.

The writing process was made possible by the support provided by our universities and institutions; we would like to thank the Mexican National Council of Science and Technology (CONACyT), the Centre for Research and Advanced Studies in Social Anthropology (CIESAS), and Kingston University and St George's, University of London. A heartfelt thanks to Georgina Sims (head of midwifery), Kirstie Coxon and Dimitra Nikoletou (leads of the Inclusive Health and Wellbeing Research Group) at Kingston University and St George's for research funding, which allowed Melania to attend the Conference of the Society for Medical Anthropology. This offered another important opportunity to continue our conversation in Cuba last year.

Together with the institutional support, none of this would have been possible without the love and life-sustaining, everyday care practices of our husbands, families and friends. Thank you for your interest in this project, and for supporting us throughout these years.

Introduction
Managing chronicity in unequal states: Ethnographic perspectives on caring

Laura Montesi and Melania Calestani

Living with chronic conditions requires careful, ongoing management, or what Annemarie Mol (2008) has defined as 'tinkering'. This means continually making adjustments, and not only to the fluctuating symptoms and moods, but also to the presence and action of the multiple, significant actors involved in the field of care. Anthropological research on chronicity and care has shown that 'institutional, economic and other circumstantial factors' have as profound an impact on the experiences of chronicity in highly industrialised settings as in resource-poor ones (Manderson and Warren 2016, 479). Chronic disease, as reflected by Moran-Thomas's (2019a, 8) work on diabetes in Belize, signals a 'global story', while also taking 'specific shape in each life, family, and nation'. Power differentials, which have crystallised into coloniality at a global level, have enduring effects resulting in embodied social inequalities with transgenerational potential (Kuzawa and Sweet 2009). Thus, processes of health and disease emerge as clear evidence of a society's contradictions (Berlinguer, cited in Menéndez 2015), with care practices undoubtedly being an integral part of them. Ethnography is ideally suited to addressing these contradictions, and to showing their impact on societies up- and downstream – from social and economic structures down to the most intimate relationships between individuals.

Upstream, within the global context of late capitalism, anthropologists have documented how contradictions get 'under the skin' (Leatherman and Goodman 2011) of specific classes of individuals and populations, and how some 'bodies' become more worthy of care than others. Some individuals become invisible to wider society, as in the case of the 'nobodies' (Green 2011), particularly those assumed to be 'disposable' people, such as illegal migrants. At this point, it has become largely acknowledged that social inequalities are the greatest determinants of ill health (Mackenbach 2012): socially constructed, they become embodied (Venables and Manderson 2015; Kierans 2019; Singer and Baer 1995), and often end up in 'stigmatised biologies' (Horton and Barker 2010) or despised corporalities. By strengthening racism, classism, sexism and many other 'isms', this process further exacerbates the social inequalities that determined stigmatised biologies in the first place. As Lesley Doyal (1983, 23) warned decades ago, 'the health needs of the mass of the population continue to come into frequent conflict with the requirements of continued capital accumulation. This produces contradictions which are ultimately reflected in historical changes in patterns of morbidity and mortality.'

Downstream, descriptions of 'perceptions of care', 'individual values, motives of care, gender roles, and relevant life circumstances' (Manderson and Warren 2013, 180) have provided an equally important picture of how care relationships and activities are driving forces for what, within the context of chronic conditions, people consider a 'good life' or a 'good death', themes which are resonant in Kennedy's and Andrade Neves's ethnographic contributions on dementia and tetraplegia in this volume.

Thus, engaging with up- and downstream forces simultaneously is central to this collection, showing how history and public policy influence state interventions and local (and personal) formations of care. Public and private institutions shape how care is provided, and how power relations play out in everyday practices of care (Darling 2011), leading to the formation of new and different 'assemblages' of care (Lancione 2014; Lamb 2020; Van Eeuwijk 2020). These care assemblages can strongly affect new and old forms of 'kinship' (Buch 2015), as Ballesteros's and Takahashi's chapters describe in this book.

This up- and downstream approach is of particular relevance in this historical moment, marked by the open wounds of the COVID-19 pandemic, a seismic and global crisis whose origins, meanings and consequences we are still largely unable to grasp. Yet, if epidemics can be said to have a 'merit', it is their capacity to expose the contradictions of the systems in which we live.

The SARS-CoV-2 virus, the strain that causes COVID-19, has revealed the frailty of the social contract between civil society and the state. The *Concise Oxford English Dictionary* (2001) defines 'social contract' as 'an implicit agreement among the members of a society to cooperate for mutual social benefit, for example by sacrificing some individual freedom for state protection (originally promoted by theorists such as Thomas Hobbes, John Locke, and Jean-Jacques Rousseau)'.[1] In particular, we are interested in looking at the role of the state in contributing to (in)effective health-care systems, whether they be tax-funded, social or private-insurance-funded (Saltman 2002), as well as disclosing how individuals within their networks craft their own strategies of care.

When it comes to the social contract in the time of COVID, this pandemic has unveiled decades of financial cuts to national health-care systems, and made inequalities visible both globally between countries and nationally within countries. In the latter case, lockdown measures have affected citizens differently. Some have lost their jobs, while others have been able to work from home and be less exposed to the virus.

Key or essential workers have been the most in danger of catching the virus. The mortality of health-care professionals in many countries has grown as we write. In the UK, the media have written extensively about the criticisms made by health-care professionals regarding personal protective equipment (PPE) (Stewart and Campbell 2020), as illustrated by the case of Serena, a European nurse in her forties interviewed by Melania in the middle of the first wave of the pandemic (Gamlin et al. forthcoming).

Serena had been living in the UK for more than 20 years, and she worked in an NHS hospital in London as a nurse in a high-dependency unit. She was happy in the UK, but with the COVID-19 outbreak, she started to worry about her safety: 'I didn't feel safe at work anymore because the PPE was only provided if the patient was positive. I felt exposed to the virus', she said. After a night shift, she developed symptoms similar to those from which a day-shift nurse, who had cared for the same patient as Serena, was suffering. However, neither of them was tested for COVID-19. Therefore, she decided to leave London and her job: 'I didn't feel supported by the system. It felt like a bit of a must, such high expectations on the nursing staff. Of course, health-care professionals, cleaners and everyone, it's been just literally expected that we go [to work].'

The point that Serena made during her interview is that since they were key workers, they were 'obliged' to go to work – but they did not 'deserve' to be tested or protected. These are workers we depend on daily during this pandemic and yet, because of chronic underfunding that has adversely affected national health systems in favour of the private sector (Pfeiffer and Nichter 2008), the value placed on their health and protection is limited. This requires analysis framed by critical medical anthropology theory that emphasises 'the importance of political and economic forces, including the exercise of power, in shaping health, disease, illness experience, and health care' (Singer and Baer 1995, 5).

Since the nineteenth century, the role of the modern state has been the implementation of policies to protect the body politic (Castro and Singer 2004). However, even in the case of universal health coverage, as in the UK, we have seen that neoliberal political and economic forces are fuelling postcode inequalities in access to health services (Wraight et al. 2007; Bungay 2005; Graley et al. 2011). The issue of scarce healthcare resources caused by underfunding led Serena to blame what she perceived as 'intransigence' for the difficulties that key workers faced in trying to access PPE and COVID-19 testing. These top-down decisions, often driven by a profit-making motive (Bales 2012), have dramatic consequences for front-line workers, imposing what they consider to be a form of 'structural violence' (Farmer 2004), and transforming them into 'disposable people'.

Because of COVID-19, hidden societal value systems based on 'distributed intensities of worth' have emerged, not only in regard to front-line workers, but also in regard to patients. What this highly contagious virus has revealed is the importance of 'care' as a complex human activity where moral, affective and sociopolitical forces intersect, coalesce and collide. In nursing homes and hospitals, unsettling dilemmas have surfaced about who deserves to be saved. Medical doctors have found themselves in the difficult position of first determining which patients are more likely to survive, and then allocating their limited medical resources to them.

Many national health-care systems were unprepared to deal with COVID-19, despite past and present experiences with HIV/AIDS, SARS, influenza A and MERS, as well as scientists' warnings about the high probability of infectious epidemic outbreaks brought about by rampant ecosystem disruption and globalisation. In the past few decades of neoliberalism, public health-care systems have undergone massive financial cuts, leaving the private sector with greater margins of manoeuvre (see the example of Italy, as described by Armocida et al. 2020). According to some experts, the strong presence of private health-care facilities in some countries has contributed to greater numbers of people being hospitalised and fewer receiving home treatment, which has led to a major increase in infections (Johnson 2020; Binkin et al. 2020).

Facing scarcity of medical equipment, several countries worldwide have drawn up bioethical guidelines establishing resource-assignment criteria, which, it turns out, also reveal hidden hierarchies of human worth. Human rights organisations have denounced discrimination in the US against people who are elderly, in poor health or intellectually disabled; some states have singled out certain people as less worthy of access to ventilators in the event of rationing, shifting the decision from clinical need to specific human characteristics (*The Arc* 2020). Are people with moderate or severe dementia, or intellectual disabilities, less worthy of treatment? In Mexico, a first draft of the 'Bioethical Guide for the Assignment of Resources in Critical Medicine' privileged young patients over old ones, causing widespread criticism (Elvira Vargas 2020). Specialists were forced to reformulate it, and explicitly to express that age, disability and other characteristics 'shall not be taken into consideration when assigning scarce resources of critical medicine' (Consejo de Salubridad General 2020, 5). The Bioethical Guide had initially been working under two main principles: saving as many lives as possible, and saving as many years of life as possible (Saldaña 2020). But do these bioethical guidelines end up, albeit unintentionally, discriminating against people with chronic conditions, since pre-existing comorbidities such as diabetes and hypertension seem to play a key role in COVID-19 lethality? In this respect, Saldaña (2020) points out that the people most affected by chronic diseases belong to disadvantaged sectors of society because of 'racism, poverty, and social injustice', and concludes that, even in normal times, the system in which we live makes 'some lives more possible than others'. Thus, as she contends, medicine-based bioethics is insufficient in contexts marked by profound inequalities – ultimately, 'responsibility belongs to the state'.

While it seems to be a generally acknowledged fact that people with pre-existing comorbidities are biologically vulnerable to COVID-19, much less attention is being paid to social vulnerabilities, structural violence and fragile regimes of care under strain from the pandemic. In this regard, Manderson and Wahlberg (2020, 429) call for paying 'careful attention … to the long-term effects [of the pandemic] on the lives of those living with (multiple) medical conditions as well as to the survivors of serious cases of COVID, who may have had multiple organs damaged permanently'.

The COVID-19 crisis is therefore revealing at least two things: that care is a set of activities imbued with tensions at micro and macro social levels; and that the social contract is fragile, marked by an unequal distribution of worth, which generates what we recognise as a politics of deservingness. This volume is a call to explore these dimensions together. It draws on ethnographies that analyse how care both responds to and influences current patterns of morbidity and mortality, especially chronic conditions. Based on the premise that the current political economy system has made 'chronicity' prevalent by increasing exposure to harm and, simultaneously, developing life-prolonging medical and technological interventions (Waldstein 2017, 7–8), we show how chronic conditions lead to the emergence of certain types of care, as well as how care, in turn, can shape patterns of chronicity.

In this book, we take a political economy approach (Doyal 1983) to shed light on how everyday life under late capitalism is subsumed into a stratified system where morbidity and mortality are largely socially determined (Breilh 2008). We look at people with chronic conditions in Global North and South contexts, at all rungs of the social ladder, in order to explore how state regulations and care gatekeeping shape their perceptions of good life, possibilities of choice and care strategies. We argue that the state plays a key role in how care is distributed among the population, and that the cutting back of health-care services has consolidated a logic of deservingness that assigns different 'intensities of worth' to population groups and individuals. Although we think that the operation and reach of this logic are relatively new, its origins are deeply rooted in the social history of world systems, as well as of each individual country. In fact, while late capitalism is globally dominant, national differences in philosophies regarding care, entitlements and notions of citizenship influence the formulation of each country's care system – and individuals, families and social groups find themselves having to navigate it amid unique challenges. By drawing on ethnographies from a wide range of countries and social contexts, this volume seeks to describe how deservingness and patterned forms of attention are the outcome of specific sociocultural and historical pathways currently informing policies and practices of care in relation to chronicity.

Defining and defying chronicity

Chronic diseases, mainly heart disease, stroke, cancer, chronic respiratory diseases and diabetes, account for 60 per cent of all deaths, according to the World Health Organization (WHO). In conjunction with impairments and other chronic conditions, they also account for 'a substantial portion of the global burden of disease' (WHO n.d.). Although at first sight, the definition of chronicity may appear straightforward – a long-lasting condition which cannot be cured – a closer look at the wide range of enduring distressful human experiences complicates the picture.

An explanatory model that, adopted by public health experts and decision makers, has had an extraordinary success in explaining 'chronicity' is the 'epidemiological transition', consecrated by Abdel Omran in 1971. The epidemiological transition theory posits that with modernisation and development, mortality tends to decrease, life expectancy increases, and a sustained shift from infectious to degenerative, 'manmade' diseases occurs. As a corollary of this model, all human societies are expected to undergo this process, with Western countries leading the way. Although appealing, the epidemiological transition (with its focus on behavioural patterns) is inadequate to account for inequities and the social determinants of health (Gómez-Arias 2001). In point of fact, the epidemiological transition has contributed to our vision of chronicity as an *inevitable* result of modernisation. It fosters a unilineal and evolutionary (ultimately neocolonial) vision of morbidity and mortality (Yates-Doerr 2015; Gómez-Arias 2001), while erasing the importance of social history and the role that inequalities and situated moral values play in shaping patterns of morbidity, mortality and care. Moreover, the epidemiological transition has somehow led to the linking of chronicity with non-communicability, serving as a contrast with the pair acute/infectious. Plenty of evidence, however, shows that infectious agents can lead to chronic diseases (certain types of cancer, for example), and that infectious and non-infectious diseases interact in synergy (Manderson and Smith-Morris 2010). COVID-19 has thrown into sharp relief the long-term impact that infectious diseases can have, both on an individual level, as in the cases of people permanently damaged by the infection or with 'long COVID' sequelae, and on a societal level, with their cascade effect on sociopolitical and economic systems. Additionally, the epidemiological transition approach ignores how 'care' – be it the highly technified biomedical interventions in intensive care units or the more mundane activities of dressing and feeding – marks life-course trajectories. Is it therefore even possible to understand chronicity in relation to modernity without being tempted to provide all-encompassing, homogenising grand narratives?

Jaime Breilh (2015, 98) proposes that health and disease processes be analysed through a dialectical lens that moves through different scales simultaneously: from the 'singular' dimension of the genotype and phenotype, to the 'particular' dimension of the lifestyles and ways of life of individuals and social groups respectively,[2] and finally up to the 'general' dimension of social reproduction, currently subsumed within the capitalist mode of production. However, in order to avoid an imposition of 'explanatory models from a distance' (Yates-Doerr 2020, 384), in addition to analysing global processes, we need to 'understand past histories and particularities' and pay close attention to 'context' (Vaughan 2019, 131). In a similar vein, Weaver and Mendenhall (2014, 97) underscore that:

> cultural contexts and chronicity dialectically shape one another, sometimes for the betterment of one's health, but other times for the worse. The ways in which people experience and understand chronic illness over time are a corollary of cultural context, but also have important implications for their health outcome.

Likewise, anthropologists Manderson and Smith-Morris (2010) have demonstrated that degenerative conditions and chronic diseases, far from being a natural or inevitable result of the epidemiological transition, are induced by a number of biological, social and economic forces. According to syndemic theory (Singer and Clair 2003), social phenomena such as unemployment, poverty and violence – made 'chronic' by the current political-economic system – can act as pathogenic forces that interact with and exacerbate infectious and non-infectious diseases. In this regard, understanding how chronic conditions are lived through, ignored or cared for is crucial.

Care is put together and carried out by multiple actors, whose interventions or omissions have tangible embodied effects. In examining experiences of care in a range of different cultural and social contexts, this volume seeks to establish a link between two threads of anthropological literature: one on chronicity and one on care. While care responses are described ethnographically in the former, the actual 'care' as such is often assumed or left undefined. Conversely, chronicity in the latter is often either the background for the caregiving or the reason it is sought, but the experience of chronicity itself is not elaborated upon. In this book, we aim to explore how chronic conditions reorganise family as well as citizen–state relations within the arena of care, while also discussing how care can lead to, shape, alleviate or complicate chronicity. As Manderson and Warren (2016, 479) contend, 'Chronic conditions are rarely an isolated problem for those who live with them.' Thus, offering ethnographically rich portraits of the challenges people face when living with a chronic condition – problematising the very notion of chronicity by listening to people's experiences – becomes imperative. This is particularly so in current times, when care has given in to the lure of the market, and the possibility of living a long *and* fulfilling life has been drastically reduced, transformed into a 'reward' for the few who have been deemed worthy of it.

Care and the politics of deservingness

Since ancient Roman times, care (*cura* in Latin) has been characterised by ambiguity, encompassing two conflicting meanings:

> On the one hand, it meant worries, troubles, or anxieties, as when one says that a person is 'burdened with cares'. On the other hand, care meant providing for the welfare of another; aligned with this latter meaning was the positive connotation of care as attentive conscientiousness or devotion (Burdach 1923). (Reich 1995, 319)

Since care '*includes everything that we do to maintain, continue, and repair our "world" so that we can live in it as well as possible*' (Fisher and Tronto 1990, 40; emphasis in the original) – including mundane (often under-appreciated) activities such as cooking, feeding and cleaning – it has gone largely unnoticed and untheorised, overshadowed by 'cure', which gained cultural prominence with the consolidation of biomedicine as the hegemonic model of care (Menéndez 1983). In the 1970s and 1980s, however, care did begin to surface as an interesting object of thought and contention, given the rise of chronic diseases and conditions worldwide, and thanks to the debates generated by feminist and disability-rights movements.

Struggling to make care visible, feminist theorists and activists showed that women have been historically burdened with the weight and responsibility of caregiving, all the while being ignored and undervalued. As Italian feminist Carla Lonzi (1978, 763) wrote, practices of care are 'gestures in the air, like equilibrists' gestures made of air. Upon these gestures with no final concretisation, our life is built' (our translation). The feminist visualisation of care as a historically consolidated feminine activity has also been riddled with ambiguity, as the discussions sparked by Gilligan's work *In a Different Voice* (1982) show. Here, she revendicated care as a uniquely feminine orientation marked by moral development, in contrast with the abstract notion of justice upheld by males. Thus, care was celebrated as a possible means to disrupt the patriarchal order of warfare and competition, which could be accomplished first by recognising 'the worthiness of caring' (Fisher and Tronto 1990, 36). However, as Fisher and Tronto (1990, 36) remark, 'recognition alone does not automatically improve the status of caring', and its celebration can even end up 'reinforcing the status quo of caring as women's work'. Care was seen, therefore, under a darker light, as the materialisation of gender, class and race inequalities. These discussions show that the concept of care is permeated by moral and political tensions.

Meanwhile, the rise of chronic diseases and long-term conditions (in tandem with the political positioning of disability-rights movements) aided in challenging the hegemony of cure over care, thus showing the necessity to overcome what Fuller (2017) terms 'fractured care', or the biomedical tendency to see and treat disease as distinct biological dysfunctions, a liability that hampers care provision, especially in the case of complex medical conditions such as paediatric acute-onset neuropsychiatric syndrome (PANS), described by LaRusso and Abadía-Barrero in this volume. Syndemic theory, developed by Merrill Singer in the mid-1990s, works in this direction by positing that disease is not a single biological entity (Singer and Clair 2003), but a dynamic biosocial phenomenon interacting synergistically with other disorders. As we saw above, the pathophysiology of SARS-CoV-2 undergoes changes depending on several biosocial factors, including multimorbid conditions and multipharmacological regimes (Ecks 2020).

The rising numbers of ageing people, and people with disabilities or chronic diseases, together with the multiple economic and societal changes that make caregiving more challenging, have put care under the spotlight of governments, institutions, publics and the market. Moreover, the intensification of global flows has determined a global care economy, where some underprivileged bodies become caregivers of more privileged yet fragile bodies (Ibarra 2002; Francisco-Menchavez 2018; Raghuram 2012).

Anthropological scholarship on care has flourished recently. Attention is being paid to how care is a constitutive human activity, one urgently needed at times of crisis, but permanently unfolding, as it both repairs and enables life. Life itself is premised on vulnerability (Butler 2004), or the 'common human fate of depending upon others' (Tronto 2006, 17). Similarly, Kleinman and van der Geest (2009, 161) have described caregiving as 'all the emotional and practical acts that enable life', ultimately 'an interpersonal experience'.

The attention to the interpersonal character of caregiving and care receiving has produced detailed ethnographic descriptions of how care materialises through emotional and practical acts. For example, Ahlin's work (2017) has shown how transnational families cultivate care through communication technologies; Chudakova's (2016) how elderly patients, in offering advice for self-care to their fellow sufferers, form a 'bodily collectivity' with them; and Heinemann's (2013) how patients decide to undergo organ transplants out of the desire to resume their roles as family member caregivers, showing the importance of morality and ideals of kin obligations in medical decisions.

Kin and care relationships constitute a key theme across the chapters of our volume. For decades, anthropologists have debated about 'kinlike' relationships (Stone 2002, 3) that do not correspond to biological bonds (Holy 1996; Schneider 1984). Fictive kin relationships have sometimes been referred to as 'alternative families', especially when it comes to caring for people affected by chronic afflictions (Heslin et al. 2011). Families and their struggles are described in Kennedy's, LaRusso and Abadía-Barrero's, and Ballesteros's contributions to this volume. In addition, Takahashi reflects upon the impact of 'kinlike' relationships with 'informal' carers in Finland. In this case, the state recognises their invaluable work and formalises their fictive kin role, which broadens support networks when there is a shortage of paid carers. It is therefore the political economy of a state that determines whether a care relationship is morally acceptable or not.

Morality stands out as a structuring force in care relationships. However, what is 'moral' cannot be taken as a given. According to its etymology, the word morality refers to customs that reflect what is held (im)proper and (un)valuable in a particular cultural and historical context. Thus, it is especially important to take into consideration a broader understanding of value (Graeber 2001) and to analyse how care, with the act of caregiving, may be linked to moral obligation and sacrifice (Pratt et al. 1987; Holroyd 2001; Mendez-Luck and Anthony 2016), especially towards family members.

In this sense, morality is intimately linked with care, because both depend on specific ideological regimes, and both have the power to reveal 'what is locally at stake' for people, or 'what matters most' (Kleinman 1999, 70). In addition to showing 'what' really matters, care also unveils 'how' it matters and 'who' really matters. This applies at both micro- and macro-social levels, including national health-care systems, whose organisation and structure mirror national projects that are at once political and moral: 'The struggle for resources and control, what we call "politics", is always about translating moral values into life' (Sampson 2014, n.p.).

Thus, a country's legislation serves to crystallise moral idea(l)s of life and death, sometimes in contrast with its citizens' incarnated experiences, as Andrade Neves contends in his chapter. This is why it is so important to acknowledge the social histories and moral tensions permeating both health-care systems and informal care networks.

Although most national health-care systems worldwide were consolidated during and after the Second World War, they are heirs of more profound legacies. Some authors have noticed that early organised efforts to offer health-care protection to the poor and the vulnerable were motivated by 'charity' and, in fact, religious bodies were usually the ones in charge of health care at the time (Narváez 2013). With the advent of modern times and the consolidation of 'citizenship', nation states gradually took over this role of benefactor. In the eighteenth century, states realised that population size was connected to military and political power (Hays 2009, 283), and started investing more in health care and public health actions. This trend solidified in subsequent centuries thanks to several factors, including the consolidation of biomedicine and states' surveillance capacities. Since the advent of capitalist industrialisation, modern political economy and society as a whole – but health-care systems in particular – have tended to pursue two conflicting goals: health and profit (Doyal 1983, 44). This conflict manifests itself in the way resources are allocated, for example: in terms of geographical coverage or eligibility criteria, with the poorest receiving fewer and worse medical services; in the prominence given to specialised/technified care over prevention; and in 'the continued existence of a private market in medical care' (Doyal 1983, 188). In Global South countries, this situation is direly evident.

Even though inequalities have been decreasing in many countries worldwide (Gwatkin 2017), disparity in access to health care due to social, cultural and economic barriers is still persistent, and is one of the major drivers behind poor health and shorter life expectancy. This is even more disconcerting when we know that health-care coverage and accessibility have a greater impact on people's health than higher incomes (Orach 2009, S49). In light of their fragmented, segmented and unequal health-care systems, several 'developing' countries have sought to 'reach the poor' through specific development programmes and care-packages – see Brocco's contribution in this volume – generating charity-welfare schemes with nostalgic colonial moral sentiments. Conditional cash-transfer programmes, for example, widely implemented in Latin American and Asian countries (Seki 2015; Valencia Lomelí 2008; Rossel et al. 2019), are the ultimate manifestation of assistentialism and, simultaneously, of the idea that monetary 'help' for health care, nutrition and education needs is a recompense for the 'deserving' poor, those who show responsibility by attending health talks and showing up at local clinics. Their right to monetary help is temporary and conditioned – and revocable if compliance is unsatisfactory – while the discriminatory line between the insured and the uninsured, the deserving and the undeserving, remains largely untouched. There exist, therefore, special types of 'care' for the poor, who, as the recipients of assistance programmes, are permanently kept in a position of dependence. Care for 'disenfranchised' people is premised on a 'damage-centred' approach (Tuck 2009, 420, 409), delivering 'reparations' that ignore 'complex personhood', and instead reinscribe 'a one-dimensional notion of these people as depleted, ruined, and hopeless'.

In the northern European context, with stronger welfare states, recent policy reforms regulating state benefits are redrawing the lines between the deserving and undeserving recipients of state support. Bambra and Smith (2010) illustrate that, in the UK, there has been a shift from a welfare to a 'workfare' regime, where people with disabilities and/or chronic conditions are required to demonstrate that they are actually unable to work in order to be eligible for increasingly conditional state benefits. This political shift is augmenting the general perception that living on benefits is tantamount to moral failure (Bambra and Smith 2010, 75). Overall, these kinds of reforms are restricting deservingness to more and more specific types of individuals, engendering notions of ('morally worthy') deserving and undeserving citizens (Bambra and Smith 2010, 77) – see, for example, Kottai and Ranganathan's, Bresciani's, and Motta-Ochoa and Arruda's chapters in this book.

What we have illustrated so far shows that the way societies are organised – despite claims of equity among citizens – often makes some citizens more equal than others. Analysing racism in Mexico, Mónica Moreno Figueroa (2010) argues that this form of discrimination works in everyday life through 'distributed intensities': often it goes unnoticed (having been naturalised into the social fabric), and sometimes it emerges unequivocally. Taking our cue from Moreno Figueroa (2010), we use the concept 'distributed intensities of worth' to address how care policies and practices can sustain or deepen inequalities and shape (un)deserving subjectivities, while simultaneously normalising this stratification. In neoliberal capitalism, these distributed intensities of worth materialise through the politics of deservingness.

The notion of 'deservingness' unfolds in the anthropological study of migration, which has described the discrimination that migrants suffer in host countries, particularly when they are undocumented, as well as the tortuous formal and informal steps they take to gain access to rights. Several authors have demonstrated that the health-care system can play a key role in shaping differential citizenships, often based on migrants' alleged merits or moral worthiness. Horton (2004), for example, has shown that in the US, Cuban immigrants are perceived as more deserving than Mexicans, as the former are seen as educated, responsible and outspoken, while the latter are seen as passively dependent on public assistance. Fassin (2012, 1) has highlighted how 'Moral sentiments have become an essential force in contemporary politics,' and determined that the administrative and bureaucratic management of 'illegal' migrants operates by acknowledging 'humanitarian reasons', which means, for example, that the sick body is judged more deserving of legalisation than the poor body. In this context, life trajectories are scrutinised by medical and legal experts, who 'translate' biographical events into state-recognised categories; in other words, they evaluate whether people are 'worthy of receiving legal rights' (Giordano 2014, 1). This politics of deservingness often goes hand in hand with extraordinariness: people are increasingly compelled to demonstrate extraordinary merits or needs to be considered worthy of care. Thus, refugees are more welcome than economic migrants, as they embody the image of the victim and enable the state to come across as a benefactor for granting them recognition through what could be perceived as more of an act of charity than of duty. Likewise, illegal migrants are granted 'honorary' citizenship after the performance of heroic acts, as in the case of the Malian man who scaled a building in Paris to save a boy in danger of falling (Reuters 2018). Extraordinariness allows the state to bestow rights from a position of power and moral superiority.

Yet the politics of deservingness, so tangible within the context of migration, has much wider ramifications stemming from long-established racial, gender and class hierarchies. It has achieved a strong grip on society, facilitated by the 'state of permanent crisis' (de Sousa Santos 2020, 19) caused by neoliberal capitalism, which produces resource scarcity and makes deservingness seem an inevitable criterion of distribution. The politics of deservingness expresses itself across multiple regimes, including the 'regimes of care' (Kierans 2019) through which states organise care, protection and assistance in ambivalent ways. Over the last four decades, states have played a crucial role in the biopolitical management of lives in conjunction with a larger set of social actors, especially supranational bodies (for example, the World Health Organization, the World Bank and the International Monetary Fund) and private organisations such as charities, non-governmental organisations (NGOs) and foundations, to the point that 'The institutional boundaries of what constitutes a healthcare system' have become 'up for grabs' (Beckfield et al. 2013, 128). In this volume, we seek to analyse chronicity, care and deservingness as an entangled whole, contending that there are multiple interactions between the three. The logic of deservingness has achieved a certain cultural hegemony, permeating interpersonal (even intimate) relationships. Through caregiving/receiving practices, however, individuals and group formations have carved room for resistance, deviation, co-optation or simply adjustment. Moran-Thomas's work (2019b) in Belize, where diabetes has become a leading cause of death, ethnographically traces patient-driven health-care protests and activism. It examines patients' and caregivers' struggles to access dialysis in a country where basic health-care access has not historically been framed as a natural right of citizens. It also considers the challenges posed for small countries now facing rising issues of diabetes-related injuries and chronic complications.

Through other compelling accounts of life with chronic conditions, such as AIDS in South Africa (Fassin 2007) or 'affliction' in low-income households in Delhi (Das 2015), anthropological perspectives on care and chronicity have analysed different types of networks, relations and institutions (Buch 2015). As Lameire et al. (1999, 4) write:

> Like other human service systems, healthcare services often reflect deeply rooted social and cultural expectations of the citizenry. Although these fundamental values are generated outside the formal structure of the healthcare system, they often define its overall character and capacity. Healthcare systems are therefore different all over the world and are strongly influenced by each nation's unique history, traditions and political system. This has led to different institutions and a large variation in the type of social contracts between the citizens and their respective governments.

Who deserves to be included in the body politic, and the how and why of such inclusion, are therefore important questions that need to be disentangled in contested and ambiguous carescapes, while, at the same time, issues of health inequities need to be seen as part and parcel of cultural and political economies of care – as products of a specific social history, each with its own legacy of deservingness.

Structure of the book

This volume draws together the contributions of several authors exploring how people in specific sociocultural contexts experience and make sense of chronicity. Taking an upstream and downstream approach, as outlined in the first section of this introduction, they describe the relevant politics, (post)colonial history and social formation, while also attending to the concerns, anxieties and hopes of the individuals and their families. All the authors reflect on how 'caring for and about' (Manderson and Warren 2013) comprises a complex social field giving rise to tensions, ambiguities and contradictions. In such a field, nation states work as providers, sanctioners and gatekeepers of care, while people living with chronic illnesses or conditions fashion their own (sometimes counterintuitive) ways to care for themselves and others. Within these circumstances, kinship relationships are particularly salient: care 'work' is often performed by family members. Yet the question of who counts as 'family' is not a natural fact, but one defined and framed through complex negotiations across multiple actors and regulations.

The volume has a distinctive feature when it comes to the methodological orientation adopted. All chapters are based on ethnographic research and engage with one or a handful of experience-near accounts (Wikan 1991), including autoethnography, an outcome of our focus on chronicity and care, which privileges subjective interpretations of chronic conditions and everyday struggles. Each story opens a window on a specific set of experiences marked by persistent, recurrent, periodic or degenerative affliction, broadening our understanding of what constitutes 'chronicity' and the different ways it manifests itself. Personal accounts of the lives of people with chronic conditions, and the support they receive or offer to others, shed light on worlds of affliction and suffering (Robinson 2002), as well as of hope and desire. Even though the ethnographic descriptions seem so person-centred, they are nevertheless premised on a 'relational approach' (Menéndez 2009), where subjects and structures are intertwined; the individuals or families described in these chapters are always embedded in wider and complex fields of care.

The volume opens with Lisa Ballesteros's exploration of how families with medically complex children experience chronicity and everyday life in the UK, engaging with the challenges families face when dependent on paid carers for 24/7 waking care. She initially focuses on the families' adaptation to a 'new normal' after their medically complex child is born, and how the concept of the 'good life' is reworked and inextricably linked with the lives and experiences of the carers. Initially perceived as strangers, they often become part of the family at a later stage. With paid carers being a precariously employed group in society, the author shows how carers' experiences are often shaped by political-economic fluctuations, and post-colonial and gendered fields of practice or the afterlife of colonialism (Gamlin and Osrin 2018). Finally, she addresses issues of public policy and politics of deservingness by arguing that creating a better future for medically complex children and their families means making sure that carers themselves are able to live a life where they feel valued, secure and supported. All this emphasises the relevance of providing better working and living conditions for those employed in the care sector in unequal states that often do not fairly reward their invaluable contribution.

Devin Flaherty describes the challenges of asserting the right to live well when older. Through a vivid ethnographic description of chronic living in St Croix, an island in the US Virgin Islands, Flaherty shows how older Crucian residents with severe chronic illnesses have little choice but to recur to hospice care. Patients remain entrapped in a bureaucracy where medical equipment and services are only accessible through a reimbursement scheme that, designed with the continental US in mind, becomes largely inoperable on the American periphery. Flaherty draws attention to the silent workings of deservingness, demonstrating that St Croix residents are 'not quite US citizens', and thus fall into the category of the legally deserving but de facto undeserving. In this case, their claims to deservingness are not so much denied as they are simply not taken into consideration – Crucians being residents of an unincorporated territory of the US, and therefore 'second-class citizens' experiencing disparities in access to health care and welfare assistance (see, for instance, Matos-Desa 2010; Roman-Basora and Bland 2021). The author concentrates on ideas of deservingness, showing that the type of care that Crucians receive is the outcome of the colonial history of the island in relation to the US government and its lack of concern or disregard for older adults and their chronic conditions.

Similarly, although in a different social and political context, Erika Takahashi examines elderly care in Finland. By describing the neoliberal reform of the social-democratic welfare regime, she analyses elderly institutional care and how it has been shifted towards 'informal' home care through the Relative Care Support Act, whereby the state provides a financial allowance and respite services for carers. By ensuring the rights of relative caregivers, this law regards them to some extent as formal workers with specific criteria that intersect with the politics of deservingness. Moreover, this Act broadens the definition of 'relative' to anyone – with or without consanguineal/conjugal ties – who can prove that they provide caregiving. Neighbours and friends may then become part of the care networks providing support. However, there are various conditions that affect the decision on who deserves to be a 'relative' caregiver, with certification criteria being less stringent in rural areas than in urban ones. The state, in fact, interacts differently with its citizens according to local political economies of care, becoming more demanding in areas less affected by care shortages and the lack of care workers. This state interference is not always welcome, because some carers perceive it as an intrusion into their private sphere.

In her contribution, Lilian Kennedy looks at the strategies that people with dementia and their carers implement in the UK to understand and procure state-funded support. In an effort to achieve a 'good life' within the context of living with dementia, people suffering from it and their carers face complex challenges when navigating the confusing bureaucratic and legal systems of an increasingly privatised National Health Service. Kennedy focuses on 'the hassle' of trying to 'get the power of attorney sorted' and to 'do the Carers Assessments right', procedures that require translating intimate details of the relationship between caregiver and care receiver into the language of governmental paperwork. This perceived 'intrusion' into one's privacy dramatically intersects with the temporality of waiting for governmental services, which are often perceived to be inadequate, uneven and unable to deliver personalised care. The state becomes identified as a 'bad relative', who, by neglecting its citizens' care needs, fails to meet expected moral obligations and reciprocities of care. In this carescape, trust is compromised and the social contract partially undermined.

The four chapters following Kennedy's contribution describe the key role that non-state actors play in the provision of care for so-called 'vulnerable' subjects: they either compensate for the state's negligence in providing quality care, or work as its right arm. It is here, at the margins of post-colonial societies, that care is assembled, and the state is then free to deny, impose or offer it as a biopolitical way to control deviant or undervalued bodies. In objecting to this exercise of disciplinary power, deviant bodies formulate their own ways of (self)caring. The 'margins' are, in fact, not 'inert spaces and populations', but 'bristling with life' (Das and Poole 2004, 30). The state clearly does not operate alone; it has ambivalent ties with many other actors, such as churches, NGOs and community-based organisations, driven by the commitment to 'do good' (Fisher 1997) through caregiving. These non-state actors influence notions and practices of (un)care, as well as how (and to what extent) the very experience of chronicity at the so-called margins is transformed.

By describing assemblages of care in contemporary, neoliberal Tanzania, Giorgio Brocco portrays the ideological and practical effects that the 'NGOisation' of carescapes has on people with albinism. Following the life and care trajectories of a woman and a man with albinism, the author describes how they master and resignify the notions of 'disability', 'rights', 'development' and 'empowerment' that they apprehend from humanitarian organisations, the state and the media. Although at first sight these notions might simply seem to be products of a neoliberal humanitarian ethos, the lives and (self)care practices of people with albinism show instead that they are polysemic and unstable, reflecting the specific and contingent ways in which people with albinism construct their identities and strive for acceptance in society. The care practices of people with albinism are defined by state and non-state organisations and structures, funding opportunities and networks. This chapter also illustrates how defining a way of being as a chronic condition that requires intervention paves the way for the medicalisation of albinism.

In her chapter on an Indigenous community in southern Mexico, Chiara Bresciani analyses the historical (post)colonial reasons and persistent health inequalities underlying alcohol overconsumption. Mexico, like Tanzania, has been significantly affected by structural adjustment programmes. Exploring the Mexican politics of care in rural, marginalised areas, she describes how the chronically underfunded health system fails to treat alcohol overconsumption and addiction, and how her research participants resort to alternative strategies of care and healing, such as religious conversions to evangelical churches. By demanding continuous participation in church affairs, and commitment to sanctity, these institutions offer a spiritual and material option that transfers 'chronicity' from the disease to the act of healing.

By contrast, Sudarshan Kottai and Shubha Ranganathan dissect how the care provided by mental health NGOs, working under the auspices of the Indian government, leads to chronicity and dependency. The authors show how psychiatric treatment for homeless people in India serves the purpose of controlling them. Through a complex assemblage of NGOs, mental health professionals, social workers and shopkeepers, the state is able to benefit from deviancy: 'beggars' under psychiatric treatment are entrusted to shopkeepers who become their caregivers, responsible for administering them drugs and including them in productive activities. Kottai and Ranganathan show us how the biopsychiatrisation of homelessness and the medicalisation of care can increase vulnerability, which is, in fact, functional to a post-colonial, neoliberal regime.

Based on research in Canada, Rossio Motta-Ochoa and Nelson Arruda vividly describe how drug users, often homeless or roughly housed, simultaneously manage multiple addictions skilfully as a form of self-care. Far from being indifferent, purely self-destructive individuals, as dominant narratives often portray them, addicts become 'parapharmacologists', even advising less expert users on how to manage drugs. In disrupting classic ideas of care as a life-sustaining practice, they compel us to consider its unsettling ambivalences. The authors also describe how difficult it is – despite the fact that Canada has a robust welfare system – for addicts to access support benefits and services such as housing or employment. It is actually easier for them to get pharmacological treatment for psychiatric issues and, ironically, their psychiatrisation adds to the diversity and number of drugs at their disposal.

The last two chapters of the volume show how the state, through the regulation of medical care (often in conjunction with private, market-based actors), functions as a gatekeeper, both enabling and obstructing citizens' access to medical resources and procedures. It is through bureaucracy that the state often exercises its power over people's bodies and decisions to live or die. Living with medical conditions that may be rare or complex, patients and their families are forced to deal with the complexities of bureaucratic red tape to assert their rights to access health care in order to cure, manage or end their chronic conditions.

Maria LaRusso and César Abadía-Barrero examine how the emergence of complex paediatric syndromes such as paediatric acute-onset neuropsychiatric syndrome (PANS) defies long-established medical nosologies and diagnostic practices, and how the US insurance-based medical system in turn hinders the provision of effective and humane medical attention to the children needing it. Following the care itineraries of two families, the authors show how diagnostic 'uncertainty', controversy, hope and prognosis shape medical encounters and end up making PANS chronic. They also illustrate how unequal and inadequate welfare systems, largely subsumed into market rules, transform emerging syndromes into triggers of poverty and undeservingness.

By describing the vicissitudes of Paul Lamb, a tetraplegic man from Leeds whose fight for assisted dying made newspaper headlines, Marcos Freire de Andrade Neves questions what care and health mean. Subjected to a drug-based regimen in order to manage his pain, Lamb inhabits a world that he names 'zombieland', characterised by suffering, confusion and depersonalisation. Lamb's condition is defined and controlled by the state, and decided on by his doctors. This prioritisation of physical health over emotional and cognitive wellbeing generates an irreconcilable fracture between Lamb and his caregivers. When Lamb brings his case to court in order to demand the right to die, he finds himself having to show the judges his suffering body in the hope of being granted this right. This is a powerful account that deals with the management of pain, care and chronicity as intersected by conflicting moral meanings, with medicine and law intertwined.

In sum, all the chapters, each with its own context, address how the managing of care gives rise to a vast variety of challenges, and how care relationships are built around entitlement rights that are constantly being renegotiated with state and non-state actors. This entitlement to care may be based upon difference (Brocco on albinism), loss of function (Kennedy on dementia, and Andrade Neves on tetraplegia), illness versus social disenfranchisement (Kottai and Ranganathan on homelessness, Bresciani on alcoholism, and Motta-Ochoa and Arruda on drug use) or level of care (Flaherty and Takahashi on elderly care, LaRusso and Abadía-Barrero, and Ballesteros on medically complex children). Overall, these entitlements to care are shaped by political-economic factors that powerfully intersect with capability assessments, affordability, citizenship rights and access to health-care services. The marginalisation of particular population groups and individuals from public areas – see Kottai and Ranganathan, and Motta-Ochoa and Arruda in this volume, via gentrification and 'social cleansing' policies (Lees and White 2020) – suggests that a strategy of managing care needs through concealment. These individuals and population groups could become difficult to classify and categorise, and therefore to take care of, acquiring an invisible liminal state (Little et al. 1998).

Concluding remarks

It could be argued that there is an 'aura of invisibility' that surrounds the significance of care in everyday life (Bowden 1997, 6). 'By not noticing how pervasive and central care is to human life, those who are in a position of power and privilege can continue to ignore and to degrade the activities of care and those who give care' (Tronto 1993, 111). In addition, the 'autonomy myth' (Finemann 2004) suits politicians and policy-makers seeking to promote individual rather than collective responsibility for welfare and wellbeing. When someone becomes 'dependent', they are then identified as of lesser worth (Fraser and Gordon 1994), with profound implications for the politics of deservingness. However, in the logic of care, as outlined by Mol (2008, 12), 'We do not start out as individuals, but always belong to collectives already – and not just a single one, but a lot of them.' These collectives, subject to the political economy of health and care, as shown in the ethnographies assembled in this book, need to be continuously (re)crafted and (re)negotiated.

How individuals manage their care circumstances, and how they access the informal and formal resources, as well as how they react to official diagnoses and decisions, are all important aspects that influence how people come to terms with their chronic conditions, negotiate restrictions, and deal with issues of power and (inter)dependency in relationships of inequality and proximity. In considering different care contexts, we therefore explore the interrelations between the private level of personal and family situations, the social level of informal networks, and the public (state) level of structures and resources.

The ethnographies in this book shed some light on what living with chronic conditions means today in specific social and cultural contexts, and on the importance of close relationships in managing chronicity. Cultivating relationships with others is fundamental for making something of oneself within the limits set by one's environment (Jackson 2011) and chronic condition. Undoubtedly it may often be a complex coexistence. Although taking care of oneself and others is key to belonging and wellbeing, profound and distressful tensions often arise.

Notes

1. See Lazar's (2013, 7) discussion of the social contract philosophers for more details on what the social contract implies and how it may frame the concept of 'citizenship'. She describes very clearly why this has relevance for political anthropology and the anthropology of citizenship.
2. Breilh (2015) distinguishes between 'lifestyles' and 'ways of life': the former refers to patterns of behaviour at the individual level, while the latter refers to the patterns of behaviour of collectivities (similar to the concept of culture).

References

Ahlin, Tanja. 2017. 'Only near is dear? Doing elderly care with everyday ICTs in Indian transnational families', *Medical Anthropology Quarterly* 32 (1): 85–102. https://doi.org/10.1111/maq.12404.

Armocida, Benedetta, Beatrice Formenti, Francesca Palestra, Silvia Ussai and Eduardo Missoni. 2020. 'COVID-19: Universal health coverage now more than ever', *Journal of Global Health* 10 (1): 1–4. https://doi.org/10.7189/jogh.10.010350.

Bales, Kevin. 2012. *Disposable People: New slavery in the global economy*. Berkeley: University of California Press.

Bambra, Clare and Katherine E. Smith. 2010. 'No longer deserving? Sickness benefit reform and the politics of (ill) health', *Critical Public Health* 20 (1): 71–83. https://doi.org/10.1080/09581590902763265.

Beckfield, Jason, Sigrun Olafsdottir and Benjamin Sosnaud. 2013. 'Healthcare systems in comparative perspective: Classification, convergence, institutions, inequalities, and five missed turns', *Annual Review of Sociology* 39: 127–46. https://doi.org/10.1146/annurev-soc-071312-145609.

Binkin, Nancy, Federica Michieletto, Stefania Salmaso and Francesca Russo. 2020. 'Lombardia e Veneto: Due Approcci a Confronto'. *Scienza in Rete*, 18 April. Accessed 15 May 2021. https://www.scienzainrete.it/articolo/lombardia-e-veneto-due-approcci-confronto/nancy-binkin-federica-michieletto-stefania.

Bowden, Peta. 1997. *Caring: Gender-sensitive ethics*. London: Routledge.

Breilh, Jaime. 2008. 'Latin American critical ("social") epidemiology: New settings for an old dream', *International Journal of Epidemiology* 37 (4): 745–50. https://doi.org/10.1093/ije/dyn135.

Breilh, Jaime. 2015. *Epidemiología Crítica: Ciencia Emancipadora e Interculturalidad*. Buenos Aires: Lugar Editorial.

Buch, Elana D. 2015. 'Anthropology of aging and care', *Annual Review of Anthropology* 44: 277–93. https://doi.org/10.1146/annurev-anthro-102214-014254.

Bungay, Hilary. 2005. 'Cancer and health policy: The postcode lottery of care', *Social Policy & Administration* 39 (1): 35–48. https://doi.org/10.1111/j.1467-9515.2005.00423.x.

Burdach, Konrad. 1923. 'Faust und die Sorge', *Deutsche Vierteljahrsschrift für Literaturwissenschaft und Geistesgeschichte* 1 (1): 1–60.

Butler, Judith. 2004. *Precarious Life: The powers of mourning and violence*. London: Verso.

Castro, Arachu and Merrill Singer, eds. 2004. *Unhealthy Health Policy: A critical anthropological examination*. New York: Rowman Altamira.

Chudakova, Tatiana. 2016. 'Caring for strangers: Aging, traditional medicine, and collective self-care in post-socialist Russia', *Medical Anthropology Quarterly* 31 (1): 78–96. https://doi.org/10.1111/maq.12276.

Concise Oxford English Dictionary, ed. Judy Pearsall. 2001. Oxford: Oxford University Press.

Consejo de Salubridad General. 2020. *Guía Bioética para Asignación de Recursos Limitados de Medicina Crítica en Situación de Emergencia*. Accessed 5 July 2021. http://www.csg.gob.mx/descargas/pdf/index/informacion_relevante/GuiaBioeticaTriaje_30_Abril_2020_7pm.pdf.

Darling, Jonathan. 2011. 'Giving space: Care, generosity and belonging in a UK asylum drop-in centre', *Geoforum* 42 (4): 408–17. https://doi.org/10.1016/j.geoforum.2011.02.004.

Das, Veena. 2015. *Affliction: Health, disease, poverty*. New York: Fordham University Press.

Das, Veena and Deborah Poole. 2004. *Anthropology in the Margins of the State*. Santa Fe, NM: School of American Research.

de Sousa Santos, Boaventura. 2020. *La cruel pedagogía del virus*. Buenos Aires: CLACSO.

Doyal, Lesley. 1983. *The Political Economy of Health*, with Imogen Pennell. London: Pluto Press.

Ecks, Stefan. 2020. 'We urgently need to understand the medication histories of COVID-19 victims', *Somatosphere*, 31 March. Accessed 15 May 2021. http://somatosphere.net/2020/we-urgently-need-to-understand-the-medication-histories-of-covid-19-victims.html/.

Elvira Vargas, Rosa. 2020. 'Persiste la polémica por la guía médica que discrimina enfermos', *La Jornada*, 17 April. Accessed 24 May 2021. https://www.jornada.com.mx/2020/04/17/politica/006n1pol.

Farmer, Paul. 2004. 'An anthropology of structural violence', *Current Anthropology* 45 (3): 305–25.

Fassin, Didier. 2007. *When Bodies Remember: Experiences and politics of AIDS in South Africa*. Berkeley: University of California Press.

Fassin, Didier. 2012. *Humanitarian Reason: A moral history of the present times*, translated by Rachel Gomme. Berkeley: University of California Press.

Fineman, Martha. 2004. *The Autonomy Myth: A theory of dependency*. New York: New Press.

Fisher, Berenice and Joan Tronto. 1990. 'Toward a feminist theory of caring'. In *Circles of Care: Work and identity in women's lives*, edited by Emily K. Abel and Margaret K. Nelson, 36–54. New York: SUNY Press.

Fisher, William F. 1997. 'Doing good?: The politics and antipolitics of NGO practices', *Annual Review of Anthropology* 26 (1): 439–64. https://doi.org/10.1146/annurev.anthro.26.1.439.

Francisco-Menchavez, Valerie. 2018. *The Labor of Care: Filipina migrants and transnational families in the digital age*. Urbana: University of Illinois Press.

Fraser, Nancy and Linda Gordon. 1994. 'A genealogy of dependency: Tracing a keyword of the US welfare state', *Signs: Journal of women in culture and society* 19 (2): 309–36. https://doi.org/10.1086/494886.

Fuller, Jonathan. 2017. 'The new medical model: A renewed challenge for biomedicine', *Canadian Medical Association Journal* 189 (17): E640–E641. https://doi.org/10.1503/cmaj.160627.

Gamlin, Jennie and David Osrin. 2018. 'Preventable infant deaths, lone births and lack of registration in Mexican indigenous communities: Health care services and the *afterlife of colonialism*', *Ethnicity & Health* 25 (7), 925–39. https://doi.org/10.1080/13557858.2018.1481496.

Gamlin, Jennie, Sahra Gibbon and Melania Calestani. Forthcoming. 'The biopolitics of COVID-19 in the UK: Racism, nationalism and the afterlife of colonialism'. In *Viral Loads: Anthropologies of urgency in the time of COVID-19*, edited by Lenore Manderson, Nancy J. Burke and Ayo Wahlberg. London: UCL Press.

Gilligan, Carol. 1982. *In a Different Voice: Psychological theory and women's development*. Cambridge, MA: Harvard University Press.

Giordano, Cristiana. 2014. *Migrants in Translation: Caring and the logics of difference in contemporary Italy*. Berkeley: University of California Press.

Gómez-Arias, Rubén Darío. 2001. 'La transición en epidemiología y salud pública: ¿explicación o condena?', *Revista Facultad Nacional de Salud Pública* 19 (2): 57–74. Accessed 24 May 2021. https://clasesantoniolc.files.wordpress.com/2021/03/la-nocion-de-transicion-en-epidemiologia.pdf.

Graeber, David. 2001. *Toward an Anthropological Theory of Value: The false coin of our own dreams*. Basingstoke: Palgrave Macmillan.

Graley, Clare E.M., Katherine F. May and David C. McCoy. 2011. 'Postcode lotteries in public health: The NHS Health Checks programme in North West London', *BMC Public Health* 11 (1): 738. https://doi.org/10.1186/1471-2458-11-738.

Green, Linda. 2011. 'The nobodies: Neoliberalism, violence, and migration', *Medical Anthropology: Cross-cultural studies in health and illness* 30 (4): 366–85. https://doi.org/10.1080/01459740.2011.576726.

Gwatkin, Davidson R. 2017. 'Trends in health inequalities in developing countries', *The Lancet* 5 (4): e371–e372. https://doi.org/10.1016/S2214-109X(17)30080-3.

Hays, J.N. 2009. *The Burdens of Disease: Epidemics and human response in Western history*. New Brunswick, NJ: Rutgers University Press.

Heinemann, Laura Lynn. 2013. 'For the sake of others: Reciprocal webs of obligation and the pursuit of transplantation as a caring act', *Medical Anthropology Quarterly* 28 (1): 66–84. https://doi.org/10.1111/maq.12060.

Heslin, Kevin C., Alison B. Hamilton, Trudy K. Singzon, James L. Smith and Nancy Lois Ruth Anderson. 2011. 'Alternative families in recovery: Fictive kin relationships among residents of sober living homes', *Qualitative Health Research* 21 (4): 477–88. https://doi.org/10.1177/1049732310385826.

Holroyd, Eleanor. 2001. 'Hong Kong Chinese daughters' intergenerational caregiving obligations: A cultural model approach', *Social Science & Medicine* 53 (9): 1125–34. https://doi.org/10.1016/s0277-9536(00)00406-8.

Holy, Ladislav. 1996. *Anthropological Perspectives on Kinship*. Edmonton: University of Alberta.

Horton, Sarah. 2004. 'Different subjects: The health care system's participation in the differential construction of the cultural citizenship of Cuban refugees and Mexican immigrants', *Medical Anthropology Quarterly* 18 (4): 472–89. https://doi.org/10.1525/maq.2004.18.4.472.

Horton, Sarah and Judith C. Barker. 2010. 'Stigmatized biologies: Examining the cumulative effects of oral health disparities for Mexican American farmworker children', *Medical Anthropology Quarterly* 24 (2): 199–219. https://doi.org/10.1111/j.1548-1387.2010.01097.x.

Ibarra, Maria. 2002. 'Emotional proletarians in a global economy: Mexican immigrant women and elder care work', *Urban Anthropology and Studies of Cultural Systems and World Economic Development* 31 (3/4): 317–50.

Jackson, Michael. 2011. *Life Within Limits: Well-being in a world of want*. London: Duke University Press.

Johnson, Miles. 2020. 'Fewer deaths in Veneto offer clues for fight against virus', *Financial Times*, 5 April. Accessed 24 May 2021. https://www.ft.com/content/9c75d47f-49ee-4613-add1-a692b97d95d3.

Kierans, Ciara. 2019. *Chronic Failures: Kidneys, regimes of care, and the Mexican state*. New Brunswick, NJ: Rutgers University Press.

Kleinman, Arthur. 1999. 'Moral experience and ethical reflection: Can ethnography reconcile them? A quandary for "the new bioethics"', *Daedalus* 128 (4): 69–97. http://hdl.handle.net/10822/760101.

Kleinman, Arthur and Sjaak van der Geest. 2009. '"Care" in health care: Remaking the moral world of medicine', *Medische Antropologie* 21 (1): 159–68. Accessed 24 May 2021. https://www.sjaakvandergeest.socsci.uva.nl/pdf/medical_anthropology/kleinman_vdgeest_2009.pdf.

Kuzawa, Christopher W. and Elizabeth Sweet. 2009. 'Epigenetics and the embodiment of race: Developmental origins of US racial disparities in cardiovascular health', *American Journal of Human Biology* 21 (1): 2–15. https://doi.org/10.1002/ajhb.20822.

Lamb, Sarah. 2020. 'Assemblages of care and personhood: "Successful ageing" across India and North America'. In *Caring for Old Age: Perspectives from South Asia*, edited by Christiane Brosius and Roberta Mandoki, 321–38. Heidelberg: Heidelberg University Publishing.

Lameire, Norbert, Preben Joffe and Michael Wiedemann. 1999. 'Healthcare systems – an international review: An overview', *Nephrology Dialysis Transplantation* 14 (6): 3–9. http://hdl.handle.net/1854/LU-175051.

Lancione, Michele. 2014. 'Assemblages of care and the analysis of public policies on homelessness in Turin, Italy', *City* 18 (1): 25–40. https://doi.org/10.1080/13604813.2014.868163.

Lazar, Sian. 2013. *The Anthropology of Citizenship: A reader*. London: John Wiley & Sons.

Leatherman, Tom and Alan H. Goodman. 2011. 'Critical biocultural approaches in medical anthropology'. In *A Companion to Medical Anthropology*, edited by Merrill Singer and Pamela I. Erickson, 29–47. Chichester: Wiley-Blackwell.

Lees, Loretta and Hannah White. 2020. 'The social cleansing of London council estates: Everyday experiences of "accumulative dispossession"', *Housing Studies* 35 (10): 1701–22. https://doi.org/10.1080/02673037.2019.1680814.

Little, Miles, Christopher F.C. Jordens, Kim Paul, Kathleen Montgomery and Bertil Philipson. 1998. 'Liminality: A major category of the experience of cancer illness', *Social Science & Medicine* 47 (10): 1485–94. https://doi.org/10.1016/S0277-9536(98)00248-2.

Lonzi, Carla. 1978. *Taci, anzi parla: Diario di una femminista*. Milan: Rivolta Femminile.

Mackenbach, Johan P. 2012. 'The persistence of health inequalities in modern welfare states: The explanation of a paradox', *Social Science & Medicine* 75 (4): 761–9. https://doi.org/10.1016/j.socscimed.2012.02.031.

Manderson, Lenore and Carolyn Smith-Morris. 2010. *Chronic Conditions, Fluid States: Chronicity and the anthropology of illness*. New Brunswick, NJ: Rutgers University Press.

Manderson, Lenore and Ayo Wahlberg. 2020. 'Chronic living in a communicable world', *Medical Anthropology* 39 (5): 428–39. https://doi.org/10.1080/01459740.2020.1761352.

Manderson, Lenore and Narelle Warren. 2013. '"Caring for" and "caring about": Embedded interdependence and quality of life'. In *Reframing Disability and Quality of Life: A global perspective*, edited by Narelle Warren and Lenore Manderson, 179–93. Dordrecht: Springer.

Manderson, Lenore and Narelle Warren. 2016. '"Just one thing after another": Recursive cascades and chronic conditions', *Medical Anthropology Quarterly* 30 (4): 479–97. https://doi.org/10.1111/maq.12277.

Matos-Desa, Mónica. 2010. 'Second class citizens: The case against unequal military healthcare benefits for Puerto Rican veterans', *Cardozo Journal of Law & Gender* 16 (2): 291–313. Accessed 24 May 2021. https://4048580a-6877-4460-b15c-ac5c8ebbccbb.filesusr.com/ugd/a6e465_e53bb42197844b059bf1d96f4b54e6bd.pdf.

Mendez-Luck, Carolyn A. and Katherine P. Anthony. 2016. '*Marianismo* and caregiving role beliefs among US-born and immigrant Mexican women', *Journals of Gerontology Series B: Psychological sciences and social sciences* 71 (5): 926–35. https://doi.org/10.1093/geronb/gbv083.

Menéndez, Eduardo. 1983. *Hacia una práctica médica alternativa: Hegemonía y autoatención (gestión) en salud*. Mexico: Cuadernos de la Casa Chata.

Menéndez, Eduardo. 2009. *De sujetos, saberes y estructuras: Introduccion al enfoque relacional en el estudio de la salud colectiva*. Buenos Aires: Lugar Editorial.

Menéndez, Eduardo. 2015. 'Las enfermedades ¿son solo padecimientos?: biomedicina, formas de atención "paralelas" y proyectos de poder', *Salud Colectiva* 11 (3): 301–30. Accessed 24 May 2021. https://scielosp.org/article/scol/2015.v11n3/301-330/es/.

Mol, Annemarie. 2008. *The Logic of Care: Health and the problem of patient choice*. London: Routledge.

Moran-Thomas, Amy. 2019a. *Traveling With Sugar: Chronicles of a global epidemic*. Oakland: University of California Press.

Moran-Thomas, Amy. 2019b. 'Struggles for maintenance: Patient activism and dialysis dilemmas amidst a global diabetes epidemic', *Global Public Health* 14 (6–7): 1044–57. https://doi.org/10.1080/17441692.2019.1596292.

Moreno Figueroa, Mónica. 2010. 'Distributed intensities: Whiteness, mestizaje and the logics of Mexican racism', *Ethnicities* 10 (3): 387–401. https://doi.org/10.1177/1468796810372305.

Narváez, Gregorio. 2013. *Un sistema en busca de salud: Desarrollo, declive y renovación del sistema de salud mexicano*. Mexico City: Fondo de Cultura Económica.

Omran, Abdel R. 1971. 'The epidemiologic transition: A theory of the epidemiology of population change', *Milbank Memorial Fund Quarterly* 29: 509–38. https://doi.org/10.1111/j.1468-0009.2005.00398.x.

Orach, Christopher Garimoi. 2009. 'Health equity: Challenges in low income countries', *African Health Sciences* 9 (2): S49–S51. Accessed 24 May 2021. https://www.ncbi.nlm.nih.gov/pmc/articles/PMC2877288/.

Pfeiffer, James and Mark Nichter. 2008. 'What can critical medical anthropology contribute to global health?: A health systems perspective', *Medical Anthropology Quarterly* 22 (4): 410–15. https://doi.org/10.1111/j.1548-1387.2008.00041.x.

Pratt, Clara, Vicki Schmall and Scott Wright. 1987. 'Ethical concerns of family caregivers to dementia patients', *The Gerontologist* 27 (5): 632–8. https://doi.org/10.1093/geront/27.5.632.

Raghuram, Parvati. 2012. 'Global care, local configurations: Challenges to conceptualizations of care', *Global Networks* 12 (2): 155–74. https://doi.org/10.1111/j.1471-0374.2012.00345.x.

Reich, Warren T. 1995. 'History of the notion of care'. In *Encyclopedia of Bioethics*, revised edition, edited by Warren Thomas Reich, 319–31. 5 volumes. New York: Simon & Schuster Macmillan.

Reuters. 2018. 'France offers citizenship to Malian immigrant who scaled building to save child', *Reuters World News*, 27 May. Accessed 24 May 2021. https://www.reuters.com/article/us-france-hero/france-offers-citizenship-to-malian-immigrant-who-scaled-building-to-save-child-idUSKCN1IS0UF.

Robinson, Ian. 2002. 'Personal narratives, social careers and medical courses: Analysing life trajectories in autobiographies of people with multiple sclerosis', *Social Science & Medicine* 30 (11): 1173–86. https://doi.org/10.1016/0277-9536(90)90257-S.

Roman-Basora, Manuel and James Travis Bland. 2021. 'Separate and unequal: A sample of disparities in five American unincorporated territories', *Public Integrity* 23. https://doi.org/10.1080/10999922.2020.1859241.

Rossel, Cecilia, Denise Courtoisie and Magdalena Marsiglia. 2019. 'How could conditional cash transfer programme conditionalities reinforce vulnerability?: Non-compliers and policy implementation gaps in Uruguay's family allowances', *Development Policy Review* 37 (1): 3–18. https://doi.org/10.1111/dpr.12327.

Saldaña, Abril. 2020. 'Vidas posibles: la guía bioética sobre asignación de recursos médicos en casos de emergencia', *Zona Franca*, 19 April. Accessed 24 May 2021. https://zonafranca.mx/opinion/vidas-posibles-la-guia-bioetica-sobre-asignacion-de-recursos-medicos-en-casos-de-emergencia/.

Saltman, Richard B. 2002. 'Regulating incentives: The past and present role of the state in health care systems', *Social Science & Medicine* 54 (11): 1677–84. https://doi.org/1677–84. 10.1016/s0277-9536(01)00335-5.

Sampson, Steven. 2014. 'Politics and Morality'. PhD course, Department of Anthropology, Stockholm University. Accessed 24 May 2021. https://www.socant.su.se/english/education/phd-studies/resa/politics-and-morality/politics-and-morality-1.202136.

Schneider, David Murray. 1984. *A Critique of the Study of Kinship*. Ann Arbor: University of Michigan Press.

Seki, Koki. 2015. 'Capitalizing on desire: Reconfiguring "the social" and the government of poverty in the Philippines', *Development and Change* 46 (6): 1253–76. https://doi.org/10.1111/dech.12200.

Singer, Merrill and Hans Baer. 1995. *Critical Medical Anthropology*. Amityville, NY: Baywood.

Singer, Merrill and Scott Clair. 2003. 'Syndemics and public health: Reconceptualizing disease in bio-social context', *Medical Anthropology Quarterly* 17 (4): 423–41. https://doi.org/10.1525/maq.2003.17.4.423.

Stewart, Heather and Denis Campbell. 2020. 'NHS workers angered at Hancock's warning not to overuse PPE', *The Guardian*, 10 April. Accessed 24 May 2021. https://www.theguardian.com/society/2020/apr/10/matt-hancock-urges-public-not-to-overuse-ppe.

Stone, Linda, ed. 2002. *New Directions in Anthropological Kinship*. London: Rowman & Littlefield.

The Arc. 2020. *HHS-OCR Complaints Re COVID-19 Medical Discrimination*, March 23. Accessed 24 May 2021. https://thearc.org/resource/hhs-ocr-complaint-of-disability-rights-washington-self-advocates-in-leadership-the-arc-of-the-united-states-and-ivanova-smith/.

Tronto, Joan C. 1993. *Moral Boundaries: A political argument for an ethic of care*. London: Routledge.

Tronto, Joan. 2006. 'Vicious circles of privatized caring'. In *Socializing Care: Feminist ethics and public issues*, edited by Maurice Hamington and Dorothy C. Miller, 3–26. Oxford: Rowman and Littlefield.

Tuck, Eve. 2009. 'Suspending damage: A letter to communities', *Harvard Educational Review* 79 (3): 409–28. Accessed 24 May 2021. https://www.hepg.org/her-home/issues/harvard-educational-review-volume-79-issue-3/herarticle/a-letter-to-communities_739.

Valencia Lomelí, Enrique. 2008. 'Conditional cash transfers as social policy in Latin America: An assessment of their contributions and limitations', *Annual Review of Sociology* 34: 475–99. Accessed 24 May 2021. https://ssrn.com/abstract=1142102.

Van Eeuwijk, Peter. 2020. 'Precarity, assemblages, and Indonesian elder care', *Medical Anthropology* 39 (1): 41–54. https://doi.org/10.1080/01459740.2019.1640694.

Vaughan, Megan. 2019. 'Conceptualising metabolic disorder in Southern Africa: Biology, history and global health', *Biosocieties* 14: 123–42. https://doi.org/10.1057/s41292-018-0122-3.

Venables, Emilie and Lenore Manderson. 2015. 'Exploring bodies in Southern and East Africa', *Medical Anthropology* 34 (4): 297–304. https://doi.org/10.1080/01459740.2015.1045141.

Waldstein, Anna. 2017. *Living Well in Los Duplex: Critical reflections on medicalization, migration and health sovereignty*. Durham, NC: Carolina Academic Press.

Weaver, Lesley Jo and Emily Mendenhall. 2014. 'Applying syndemics and chronicity: Interpretations from studies of poverty, depression, and diabetes', *Medical Anthropology* 33 (2): 92–108. https://doi.org/10.1080/01459740.2013.808637.

WHO (World Health Organization). n.d. *Chronic Diseases and Health Promotion. Overview – Preventing Chronic Diseases: A vital investment*. Accessed 24 May 2021. https://www.who.int/chp/chronic_disease_report/part1/en/index1.html.

Wikan, Unni. 1991. 'Toward an experience-near anthropology', *Cultural Anthropology* 6 (3): 285–305. https://doi.org/10.1525/can.1991.6.3.02a00020.

Wraight, William M., Sherilyn K.L. Tay, Charles Nduka and John A. Pereira. 2007. 'Bilateral breast reduction surgery in England: A postcode lottery', *Journal of Plastic, Reconstructive & Aesthetic Surgery* 60 (9): 1039–44. https://doi.org/10.1016/j.bjps.2007.03.002.

Yates-Doerr, Emily. 2015. *The Weight of Obesity: Hunger and global health in postwar Guatemala*. Oakland: University of California Press.

Yates-Doerr, Emily. 2020. 'Reworking the social determinants of health: Responding to material-semiotic indeterminacy in public health interventions', *Medical Anthropology Quarterly* 34 (3): 378–97. https://doi.org/10.1111/maq.12586.

1

A house of cards: Chronicity, care packages and a 'good life'

Lisa Ballesteros

Tuesday 8.00 a.m., November 2017, south-east London. The morning routine was in full swing. T, aged 3, was sitting in a sea of books and toys, contentedly sucking his fingers as he flicked through *The Gruffalo*, a book about a woodland monster that he had been obsessed with since he was a baby. His ventilator beeped as he gave a squeak of joy at a favourite page, and frantically bum-shuffled across the living room to match it with the appropriate stuffed animal. His father, B, jumped up just in time to adjust the long plastic tube snaking out of a hole in T's neck, through which a steam nebuliser was running. Crisis averted, B went back to correcting essays for his freelance job as an online English tutor for Chinese teenagers, the only employment he had been able to find that fitted around T's medical needs. The next intervention was not due for another half hour, after which it would be time to pack up T's specially adapted buggy to go to nursery: ventilator, emergency bag, oxygen, posterior walker, suction catheters, suction machine, resuscitation bag, feed pump, gastrostomy connector, medications, urinary catheters, nappy bag. Oh, and a copy of *The Gruffalo* for the journey.

T is my son. I had planned to spend the day writing up my PhD in a corner of T's room, the only place available to work in our two-bedroom flat. My desk was wedged between an oxygen concentrator and a pile of bowel irrigation supplies, bundles of medical gauze taped to its corners in an attempt to protect T's head during his wobbly attempts to walk. I had done my fieldwork in between looking after T, although at this point in our lives B was doing the bulk of the childcare. T had been discharged from hospital at 11 months old, with tubes embedded in his brain and sticking out of his throat and stomach. Surviving the first year had been a big achievement, but nobody with his set of conditions had lived long enough to take anything for granted and the first year of his life at home passed by in a blur of life-support interventions. These were punctuated by occasional admissions to various London hospitals for chest infections, neurological surgery and investigative admissions. Although the secondary school where B taught was initially sympathetic, after several months of leaving early to get to the hospital, they had not renewed his contract. Money was tight, but we had decided to try to get by on a combination of my PhD stipend, disability benefits and whatever freelance work B could get.

Life had become easier when T turned 2, became more medically stable and eligible for 15 hours a week of government-funded nursery care. This was available a year earlier than for many other children, as he received the highest level of Disability Living Allowance (DLA).[1] With his right to education protected through the 2010 Equality Act, our local Clinical Commissioning Group (CCG), the arm of the UK's free National Health Service (NHS) responsible for commissioning local health services for those eligible for continuing health care (Department of Health 2016a), was legally obliged to provide a carer to attend nursery with him. The tracheostomy in T's windpipe, which connected to the ventilator on which he was totally dependent to breathe, was at risk of blocking or popping out when least expected, as had nearly happened during the morning's Gruffalo-chasing mission. Failure to securely replace it would mean T could die in minutes, his airway deflated and fragile lungs collapsed.

Carers were, and still are, part of our lives. After almost a year of being moved between various hospitals, we were told that for T to safely come home, we would need a government-funded package of continuing health support to assist us in providing 24-hour waking care. The realisation that life as I knew it had come to an end was a turning point. 'You'll get used to it,' the nurses said. 'It'll become your new normal. Twenty years ago you would have had to stay in hospital until he either got better, or, you know …'. I did know. During that year, I had seen enough hollow-eyed parents going home empty handed that, despite T not being likely to 'get better' any time soon, there was an alternative I dreaded even more.

Eventually, having strangers in our home went from being a horrifying prospect to something I depended on and felt grateful for, albeit with moments where I swung between resentment for the lack of privacy and control, and frustration when things did not happen the way they were supposed to. A carer not coming for the nursery shift meant that either T did not go in, or B or I cancelled our plans for the day and went with him.

A non-arrival at night meant one of us had to try and stay awake all night after being awake all day.

Becoming pregnant during my PhD had seemed like a minor set-back. I planned to take six months off and carry on with my fieldwork overseas as planned, family in tow. B was going to be a hands-on, stay-at-home dad anyway. A 'good life' back then meant freedom and choice: where to live, who to have in my home, taking my child to meet family around the world. As the weeks in hospital turned into months, that openness and hope was sucked into what felt like a vortex of sus-pended reality, and only gradually reconfigured into a completely differ-ent conception of what a 'good life' was. Part of that is dependence on paid care from individuals who start off as strangers. All previous notions of a 'good life' suddenly became intimately intertwined with the complex universes of people we had not met yet, and the fluctuations of public policy in austerity Britain.

In this chapter, I explore how families raising medically complex children in the UK in the early twenty-first century experience chronic-ity. I examine the extent to which changing perceptions of, and ability to live, a 'good life' intersect with the formal care system, and are mor-ally expressed through notions of deservingness and gratefulness. To this end, I argue that the inherent relationality of ongoing 'moral pro-jects of becoming' (Mattingly 2014), as lived by the families of medically complex children, and care as both a relational and institutional concept (Graham 1991; Thomas 1993; Shakespeare 2014), ensures that the lives and experiences of paid carers intertwine with those of the fami-lies with which they work. The result is a complex field of social assem-blages where moral and affective forces collide with political-economic fluctuations and post-colonial and gendered fields of practice (Bourdieu 1977). Bearing in mind the particularly precarious nature of care work in contemporary Britain (Christensen 2010), I show how institutionalised statutory care relationships by their very nature – that is, racialised and gendered fields of power which occur in the most intimate of spaces, that of the domestic sphere – are marked by tension and contradictions.

Background

As medical technology has become more sophisticated, the life expec-tancies of medically complex individuals around the world have become longer, although not necessarily more stable, moving from 'cri-sis' to 'chronic' mode. This persistence of medical precarity in time is fundamentally linked to the structural factors of modernity (Manderson and Smith-Morris 2010; Montesi and Calestani, this volume). Over the last 20 or 30 years, this has been reflected in a shift in policy regarding the long-term care of chronically fragile individuals in the social welfare democracies of northern Europe, where state-funded care has been spatially reconfigured from institutional (hospitals, hospices, care homes) to domestic settings (Shakespeare 2014; Christensen 2010), determining an increasing hospitalisation of homes.

The NHS in the UK has always been free at the point of access for eligible individuals, a status which is based on citizenship and settlement rights. Once a child with complex medical needs has been assessed and accepted for a package of care by their local CCG, commissioners decide how the care will be provided and the resources required to deliver it through multi-agency panels (Department of Health 2016a). Each CCG has access to different levels of funding through their local NHS trust, whose available income can vary hugely from area to area, and even within cities. When a package of care has been agreed on, and the budget approved, this funding is used to commission the services of care agencies.[2] After a tendering process in which various agencies bid for a new care package contract, a handful of bidders are shortlisted based on who promises to deliver the best mix of quality and price, and presented to potential clients (in this case, parents), who choose a final provider. This agency is then responsible for hiring and training staff and the ongoing management of the package. Carers are trained in whatever interventions are necessary to support families in meeting the care needs of the child in question. T's daily care routines mirrored those of many families we got to know through online communities and through frequent hospital visits: a meticulous operation of suctioning, nebulising, catheterising, and administering medicines and feeds through various artificially created points in the body, as well as always being alert to any signs of deterioration, which could quickly escalate into crisis.

CCGs are provided with a set of national guidelines via various decision-support tools and flowcharts, which are designed to assess levels of needs, ranging from 'no additional needs' to 'priority' (Department of Health 2016b). Despite such tools, however, the ultimate decision about how much care a family is capable of providing ultimately rests with individual commissioning panels, and is often guided by budgets. This means that provision of care packages for those with similar medical prognoses varies widely across NHS trusts. The inequality of this postcode lottery is a common complaint among families with medically complex children, with ventilated children in some areas receiving seven waking nights of domiciliary care a week in addition to several day shifts, while others are awarded two or three nights only. In recent years, austerity cuts have exacerbated this problem, with funding available to local NHS trusts being reduced amid rising debts (Taunt et al. 2014).

In addition to variation in provision, the ability of agencies to actually provide staff for care packages also presents challenges. Although agencies claim that a background in health care is a necessary requirement in the training of new carers, when it comes to recruitment processes, the specificities of what this means are vague, an issue which is linked to nationwide shortages of willing and competent individuals. A major factor contributing to this is the precarity of the work. Care work has always been poorly paid, unstable, undervalued and physically difficult (Christensen 2010). As a labour system, it is embedded in the UK's colonial past and long history of using migrant labour to fill skill gaps in the health sector, making it not only historically gendered (Thomas 1993; Graham 1991; Christensen 2012), but also reflective of divisions of class and race (Graham 1991). Despite the increasingly specialist skills required with the rise in the chronically medically complex population, full-time, permanent contracts which guarantee a minimum monthly salary are extremely scarce. At the time of writing, the average pay on a night shift for a London-based health-care assistant, Band 2 (their official NHS banding), was £11–14 an hour.[3] With monthly rental costs plus bills starting at around £1,000 a month for a one-bedroom flat in London's Zone 2, and going up to around £1,400 for a two-bedroom flat, care work cannot provide sufficient income to support a family as a single salary.

Simultaneously, changes in public spending following the 2012 Welfare and Reform Act have deeply affected access to supplementary forms of income. Although ostensibly a simplification of the benefits system to improve incentives to work, the Act formed part of a controversial discourse at nationwide level regarding access to benefits and who 'deserved' them (LGIU 2012). In a city well known for its expensive housing and childcare costs, this chapter shows how, in one particular employment context, these changes especially affected women of African and Caribbean backgrounds. As a group in society for which historical racialised and gendered inequalities and austerity policies, which draw on moral panics of 'deserving' and 'undeserving' recipients of social welfare, have conspired to leave precariously employed, they are disproportionately represented in the care sector in London. This precarity in turn undermines the integrity of the sector itself. In other words, financial, social and medical precarity combine into a relationally defined field of practice (Bourdieu 1977) between carers and families which is in constant danger of collapse.

Methods

The fieldwork for this paper consists of my notes and memories of the period from 2015 to early 2019, during which I lived with my son, husband and, eventually, daughter in London before moving to a different city. The spatial marking of a 'beginning' and 'end' of this period automatically lends itself to a consideration of narrative along with autoethnography as a principal methodology.

My approach to narrative is inherently temporal, that is, characterised by an awareness of time. I follow Taylor (1989, 47) in drawing on a Heideggerian temporality in that 'in order to have a sense of who we are, we have to have a notion of how we have become, and of where we are going'. Similarly, Mattingly (2014) argues for the centrality of a narrative methodology and the inherent narrativity of ethical practice in her ethnography of families caring for children with complex needs. She refers to the temporality of the projects of care as *historicity*, a self-constituting nature with a middle emerging from a continually revised beginning and multiple possibilities of foreshadowed but suspenseful endings. For Mattingly (2014, 20), narrative framing as methodology, rather than presuming an overly coherent self, is a useful approach for investigating how moral projects are 'riddled by uncertain possibilities and informed by pluralistic moral values, concerns and communities'.

Apart from my own experiences, I also draw on four years of participant observation of other families of medically complex children that I met during long hospital stays and on internet forums. The proliferation of Facebook groups dedicated to niche areas of interest extends to support groups for families of tracheostomy children, bowel management support groups and disability benefits advice forums. I engaged in, and observed, heated debates regarding carer behaviour, unreliable/dishonest care agencies, CCG policies and various other third-party actions that families see as impeding their ability to live a good life on their own terms. With this in mind, I created a survey entitled 'Chronic Conditions, Care Packages and a Good Life' in July 2019, and posted it in various groups. I use the results here to develop some of the more 'thick' descriptions which I include from my own experience.

Theoretical framework: Temporality, ethics and care

Horton and Barker (2010) advocate the anthropological approach to health as ideally placed to examine how we physically incorporate social and material environments, tracing material and lasting effects of public policies on the embodied self. Building on this approach, in this chapter I draw not only on anthropological literature on health and disability, but also on sociological and public policy research in order to emphasise the extent to which the deeply first-person methodology of autoethnography/narrative is shaped by the political and sociological implications of the UK health-care system.

Conceptually, I first advocate a strong temporal focus on chronicity in its capacity as an ongoing process of medical precarity. In defining 'temporality' as a consciousness of time, rather than a linear progression of past, present and future, I emphasise the specific temporal dimension and texture of living with chronicity. To explore this, I draw on anthropological literature on different types of 'crisis', in particular, that of the financial crisis in southern Europe in the early 2010s. The use of 'crisis' here was the suspension of future thought, an examination of hopelessness, waiting and survival after an extended period of belief in the neoliberal capitalist system in southern Europe as an arena in which one could thrive (Knight and Stewart 2016; Janeja and Bandak 2018). I argue for parallels in the lives of families with medically complex children, whose understandings of pre- and post-crisis conditions have had to adjust to a model where their expectations of the future can no longer assume a statistically average life expectancy and standard of health, as experienced by the 'healthy' population who benefit from Europe's low child mortality rates and social democratic health-care systems. I propose hope and temporality as affective strategies to create spaces of possibility within potentially catastrophic circumstances, and also ask how they interact with experiences of guilt, deservingness and gratefulness.

I link the literature discussed above to a notion of care, in its dual conceptualisation as an institutional as well as an affective practice, which is firmly rooted in the anthropology of morality. As part of the 'ethical turn', Mattingly (2014, 4, 5) refers to the suffering and challenges in the lives of families raising disabled children as a 'complex reasoning task that engenders ongoing moral deliberations, evaluations, and experiments in how to live', which propels parents into a 'new, often unexpected and unwanted project of becoming'. In reference to the 'good life' within this anthropology of ethics, as Aristotle argues, a good life is not just survival but flourishing, not a subjective notion of happiness but of leading a life worth living. A key concept here is Bernard Williams's (1981) use of 'ground projects' – commitments so deep that they make life meaningful in themselves, including 'deeply cherished and self-defining ideals, activities and personal associations' (Mattingly 2014, 12). These activities consist of small moments and routine activities that may at first glance appear repetitive, pre-reflective or inconsequential, but that 'take on depth as episodes in unfolding narratives of moral striving and as part of conscious commitments to realize particular versions of the good life' (Mattingly 2014, 205).

Discussions of deservingness within ongoing moral deliberations of ground projects have rich potential for theorisation within the anthropology of ethics, but they also appear in other disciplines. Within political science, deservingness can be found as a heuristic device to link values and political attitudes (Petersen et al. 2010). In critical public health, it appears via an analysis of how the new politics of welfare have reshaped articulations of 'deserving' versus 'undeserving' recipients of health-related benefits according to a specific political agenda (Bambra and Smith 2010). Sociology engages with the politics of deservingness through discussions of illegal migrants. Chauvin and Garcés-Mascareñas (2014), for example, locate it within a moral economy that is embedded in legalisation claims and programmes. Most significant for the purposes of this chapter, however, is how deservingness appears within the extensive literature on care available within sociology, public policy studies and disability studies. This literature ranges from the experiences of being a care worker and being cared for (Christensen 2010, 2012), different models of care (Shakespeare 2014; Ungerson 2006), the theoretical underpinnings of care as an ethical model (Shakespeare 2014; Graham 1991; Thomas 1993), the meaning/nature of formal care relationships and how they are experienced by both care workers and care users (Yamaki and Yamazaki 2004; Ungerson 2006; Woodin 2006; Kelly 2010; Leece and Peace 2010; Christensen 2010; Mladenov 2012), and the sociohistorical context of care and its implications on neocolonial, class, gender and racial relations (Graham 1991; Thomas 1993). I draw on this literature in order to link the affective experience of participating in the institutionalised statutory care system as both a service user and a care worker to the wider social and economic aspects which shape different assemblages of care. This also incorporates a consideration of the wider discourse of deservingness at a time of welfare cuts, the moral panic surrounding 'deserving' beneficiaries of care and disability benefits, and debates surrounding migration and the Other. I maintain that a reflection of the sociological context of my fieldwork complements the anthropological insistence on the question of the human condition within a particular historical and cultural space, and thus fills a gap in the literature for an analysis of affectivity and actual articulation between cared-for and caregivers, as mediated by larger structural forces. In particular,

I follow Shakespeare (2014) in calling for a theoretical underpinning within the feminist ethic of care as model for understanding care relationships in the disability sector, as well as Christensen (2010) in distinguishing different approaches to analysing the motivations of care workers. These approaches draw on a strong critique in sociology and disability studies regarding the false dichotomy and pure utilitarianism of care as public/private, waged/unwaged (Graham 1991; Thomas 1993; Shakespeare 2014). I join them in calling for a focus on relationships and emotions in order to consider the heterogeneity of people's support needs, aspirations and values.

Clarissa's struggle and the house of cards

B and I were so excited when T started nursery: three hours a day, five days a week, after two years of being unable to leave him during the day with anyone apart from each other. However, it soon became clear that a new set of challenges was beginning. The agency who had won our contract from the CCG were struggling to recruit and keep people for school hours. All our carers were women with school-age children or grandchildren, and they either had to take them to school themselves or only worked nights, as it was easier to get childcare. One carer confided in me apologetically that the amount the agency was offering for three hours' work meant that it was not really worth her while to organise childcare and drive across London. Eventually Marie,[4] a softly spoken 40-year-old woman from Ghana, agreed to take the job. She had lots of experience with medically complex children, and she learned the ventilator settings quickly. She lasted two months. Carrying the five-kilogram ventilator around all day aggravated her back condition, she explained, but she told us she had a solution and had set up her cousin Gloria with the agency. Gloria had never cared for such complex needs before, and after I saw her attempting to suction T's tracheostomy with the wrong type of catheter, we asked for someone else.

Eventually, one of the carers who did night shifts agreed to move to days. Clarissa had a raucous laugh and superb clinical skills. T loved her, and she was one of the few people to whom he gave one of his rare hugs. Over the following months, she confided in us about her life, especially her 12-year-old son, Paul, who was six feet tall and 'Looks 25! Oh my lord. God help him.' She would also refer darkly to the mysterious father of her child, who had banned her from visiting her family in Nigeria over Christmas, yet did not contribute to the rent: 'He has another family.

In Italy.' She muttered, and tossed her head: 'Paul and I, we don't need him!' Paul had been getting into trouble at school, and she was terrified of him getting involved in a gang, a big problem in that part of London, and especially so for young men of African or Caribbean backgrounds. T's nursery teacher, who worked closely alongside Clarissa, and who we often saw around the neighbourhood, had a brother who, at the age of 14, had been stabbed to death the year before in the estate just behind the nursery. Gang culture, socioeconomic inequality and institutionalised racism have long been major issues in this part of London.

Paul's form teacher at school was a former colleague of B's, and B offered to talk to her on Clarissa's behalf. Our relationship soon moved to a liminal area where B and I felt emotionally affected by what Clarissa told us, where B wrote letters to the council on her behalf, and where she would cry on the sofa after taking another phone call from school. Yet there was always an agitated feeling of limbo, that our lives were on hold while she sorted things out. Clarissa often arrived late to look after T, as she had been called into meetings when she dropped her son off, meaning that whoever out of B and I had less work to do would stay at nursery for an hour or two or three, fulfilling the role of T's carer as we waited for her to arrive.

Eventually, backup was provided by a second carer, Ngozi. Ngozi had been a nurse in Nigeria, but her qualification was not recognised in London, so she was studying nursing part time at a local university. Her children were all grown up, so she was slightly more flexible and able to swap shifts with Clarissa during emergencies, such as when Paul was suspended from school for fighting. 'I don't want to leave him alone in the house,' Clarissa told me. 'Around here, there are so many gangs. And he looks like a man, but he isn't, he's just a little boy still! He doesn't know to control his impulses.'

A few weeks later, Clarissa was off again. Gradual changes to state support since the implementation of the Welfare Reform Act meant that she was no longer eligible for contributions towards her rent. As a migrant and a single mother, Clarissa was constantly negotiating the ever-changing bureaucratic hoops she needed to jump through to access various in-work benefits, until she finally accepted that she would be unable to continue paying the £1,200 a month rent on their two-bedroom flat on a single salary. She decided to declare herself homeless and go into council-provided temporary accommodation, telling me: 'I will take matters into my own hands. This way, I can get on the list for housing.' This involved Clarissa having to sit in the council office for two days in a row before she and her son were eventually sent to a one-bedroom flat in another part of the city. For a few weeks, she could still manage the commute to T's nursery after doing the school run, but she was then told that she was going to be moved much further away. She looked exhausted as she explained that she would have to have some time off to move house and look for a new school for her son. Unsure whether we would ever see her again, I felt my insides twist at the unfairness of what had happened to her, and a large dose of self-pity that once again our precious respite hours were being taken away. I had already spoken to the care agency, who were unable to provide cover for the rest of the week as Ngozi was now on her nursing placement. There was only one other carer on the package, Lily, a tall and striking 28-year-old Sudanese refugee with two children who had done the odd cover day, but who was already doing four nights with us that week, in between her paramedic exams. The agency asked if I preferred night cover or day cover, and I angrily told them that I preferred to sleep, and to look after T myself during the day.

Adapting to our new lives and adjusted parameters of possibility felt like living in a house of cards. There was beauty in its complexity when everything was working well, and every day that T was healthy and we were able to live out our 'new normal' was a gift for which I was deeply grateful. Then, in a moment, it could suddenly compress and seem like the world had collapsed when the slightest thing failed. Everyday life felt like it was suspended while our carers sorted their lives out. Empathy for what Clarissa was going through mingled with frustration that there was no one else available to help, and that I would have to indefinitely suspend all the little daily routines in which I had learned to find happiness in the absence of an ability to plan for a future that assumed my child would survive. Then, crashing guilt that, in her own way, Clarissa was in an even more precarious position than I was. Living in London, the same city to which my mother had migrated four decades earlier, and where I had friends and acquaintances of different racial backgrounds, I was aware of the privilege afforded by my light skin tone, citizenship status and middle-class upbringing, despite the restrictions that chronic illness had brought into my life. Clarissa, like all the other carers on our package, had arrived in London from one of Britain's former colonies in Africa and the Caribbean, reflecting transnational care migration trends which have historically relied on low-paid, usually female, migrant workers (Williams 2001; Ungerson 2006; Graham 1991). All of our carers had been in the UK long enough to be granted permanent residency and the legal status to work and live, although the nature of the work available was overwhelmingly precarious and focused on the service industries. Indeed, Graham (1991) argues that divisions of gender, class and race via the historical employment in domestic settings (both paid and unpaid) of colonial (black) subjects as well as the white working class in Britain have been central to the development of the middle-class home as a location of family care in Britain. As the twentieth century progressed, this domestic element of care became increasingly institutionalised as the expanding NHS increased the demand for what had previously been considered domestic labour *outside* of private homes, while post-war labour shortages in Britain ensured a continued racial element to the provision of such care via large recruitment drives in Britain's former colonies in the Caribbean (Graham 1991).

Like Clarissa, I received benefits, but I had always been assured by those around me that 'you deserve them', as they were linked to T's disabilities. At the same time, moralised discourses in the media were raging around people such as Clarissa, who, despite being in skilled employment, was attempting to claim state support as she was not paid enough to cover her rent and provide for her son. In turn, the inability of the care sector to adequately sustain our house of cards meant that, despite T being stronger, B was unable to return to the job he loved in a local secondary school, where as a teacher he would have been part of a system that might enable individuals such as Clarissa's son to access a life outside of London's gangs.

For different reasons, then, the families of carers and those they cared for are both unable to act against a care system that does not protect those on whom it depends to keep going. Sitting there as T had a nap that afternoon, I felt trapped, guilty for feeling frustrated when at least I had a roof over my head, and overwhelmingly disempowered over my own life and future, and that of my child.

Temporal/spatial reconfiguration: a discussion

I suggest that the collapsed temporal worlds of acute crisis, when individuals are unable to conceive of anything beyond the immediate precarious present (Knight and Stewart 2016), give way, in families with complex children who attain stability, to *chronicity*. Estroff (1993, 250) defines chronicity as 'the persistence in time of limitations and suffering that results in disabilities as they are socially and culturally defined and lived'. In the context of this chapter, I suggest a conceptualisation of chronicity as less the persistence of suffering, and more the suspension of crisis as acute and hopeless (Knight and Stewart 2016); that is, chronicity as a longer-term experience of medical precarity within which a reconfiguration of some sort of ability to visualise a future/good life is possible, albeit one which is based on an adapted routine and sense of self.

The vignette in which I introduced T indicates the process by which my own initial appalled realisation that life had changed gave way to adaptation to a new normal, or ground project (Mattingly 2014). This was also reflected in the answers of the 37 families who responded to my online survey.[5] When asked about what constituted a good life before their medically complex child was born, families reflected on variations on the concept of freedom – to travel, to relax at home in private, and to make plans for one's own routine and future. When asked what a good life meant now, the focus underwent a spatial and temporal shrinking:

> It's freedom in a different way, in a much more micro-way like having small chunks of time to exercise, read, plan for the not too distant future, have the occasional night out. And enjoy my children and family without feeling crowded by health professionals but at the same time knowing my boy is safe. I definitely focus more on mini-actions in the present now than scary ideas about the future. (Respondent 1)

Many prioritise health and stability now, rather than holidays and planning. There are more references to spending time outside, making memories and sleeping:

> Now in order to have a good quality of life we have to rely on the generosity of strangers to support charities that support us. Going three months without a hospital admission. Having a little boy who lights up a room and is loved wherever we go. It means having to constantly fight and battle in order to get the bare essentials for your child so they can have a good life. (Respondent 30)

This is echoed by Respondent 33:

> Making sure our daughter has a Good Day every day is our plan. We want to see her happy, enjoying life and as healthy as can be. We want to celebrate the small achievement and have lots of happy memories.

Respondent 13 writes about 'spend[ing] precious time with our gorgeous boy who has severe complex needs as we don't know how long we have with him'. There is a strong focusing inwards: a 'good life' is the 'bare essentials', 'micro-victories' and 'small achievements', happiness materialising out of being rested, seeing smiles, staying out of hospital. Freedom is re-visualised and temporally and spatially shrunk to micro-events and the achievement of routine. Mattingly (2014) insists that for families of medically complex children in Los Angeles, seemingly mundane domestic routines are not only achievements in the face of a backdrop of crisis and trauma, but also allow possibilities for transcendence, the ongoing practical, dogged hope to create something better. She suggests that 'turbulence, uncertainty and drama are such pervasive qualities that ordinary routines are not the daily expression of a habitual way of life culturally inherited so much as a fragile achievement, a hard-won moment of mundaneness' (Mattingly 2014, 79).

Although I agree with Mattingly's (2014) suggestion of routine as offering the possibility to transcend the ongoing experience of chronicity as a micro-victory, I would expand upon this by proposing that the provision of care packages provides an extra layer of relationality which makes the fragile achievement of routine even more precarious and undermines the moral weight and symbolic density of such micro-victories. A key element within this notion of chronicity is the awareness that acute crisis, the suspension of future thought, could re-enter at any time. Although for many medically complex children this is crisis in its medical sense, a sudden medical deterioration, I suggest here that the institutional framework that provides the means for a care package is also chronically precarious and in danger of crisis at any moment, like the human body itself. The consequence of this is its disintegration into a state which leaves those who depend on it in the midst of crisis once more. This is what happened when historical, social, economic and institutional conditions converged to leave Clarissa unable to fulfil her role as carer. Her absence caused the immediate and complete collapse of the house of cards, the temporal and spatial reconfigurations of being, and a good life as acted out through routine and mini-victories against ongoing chronicity.

Relationality: a discussion

The relationality of care packages is both complex and turbulent. When asked about how they felt regarding amounts of care in general, respondents to my online survey used expressions with moral weight which link to deservingness, such as 'grateful', 'thankful' and 'lucky':

Although we're [*sic*] rather we didn't need them, we feel incredibly lucky they're there. Anyone living with a complex needs child/young adult suffers from mental/emotional & physical exhaustion on a regular basis, with carers life is bearable, without carers it can be unbearable. (Respondent 21)

Linked to this notion of gratefulness is the feeling that provision of a successful package is crucial to a sense of self and inter-family relationships. This ideal sense of self as a familial being significantly differentiates between technical care activities and notions of care grounded in love and 'normal parenting':

We as Phoebe's parents would not be able to be ourselves in the slightest without care. We lose our sense of self. We become a carer, a nurse. Not a parent. We constantly suction, or jej feed, or medicate, or physio, or splint, or change pads, or hoist etc. ... we become so routine in our delivery of care we forget to cuddle, kiss, parent. We become robotic in our duties because we're so damned tired. We have no time or inclination for anything. (Respondent 17)

If our care package actually happened my husband and I could sleep in the same bed five nights a week, I could give my younger daughter the attention she needs and deserves. It would mean my daughter could enjoy the summer holidays like most five year olds rather than having to be stuck indoors because it's too hot for her brother. (Respondent 30)

The care package provided is essential to my son's ability to stay alive. I could not care for him alone 24/7 as he now needs two trained people to see to his needs when awake and one trained person (and me in bed on call) at night. Occasionally I am given a double up where I have two trained so I can go out and leave them to care for my son but I usually use this time to spend time with my son as his mummy rather than his carer. (Respondent 26)

In this context, the concept of care as paid work done by strangers, as opposed to emotional, unpaid work done by kin, is defined by the provision of the care relationship itself by the state. The nature of this institutionally defined relationship is subject to two poles of interpretation within families. On the one hand is a sense of a lack of control and helplessness, which manifests as existential frustration and resentment:

Having strangers in your house, caring for your child, is one of the hardest things you can do. You do it because you know it's best for your child but it means that your house is no longer your sanctuary. You have to fit life around your carers. We have so little control of our lives, so much is dictated by our son's condition or professionals that our home was always our sanctuary and now we don't even have that. (Respondent 30)

On the other hand, as well as frustration and resentment, there are feelings of gratefulness. As a concept, gratefulness, and the extent to which one should feel grateful to the state for providing the means to allocate more technical aspects of care to paid individuals, arises when the package is working well. Central to this is the perceived quality of the carer relationship. Generally, there is a conflict between the two ideals of being professional (that is, competent) and loving (that is, one of the family).[6] For some, a good carer is someone who becomes like kin, with whom there is a strong affective bond and who is also fully trusted:

If I have one or two carers then the precious time with my son is diluted by having staff with us. The only time this is actually 'nice' is when the carer or nurse is so perfect that they become a member of the family but of course this upsets the professional conduct situation that agencies and CCGs insist upon. (Respondent 26)

During my years of observation of online forums, I frequently saw how the overall value system which prioritised care workers who were 'like one of the family' in the sense above could be disrupted at any time by incidents of professional misconduct, most often overstepping boundaries or falling asleep on the job and putting the cared-for person at risk. On an everyday basis, therefore, while kin-like relationality is valued over cold professionalism, even the most cherished care workers were not immune to a total and sudden relational breakdown when they committed the ultimate sin of endangering their charge or the family's wellbeing. This was often expressed by affected families through narratives of betrayal. Emotional responses of frustration and guilt in reaction to the precarity of the re-conceptualised good life (which appear as gratefulness when the routine works) are fundamentally linked to relationality and the moral projects of others. Such a consideration is particularly important when considering the extent to which power interweaves with affect in care relationships. Writing about adult disabled people–personal assistant relationships in the UK, Shakespeare (2014) refers to a prevailing mode of master/servant, and cites privacy and ensuring that workers do not take over their social lives or interfere in family life as the ultimate reason for which service users cultivate such a relationship. Privacy was indeed a major issue for many families in my study, and many described a 'good carer' not so much in familial terms, but as 'dynamic', 'trustworthy' and 'professional', maintaining a distance from the family, rather than being 'one of the family'. Central to this is feeling invaded by representatives of the state intruding into the family home:

> We sometimes feel judged in the decisions we make. Privacy is important to us and very difficult to get a good balance with. We've had really good relationships with carers but gossip and Chinese whispers, expectations of duties, difficulties in recruiting and lack of sufficient management has made things very difficult at times. (Respondent 7)

Families sometimes felt as if they were 'being watched all the time as carers had to write everything down' (Respondent 9). The maintenance of such a relationship, however, leads to a distancing and emotional exhaustion between families and carers:

> We are constantly reliant on someone else. Their needs are put before ours as they are protected through employment. Pregnancy, annual leave, illness, family members becoming ill or bereavement, broken down cars, everything you can imagine from a team of carers then has an impact on us. We find it difficult to sympathise sometimes as we know when someone's pulling a fast one and can't be bothered to come to work. Our 'bullshit' filter runs on overdrive! It makes us sometimes seem very hard but our emotions are damaged. We don't express the way we used to. We're not good at the head tilt and 'poor you' which is often what people want. (Respondent 7)

This is far from the ideal of being like a member of the family, which other care package users suggest, an ideal which in itself advocates a blend of trust, competence and understanding. The two values of 'professional' and 'like family' are therefore not only qualitatively defined, but also, and more significantly, in a constant negotiation in order to achieve a good relationship. Respondent 26 writes:

> Some are ultra professional and act at all times like they are at work, forgetting their work is our home. Some are disrespectful and lazy.

Some are just perfect. The balance between the two is so important. It is so difficult to find the right people.

Referring to this constant negotiation of ideals, Christensen (2012) suggests that the way in which paid care systems are run is fundamental to how carer relationships are subsequently played out. She suggests that marketised approaches to care provision, such as those that are prevalent in the UK, are more likely to produce either extreme master–servant relationships or solidarity/emotional types of relationships, while a more regulated system, such as the Norwegian model, encourages a more sustainable hybrid relationship which combines friendship and paid care work (Christensen 2012; Shakespeare 2014). This combination encompasses the dual notion of care as described by Thomas (1993, 665) of care as '*both* the paid and unpaid provision of support involving work activities and feeling states'. An ideal hybrid in this context would consist of friendship (as an intangible relationality based on mutual affect and trust) and the professionalism inherent in the concept of paid care work, as well as the accompanying tangible clinical standards needed to keep not just the carers' charges stable, but the whole family able to live a good life.

Conclusion

I have argued in this chapter that families with medically complex children who experience chronicity do so via a spatial and temporal reconfiguration of the 'good life'. This good life is played out as ongoing moral projects which focus on the achievement of micro-victories and daily routines, a notion which has been documented in other studies of medically complex families (Mattingly 2014). However, I propose here that those who experience chronicity within the institutional structure of the state-funded, community-based care packages which are unique to northern Europe (Ungerson 2006) encounter a further layer of both precarity and relationality which works on a dual level and challenges the realisation of such moral projects and abilities to lead a good life.

This first takes the form of precarity regarding relationships with carers, and can be conceptualised as the ongoing negotiation towards a positive and mutually affective relationality within the carer–family relationship. This relationality is underscored by affective notions of deservingness and gratefulness, which can also intermingle with resentment that a care package is needed in first place. A successful relationship here is one where carers who are 'like family' but also 'professional' facilitate access to the moral project of a good life.

The second notion of precarity appears around the working conditions for carers within the care system itself as an arena of paid labour. Regardless of the relationships built between carers and families, this second form of precarity exists as the ongoing potential for the breakdown of possibilities for the micro-victories of a good life when a carer is forced into crisis. Whether through acute reasons or longer-term structural inequalities which have their roots in historical, social and economic practices, the house of cards can at any time collapse into crisis for all parties connected by the relational practices of the care package.

This dual notion of precarity has a significant impact on those families whose abilities to live a good life are already marked by the experience of chronicity. Throughout this chapter, I have suggested that a good life, as the spatial and temporal reconfiguration of what it means to flourish, is strongly enabled and shaped by the provision of structural support that enables the basic provision of human needs such as sleep, routine and basic kin relationships. The structural support provided by carers such as Clarissa, who was able to facilitate a good life for T and his family on both a relational and clinical basis, was undermined by her position within a sector of the labour market which was defined by post-colonial and gendered socioeconomic inequality. This inequality is what challenges the solution proposed by sociological research on care systems, which calls for a more regulated system in order to encourage a better hybrid carer relationship (Christensen 2012), and in turn facilitate families' potential to lead a good life. The UK care system is also burdened by the economic realities of several years of austerity policies and reduced public spending. In order to conceptualise a future for medically complex children in which they and their families can live a good life to its fullest extent, a hybrid model of care needs to be developed in which not just care recipients but also carers themselves are able to live a life where they feel valued, supported and secure.

Notes

1. Those on low incomes are also eligible for the 15 free hours at the age of 2. These latter families are means tested, whereas DLA recipients are not.
2. At the time of writing, this situation was changing, with Personal Health Budgets increasingly being awarded directly to eligible individuals, who then recruit for and manage their own care team. However, although a legal amendment to the NHS and CCG Regulations in 2013 stated that 'the families of a child or young person eligible for continuing care have a "right to have" a personal health budget' (Department of Health 2016a, 9), at the time of writing they are

still relatively uncommon, and information regarding them is difficult to access from official bodies.

3. In 2016, several agencies across London cut their rate to £11 per hour without any prior warning, explaining only that the CCGs were unable to continue paying them at the previous rate. The rate was partially reinstated some months later without explanation.

4. All carers' and survey respondents' names have been changed.

5. I also knew many of these families through online forums, and we interacted with each other's lives through commenting on each other's photographs and giving advice on the full array of aspects of life with medically complex children.

6. At the other end of the scale, of course, is neither excess professionalism nor quasi-kinship, but gross incompetence, which I do not discuss in this chapter.

References

Bambra, Clare and Katherine E. Smith. 2010. 'No longer deserving? Sickness, benefit reform and the politics of (ill) health', *Critical Public Health* 20 (1): 71–84. https://doi.org/10.1080/09581590902763265.

Bourdieu, Pierre. 1977. *Outline of a Theory of Practice*. Translated by Richard Nice. Cambridge Studies in Social and Cultural Anthropology. Cambridge: Cambridge University Press.

Chauvin, Sébastien and Blanca Garcés-Mascareñas. 2014. 'Becoming less illegal: Deservingness frames and undocumented migrant incorporation', *Sociology Compass* 8 (4): 422–32. https://doi.org/10.1111/soc4.12145.

Christensen, Karen. 2010. 'Caring about independent lives', *Disability & Society* 25 (2): 241–52. https://doi.org/10.1080/09687590903537562.

Christensen, Karen. 2012. 'Towards sustainable hybrid relationships in cash-for-care systems', *Disability & Society* 27 (3): 399–412. https://doi.org/10.1080/09687599.2012.654990.

Department of Health. 2016a. *National Framework for Children and Young People's Continuing Care*. Accessed 22 May 2021. https://assets.publishing.service.gov.uk/government/uploads/system/uploads/attachment_data/file/499611/children_s_continuing_care_Fe_16.pdf.

Department of Health. 2016b. *National Framework for Children and Young People's Continuing Care: Decision support tool*. Accessed 22 May 2021. https://www.gov.uk/government/publications/children-and-young-peoples-continuing-care-national-framework.

Estroff, Sue E. 1993. 'Identity, disability, and schizophrenia: The problem of chronicity'. In *Knowledge, Power, and Practice: The anthropology of medicine and everyday life*, edited by Shirley Lindenbaum and Margaret Lock, 247–86. Berkeley: University of California Press.

Graham, Hilary. 1991. 'The concept of caring in feminist research: The case of domestic service', *Sociology* 25 (1): 61–78. https://doi.org/10.1177/0038038591025001004.

Horton, Sarah and Judith C. Barker. 2010. 'Stigmatized biologies: Examining the cumulative effects of oral health disparities for Mexican American farmworker children', *Medical Anthropology Quarterly* 24 (2): 199–219. https://doi.org/10.1111/j.1548-1387.2010.01097.x.

Janeja, Manpreet K. and Andreas Bandak, eds. 2018. *Ethnographies of Waiting: Doubt, hope and uncertainty*. London: Bloomsbury.

Kelly, Christine. 2010. 'The role of mandates/philosophies in shaping interactions between disabled people and their support providers', *Disability & Society* 25 (1): 103–19. https://doi.org/10.1080/09687590903363456.

Knight, Daniel M. and Charles Stewart. 2016. 'Ethnographies of austerity: Temporality, crisis and affect in southern Europe', *History and Anthropology* 27 (1): 1–18. https://doi.org/10.1080/02757206.2015.1114480.

Leece, Janet and Sheila Peace. 2010. 'Developing new understandings of independence and autonomy in the personalised relationship', *British Journal of Social Work* 40 (1): 847–65. https://doi.org/10.1093/bjsw/bcp105.

LGIU (Local Government Information Unit). 2012. *Policy Briefing: Welfare Reform Act 2012*. Accessed 22 July 2020. https://lgiu.org/wp-content/uploads/2012/03/Welfare-Reform-Act-20121.pdf.

Manderson, Lenore and Carolyn Smith-Morris. 2010. 'Introduction: Chronicity and the experience of illness'. In *Chronic Conditions, Fluid States: Chronicity and the anthropology of illness*, edited by Lenore Manderson and Carolyn Smith-Morris, 1–18. New Brunswick, NJ: Rutgers University Press.

Mattingly, Cheryl. 2014. *Moral Laboratories: Family peril and the struggle for a good life*. Oakland: University of California Press.

Mladenov, Teodor. 2012. 'Personal assistance for disabled people and the understanding of human being', *Critical Social Policy* 32 (2): 242–61. https://doi.org/10.1177/0261018311430454.

Petersen, Michael Bang, Rune Slothuus, Rune Stubager and Lise Togeby. 2010. 'Deservingness versus values in public opinion on welfare: The automaticity of the deservingness heuristic', *European Journal of Political Research* 50 (1): 24–52. https://doi.org/10.1111/j.1475-6765.2010.01923.x.

Shakespeare, Tom. 2014. *Disability Rights and Wrongs Revisited*, 2nd edn. London: Routledge.

Taunt, Richard, Alecia Lockwood and Natalie Berry. 2014. *More than Money: Closing the NHS quality gap*. Policy Report by the Health Foundation. Accessed 22 May 2021. https://www.health.org.uk/sites/default/files/MoreThanMoneyClosingTheNHSQualityGap.pdf.

Taylor, Charles. 1989. *Sources of the Self*. Cambridge, MA: Harvard University Press.

Thomas, Carol. 1993. 'De-constructing concepts of care', *Sociology* 27 (4): 649–69. https://doi.org/10.1177/0038038593027004006.

Ungerson, Clare. 2006. 'Care, work and feeling', *The Sociological Review* 53 (s2): 188–203. https://doi.org/10.1111/j.1467-954X.2005.00580.x.

Williams, Bernard. 1981. *Moral Luck: Philosophical papers*. Cambridge: Cambridge University Press.

Williams, Fiona. 2001. 'In and beyond New Labour: Towards a new political ethics of care', *Critical Social Policy* 21 (4): 467–93. https://doi.org/10.1177/026101830102100405.

Woodin, Sarah. 2006. 'Social relationships and disabled people: The impact of direct payments'. PhD thesis, University of Leeds, School of Sociology and Social Policy. Accessed 22 May 2021. https://disability-studies.leeds.ac.uk/wp-content/uploads/sites/40/library/woodin-FinalThesis.pdf.

Yamaki, ChikakoKimura and Yoshihiko Yamazaki. 2004. '"Instruments", "employees", "companions", "social assets": Understanding relationships between persons with disabilities and their assistants in Japan', *Disability & Society* 19 (1): 31–46. https://doi.org/10.1080/0968759032000155613.

2

(Un)Deservingness and disregard: Chronicity, hospice and possibilities for care on the American periphery

Devin Flaherty

> She stopped here today and tell me I'm n'ont get any betta.
> I wanted to cuss her so badly, but I couldn't do it. Ya know.
> I said I am going to get betta, you might not feel I'm going to
> get betta, but I know I'm going to get better. (Ms Donovan)

When Ms Donovan said this to me, we were sitting in her living room in St Croix, an island in the US Virgin Islands. It was 2016. Ms Donovan was 71 and was suffering from a number of ailments, all of which biomedicine categorises as 'chronic': chronic heart failure, hypertension (high blood pressure), high cholesterol, diabetes and sciatica. The symptoms of these various ailments came and went, entangling with each other to create changing states of discomfort, pain and disability that shaped Ms Donovan's everyday life (see Flaherty 2018a). Most days, she appeared to be a very sick woman. And yet, despite this, Ms Donovan often made claims that she was going to get better. Soon, she would often tell me, she would be herself again.

Who, then, was this 'she' who insisted to Ms Donovan that she was not, in fact, going to get any better? Who came to her house to tell her that she was, to the contrary, nearing the end of her life? This 'she' was Wanda, Ms Donovan's hospice chaplain. At this time, Ms Donovan had been a patient with one of St Croix's two home-hospice services for about five months. This moment – in which the two women butted heads about Ms Donovan's existential fate – was one of many, many instances in which Ms Donovan's claims to future health and wellbeing clashed with the vision her hospice caregivers had for her future decline and death.

This chapter is about care, disregard and (un)deservingness, and about how their entwinement shapes possibilities for, and experiences of, end of life for older adults with chronic illness in St Croix, US Virgin Islands (USVI) (see Montesi and Calestani, this volume). To date, anthropological analyses of 'deservingness' have been limited to those without a legitimised claim to legal rights. However, in St Croix, on the penumbral periphery of the nation, citizenship is contingent, and the division between rights and deservingness is blurred. As residents of an unincorporated territory of the United States, older adults in St Croix have a legal right to Medicare, the national health insurance programme that provides health care for citizens who are 65 years old and above.[1] However, there is such a dearth of health-care services on the island that older adults with chronic illness are often not able to exercise their legal right to curative care. Many in this situation turn to hospice care instead, which, since 1982, has been free for qualifying Medicare beneficiaries. This was the context that brought Ms Donovan into conflict with her hospice caregivers.

This deficient landscape of care shifts the assumed boundary between the chronic and the terminal. Meaning simply 'of time', *chronic* indicates the extended temporal duration in which some ailments exist. Their chronicity is, of course, a product of social life (see Montesi and Calestani, this volume; Manderson and Smith-Morris 2010). These ailments continue to exist through time both because they do not quickly kill the individual who is embodying them and because they are difficult (if not impossible) to cure. The naming of an ailment as 'chronic', then, assumes a particular infrastructure of care – including drugs, services and monitoring – under which some conditions perdure through extended periods of time without killing the individual or being cured. However, in a context like St Croix, where hospice attracts patients who might otherwise seek curative care,[2] the temporal expanse of so-called 'chronic' ailments can be cut short. This is a case that demonstrates, as Montesi and Calestani argue in their introduction to this volume, how state-based care shapes and complicates patterns of chronicity through the assignment of unequal 'intensities of worth'.

I argue that this is a situation created and maintained by the mutual constitution of attention/deservingness and disregard/undeservingness as it plays out in the federal governance of St Croix. This argument is founded in a theoretical claim about deservingness: that it is a relation predicated upon particular forms of attention. This is a claim in line with, but to date not mobilised by, anthropological discussions of deservingness (see Montesi and Calestani, this volume). Deservingness is not a property, a quality that exists whether or not it is noticed, but rather a relation that necessitates a noticing in order to be constituted. Because of this, disregard can lead to what I call *de facto undeservingness*: a situation in which claims to deservingness are not so much denied as they are simply not noticed. Situations of de facto undeservingness are characterised by the same kinds of inaccessibility of care and services that characterise situations of recognised undeservingness (see Montesi and Calestani, this volume). Furthermore, de facto undeservingness can characterise not just those outside the sphere of rights, but also those within it. I suggest that a primary mechanism for maintaining disregard and undeservingness in the case of St Croix is the federal Medicare bureaucracy.

In what follows, I first present a review of recent anthropological approaches to deservingness, showing that deservingness as a relation constituted by forms of attention is an implicit concept throughout. Next, I turn to a theoretical discussion of (un)deservingness, attention and disregard, outlining their interrelations. I then turn to my ethnographic analyses, demonstrating how disregard has functioned, facilitated by the Medicare bureaucracy, along three social strata to create de facto undeservingness for older adults with chronic illness living in St Croix. I show how the health-care landscape in St Croix is a product of bureaucratic disregard predicated on assumed undeservingness; how local stakeholders' interactions with particular others within the Medicare bureaucracy disclose the systematic mechanisms that maintain the disregard shaping that landscape; and how that landscape situated Ms Donovan as someone whose claims to deservingness were subject to disregard among her hospice caregivers.

This chapter is based on 14 months (2014, 2015–16) of ethnographic research in the US Virgin Islands, principally on the island of St Croix. St Croix is a rural, 82-square-mile Caribbean island situated just south-east of Puerto Rico. The island has a population of roughly fifty thousand, the majority of whom are Afro-Caribbean. My study focused on care for older adults near the end of their lives on the island (see Flaherty 2018b for a full account of research methods, sites and participants). The scope of the study included both everyday experiences and trajectories of older adults and their caregivers, and the structural forces shaping possibilities for those experiences and trajectories. There were 70 participants in the study. Participants included 12 older adults near the end of life (9 of whom were 'focal participants' with whom I engaged in intensive data collection over several months), 12 family/friend care-givers, 17 professional care providers, 19 administrators (including health-care and political), and 10 others involved in or knowledgeable about care, ageing and end of life in St Croix. Ms Donovan was one of the 9 focal older adults who participated in the study; I engaged in intensive data collection with her over 11 months.

Deserving and undeserving of care

In recent years, anthropologists and other social scientists have examined how politics of deservingness shape the possibilities for, and trajectories of, those seen as existing in some way 'outside' of hegemonic claims to citizenship, rights or belonging. Many of these studies have focused specifically on migrants, and the processes through which they either gain or fail to gain access to citizenship, services and care in the country to which they have come (Carney 2015; Duke 2017; Holmes and Castañeda 2016; Horton 2004; Marrow 2012; Willen 2015; Willen and Cook 2016; Yarris and Castañeda 2015; see also Montesi and Calestani, this volume). As Willen (2015, 75) puts it, the basic question constituting a politics of deservingness is this: 'Who is deserving of a country's attention, investment, or concern, and who is blocked from entry into the national body and body politic?'

The answer to this question in any given community, scholars have shown, is contested, ambiguous and far from straightforward. For instance, Holmes and Castañeda (2016, 13) have pointed out that while popular and political discourses in Europe around the then contemporary refugee crisis attempt to 'morally delineat[e] the deserving refugee from the undeserving migrant', such parsing is always contested, and indeed these two categories are themselves 'often blurred, adding to the confusion regarding what is actually possible legally and practically' (Holmes and Castañeda 2016, 16; see also Montesi and Calestani, this volume). It is also clear that declarations of deservingness simultaneously delineate the limits of the responsibility of the state; admitting deservingness can in some cases even betray culpability (see Duke 2017).

Willen (2012a, 2012b; Willen and Cook 2016) has introduced the concept of 'health-related deservingness' in order to specifically analyse how migrants' deservingness of access to state health care, and to social determinants of health, is reckoned at local scales. In their conceptual analysis of 'health-related deservingness', Willen and Cook (2016) argue that the concept of deservingness is importantly defined by its distinction from rights. While claims to rights are articulated in, and engaged within, the juridical sphere in which 'fundamental equality before the law' is presumed, claims to deservingness are articulated in, and engaged within, the moral sphere governed by a mix of 'subjective attitudes and presumptions with taken-for-granted truths regarded as collective "common sense"' (Willen and Cook 2016, 96).

Anthropologists writing about deservingness seem all to be in agreement that deservingness is an assessment of moral worth (see Montesi and Calestani, this volume). The logic underpinning Willen and Cook's (2016) distinction, however, is troubled by accounts of the ambiguity integral to politics of deservingness, through which it is precisely whether or not particular groups or individuals can make legitimate claims to certain kinds of rights that is at stake. Indeed, the discursive distinctions that seek to frame migrants as either deserving or undeserving of care (for example, 'refugee' versus 'migrant') serve as meta-frames for invoking or excluding particular legal (rights-based) processes (see Holmes and Castañeda 2016, 16–18). There exists a theoretical tension, then, regarding to what extent questions of deservingness are truly delineated from questions of rights, and if indeed those who can be shown to have legal rights (for instance, to health care) have truly escaped a politics of deservingness.

I suggest that the legally liminal space of St Croix, US Virgin Islands, offers a distinctive viewpoint on this tension. As the USVI is an unincorporated territory of the US, residents of St Croix have rights that are relatively dimmer and less fixed than their co-citizens living in US states. The implications of this status stem as much from the islands' colonial history as they do from contemporary modes of US governance (see Boyer 2010; Flaherty 2018b, 2021; Goldstein 2014; Rivera Ramos 2001). Purchased by the United States from Denmark in 1917, the US Virgin Islands are a '(post)colonial' (Stevenson 2014) space on the American periphery, where institutional and political legacies of colonialism – including economic scarcity, lack of political sovereignty and a grossly insufficient health-care infrastructure – are perpetuated. While anyone born in St Croix is a US citizen, this is not a birthright citizenship, but rather one that can be revoked by an act of Congress: it is a contingent citizenship. Furthermore, USVI residents do not have a right to vote for federal representation, and they do not have a right to vote for the president.

St Croix residents are thus both US citizens and also, when compared to the normative case of citizenship, not quite US citizens (a situation of, as Montesi and Calestani in this volume, p. 13, suggest, 'mak[ing] some citizens more equal than others'). While the status of unincorporated territory situates the USVI as politically peripheral (inside the nation, but only just), the islands themselves are literally not included in the continental bulk of the country (see Flaherty 2021). This peripheral, ambiguous 'included outside' status (see Hansen and Stepputat 2006; Agamben 1998) destabilises clear conceptual distinctions between inclusion and exclusion, citizenship and illegality, rights and (un)deservingness. Indeed, it is in this context that those with legal rights to certain forms of affordable health care – particularly older adults with chronic illnesses – are rendered de facto undeserving of that care through processes of disregard.

(Un)Deservingness, attention and disregard

Attention has yet to become a seminal topic in anthropology, despite exciting work on the subject among phenomenological anthropologists (see Csordas 1993; Throop 2003, 2010; Throop and Duranti 2015). However, attention is a central undergirding constituent of intersubjective processes and social life. Our habituated patterns of selective attention (see James 1954 [1890]) delineate the world that we experience. These patterns are constituted in part through the differential distribution of prominence among objects in our everyday milieu, and the ways in which certain objects – novel or mundane – affect an 'attentional pull' on us (Husserl 2001; see also Throop and Duranti 2015), while others fall into the background, unnoticed. These patterns of attention – what we can, as well as what we do, pay attention to – become embodied through normative processes of socialisation across life course development as we become competent members of our society, take on professions and learn new skills (see Duranti 2009; Goodwin 1994; Ochs and Schieffelin 1984). Indeed, Throop and Duranti (2015, 1056) have argued for 'the organization and regulation of attention as a key dimension of our cultural existence'.

In selectively distributing attention through habitual processes of foregrounding and backgrounding, socialised patterns of attention also selectively distribute disregard. Entangled with their role in co-constituting everyday practice, these patterns of attention and disregard are socioculturally embodied enactments of care, value, concern and interest. Thinking with patterns of disregard alongside patterns of attention, it is both that objects that matter are habitually foregrounded in our attention, or affect an 'attentional pull' (Husserl 2001) on us, and that objects that matter less (or do not matter at all) are habitually objects of disregard, and do not pull our attention. Considering patterns of attention and disregard can disclose existing distributions of care and other forms of mattering (see Flaherty 2018b, 2021).

Questions of (un)deservingness are predicated on questions of attention and disregard because being constituted as deserving necessitates being paid attention to in particular ways. Without the assessment or recognition of another (such as a state actor), deservingness does not come into being. This is clear when we think again of the metaframes through which claims to deservingness and undeservingness are made: 'refugee' brings to attention different characteristics and possibilities than 'illegal immigrant' (see Horton 2004; Holmes and Castañeda 2016; Yarris and Castañeda 2015). Discourses of deservingness and discourses of undeservingness vie for attention, and the outcomes of such contests turn on what kind of attention is able to be garnered for each side. Returning to Willen's (2015, 75) central question, *'Who is deserving of a country's attention,* investment, or concern, and who is blocked from entry into the national body and body politic?' (my emphasis), we can see that the politics of deservingness is itself a method for organising the selective attention of the state. Who is the state responsible for attending to, and in what way? Who can the state disregard, and to what extent?

Patterns of attention and disregard correspond to, but also function to reproduce, patterns of care, value, interest and concern. There are many people around the world whose legal rights are unsecured, but who are excluded from a politics of deservingness because their needs and status never rise to the level of public debate: they never gain attention (see Willen and Cook 2016, 96). It is those on whose lives states place the least value who are most easily subjected to disregard (Ong 1999; see Foucault 2004). This pattern is also mirrored, however, *within* citizen populations. We now re-encounter the importance of deservingness as a dynamic that can seep into the sphere of rights. The US maintains systems of what Ong (1999, 217), in analysing a different social context, has called 'variegated citizenship': 'the unequal biopolitical investment in different categories of the population [which] results in the uneven distribution of services, care and protection; while some subjects are invested with rights and resources, others are *neglected outright*' (my emphasis; see also Montesi and Calestani, this volume). Ong's wording gestures to an argument I will make explicitly: that between the US and the US Virgin Islands, a primary mode of this process of uneven distribution is disregard. Furthermore, I argue that this uneven distribution can productively be seen as de facto undeservingness.

Joining others who have positioned state bureaucracies as not only directly implicated in, but indeed productive of, suffering among those under their jurisdiction (e.g. Gupta 2012; Kleinman et al. 1997), I suggest that the US Medicare bureaucracy is a central mechanism of disregard and de facto undeservingness for older adults living in St Croix. In proposing that the Medicare bureaucracy practises and perpetuates the US state's stance of disregard vis-à-vis the USVI, I am arguing for a new perspective on how bureaucracies can act to create and maintain structural violence: by manifesting and reproducing the patterned attention of the state.

Shaping a landscape of care through disregard

The power of disregard in shaping possibilities, trajectories and experiences for older adults with chronic illness in St Croix begins with the forced dependence of Crucian residents on the federal health-care system.[3] Because the US 'owns' St Croix, possibilities for health care are defined within federal bureaucratic logics upheld by the power of law. For older adults, this manifests primarily through Medicare and its governing institution, the Centers for Medicare and Medicaid Services (CMS).[4] It is because older Crucian residents usually have no choice but to rely on Medicare for health care that the disregard integral to Medicare's bureaucratic operations in the US Virgin Islands is so significant. In this section, I discuss how modes of disregard within the regulation of Medicare services determinatively shape the health-care landscape for older adults in St Croix, leaving hospice care as one of the only possibilities for older adults with severe chronic illnesses.

Disregarded costs and the disappearance of medical equipment

When I arrived in St Croix in September 2015, a crisis was brewing. As I was new to the island, it would be months before I came to recognise it at all. The urgent situation was regarding 'durable medical equipment' (DME), and it came to be known within administrative health-care circles on the island as the 'DME crisis'. Once I caught on, and was allowed into the many meetings, phone calls and informal discussions surrounding the DME crisis, the crisis revealed itself as disclosing modes of disregard that had been shaping health care on the island for decades.

The crux of the 'crisis' was that there was no longer any Medicare-certified supplier of durable medical equipment in the USVI. 'Durable medical equipment' is the official category for a number of material items used to support those in medical need: canes, walkers and crutches are included, as are commodes, hospital beds, wheelchairs, oxygen concentrators and many other items. To have this kind of equipment covered by Medicare – that is, in order to make it affordable – it has to be purchased through a Medicare-certified supplier. Without a Medicare-certified supplier of durable medical equipment, all older adults in St Croix only had access to the medical equipment that they could afford to pay for out of their own pockets (see Flaherty 2018b, 2021). These older residents are on average very low income (older adults in St Croix are twice as likely as those living on the mainland to be living under the poverty line (US Virgin Islands Bureau of Economic Research 2015)). In practice this meant that needed medical equipment had become out of reach for many.

How did this come to be? In investigating this question, alongside health-care administrators on the island, I came to find that it was due almost entirely to the bureaucratic mechanism of Medicare reimbursement schemes. Or, I should say, to Medicare reimbursement schemes and disregard.

Medicare reimbursement schemes are designed to standardise the reimbursement that the Centers for Medicare and Medicaid Services pay out to Medicare-certified medical equipment suppliers for the provision of a given piece of equipment (see Flaherty 2021). For instance, they might indicate that for every wheelchair of a particular type provided to an individual, a durable medical equipment supplier would be reimbursed a certain number of dollars by CMS. This reimbursement scheme determines how much it is possible for a medical equipment supplier to make for each item it provides, defining the business's possibilities for profit. These reimbursement schemes, however, failed in making it possible for medical equipment suppliers in St Croix to stay in business.[5]

In my investigation into this disjuncture, I discovered that the final Medicare-certified durable medical equipment supplier in the USVI, Apex Medical Equipment ('Apex'), explicitly identified Medicare reimbursement schemes as the main reason that they could no longer offer this service in the USVI. While I learned about this in part through ethnographic interviews with Apex employees, the company also created and circulated a document that outlined the crux of the problem: Medicare reimbursement schemes did not account for the expenses integral to providing medical equipment to a small island over 1,100 miles from the continent. These costs included the costs of transporting equipment from the mainland to the territory (freight costs, a 4 per cent excise tax and a 6 per cent duty on foreign-made goods), and those of transporting it between the territory's three main inhabited islands (including barge fees, freight fees and labour costs for the 'extra' work of coordinating deliveries between ports). It was these costs that it had become impossible for Apex to afford (see Flaherty 2021).

As a bureaucratic instrument Medicare's reimbursement schemes regulating the sale and distribution of durable medical equipment are based on an implicitly continental model. All of the costs that were left out of Medicare's reimbursement calculations were directly connected to the US Virgin Islands' geopolitical status as islands with the status of unincorporated territory (see Flaherty 2021). This accounts not only for the excise and duty taxes (which do not apply to US states), but also for the fact that none of these costs were considered when calculating the appropriate reimbursement rates for the territory. Apex's document, and the company's subsequent giving up of its Medicare certification, points directly to the role of disregard in US–USVI governance.

Without Apex as a supplier of Medicare-certified durable medical equipment, many older adults in St Croix were left with a choice: they could go without, living as long as they could without the material support that their chronic illnesses called for; or they could – if sick enough – sign on to a service that provided any medical equipment they needed free of charge. This service was Medicare-certified home-hospice care. Unlike medical equipment provision, Medicare's reimbursement schemes did make it possible for for-profit hospice services to stay in business in the territory (see Flaherty 2018b). And because medical equipment is an integral component of the palliative care that hospices deliver, eligible older adults could exercise their right to Medicare-certified hospice care as a way of obtaining access to the medical equipment they could otherwise not afford.

I do not suggest that this consequence, essentially a funnelling of older adults with chronic illness into hospice care, was malevolently planned (see Gupta 2012). Rather, it is a consequence generated by disregard: the USVI does not attract legislators' attention in the creation and maintenance of Medicare policy; when the policy is practised (through the bureaucracy), seemingly haphazard situations result. I do suggest, however, that this disregard itself was enabled, and is maintained, through background assessments of undeservingness. As I suggested earlier, I frame deservingness as a social relation that can only come into being through particular forms of attention, and as one that defines bonds of responsibility. Seen as poor, black and culturally other, the residents of the USVI are barely 'seen' at all at the level of federal governance (see Boyer 2010; Flaherty 2018b; Goldstein 2014; Rivera Ramos 2001). Ideologies of race, otherness and nationalism shape the selective attention of those in power. In the shadow of disregard, St Croix residents remain legally 'deserving', but de facto undeserving: with rights on the books, but in circumstances, shaped through disregard, that foreclose the possibility of exercising them. We might say that it is their right to chronicity – their right to live in an ongoing way with chronic illness, enabled by supportive medical equipment – that is being foreclosed.

Claims to deservingness and bureaucratic mechanisms of disregard

As the months went by, and the DME crisis wore on, health-care providers and administrators in St Croix were increasingly concerned – some were even panicked – about the unavailability of affordable medical equipment on the island. A large part of this distress came from growing numbers of patients that they had cared for, or that they had heard about from colleagues, whose lives were being severely impacted – and sometimes even cut short – by the unavailability of affordable medical equipment. For instance, around this time, a story was being circulated among health-care professionals about an older man who had come to the hospital with extremely low blood oxygen levels (see Flaherty 2021). His chronic health condition required that he be on continuous concentrated oxygen (requiring durable medical equipment), but when he arrived, he had been off it for some time. While his family had managed to afford the required equipment for a while, the oxygen had eventually run out and they could not afford more. The man's blood oxygen was so low when he arrived at the hospital that before they were able to hook him up to oxygen, he died.

Stories like these were making health-care professionals on the island ready to fight for change. However, interactions with the Medicare bureaucracy demonstrated how hard it is to elicit change while being subject to sustained and systemic disregard. Indeed, the disregard integral to the Medicare bureaucracy's governance of the US Virgin Islands was disclosed as much in the fight to stop the DME crisis as it was in the creation of the crisis itself.

In this section, I explore some of the bureaucratic infrastructure enabling the disregard central to the maintenance of a deficient health-care landscape in St Croix (see Flaherty 2021). The central locus for the effort to make Medicare-certified medical equipment available again in the USVI came from a task force made up of health-care providers and health-care administrators, which had been formed in response to the DME crisis.[6] Through my inclusion in the DME task force, I observed and participated in conversations between local health-care professionals and branches of Medicare involved in the certification of durable medical equipment suppliers and the provision of durable medical equipment more broadly. In discussing particular interactions between this task force and these branches of Medicare, I demonstrate how disregard is manifest through the systematic drawing away of the attention of Medicare bureaucrats from the realities on the ground in the USVI (see Flaherty 2021). Discussing three examples of the task force's encounters with different branches of the Medicare bureaucracy, I explore two mechanisms of disregard: illegibility and inaudibility. Seeing these mechanisms in action shows not just how disregard is perpetuated through bureaucratic means, but also how it is maintained *despite* requests for attention and claims to deservingness.

Durable medical equipment 'within reach'

The first disclosure of mechanisms of disregard in the task force's interactions with the Medicare bureaucracy emerged from conversations with representatives of the branch of Medicare in charge of provider customer service (see Flaherty 2021). This is the branch which doctors' offices (or other 'providers') are supposed to contact if they have a concern about Medicare. However, while this was presumably the most appropriate branch of Medicare for the task force – a group of health-care providers (and one anthropologist) – to be contacting with their concerns, the group encountered an immediate obstacle. While the basis of the task force's existence was the absence of any Medicare-certified medical equipment supplier in the USVI, the representatives of this branch of Medicare saw a different picture. This was due to the method on which this branch of Medicare relied to survey and assess the distribution of durable medical equipment suppliers in a given area: the online 'provider search' tool on the medicare.gov website (see Flaherty 2021). This tool allows users (including Medicare bureaucrats) to search for Medicare-certified durable medical equipment suppliers within a given geographical area. Using this tool, representatives of this branch of Medicare saw that there were several suppliers of durable medical equipment within what they assumed was a reasonable radius of the USVI's capital. Without direct local knowledge of the USVI, however, what these Medicare representatives were missing were the implications of those suppliers all being on the neighbouring, much larger island of Puerto Rico. Although the task force had previously researched the possibility of getting durable medical equipment from Medicare-certified suppliers in Puerto

Rico, they had learned that this was impossible. This was in part due to Medicare regulations: there is a required time frame with which durable medical equipment suppliers must comply when performing repairs on patients' equipment – one that would be very difficult to meet if travelling between Puerto Rico and the USVI. It was also due in part to the (non-reimbursable) costs and logistical difficulties of setting up regular shipments of durable medical equipment between Puerto Rico and the USVI, which existing suppliers were not interested in taking on. These obstacles to obtaining durable medical equipment from suppliers in Puerto Rico were not within the purview of this branch of Medicare. Through the tool at their disposal, these Medicare representatives had no way of systematically tracking what the actual availability of durable medical equipment was in the USVI. This limited view made it very difficult for them to pay attention to the DME crisis, and much easier to disregard it.

Snowbirds

The next disclosure of illegibility as a mechanism of disregard within the Medicare bureaucracy came in the task force's conversations with representatives of another branch of Medicare involved in durable medical equipment provision (see Flaherty 2021). This branch was responsible for processing all of Medicare's durable medical equipment 'claims' for the region, which get submitted as documentation by DME suppliers in order to request reimbursement when they provide a patient with medical equipment. In these conversations too, members of the task force were struggling to make clear that Medicare-certified durable medical equipment was truly unavailable in the USVI. This was in large part because the records of this branch of Medicare showed them several recent durable medical equipment claims filed by suppliers in the mainland US for sales of equipment to patients with USVI addresses. So, while these Medicare representatives understood that there was not as much availability of durable medical equipment as would be ideal in terms of serving the local population, our claims of crisis – of urgent, life-threatening emergency – did not seem believable to them.

On one conference call in particular, a group of task force members and a handful of Medicare representatives went in circles around this issue, each group trying to convince the other of their version of reality (see Flaherty 2021). While members of the task force (myself included) insisted that there was no way for residents of the USVI to access Medicare-certified durable medical equipment in the territory, the Medicare representatives assured us that some USVI residents did in fact have access to such equipment (since they had the claims to prove it). Eventually, the Medicare representatives began expressing some openness to considering that perhaps it was possible that durable medical equipment was somehow not available to residents of the USVI, despite what their records showed. Then, finally, one of the Medicare representatives offered a scenario that would explain this disjuncture: she suggested that the USVI addresses shown on the claims might not be the primary residential addresses of the patients in question. In that case, these patients might be living most of the year in the mainland US. Indeed, she was right. While the Medicare representatives had been assuming that these claims showed USVI residents accessing durable medical equipment, this was not in fact the case. Instead, patients with multiple homes (likely wealthy retirees) were using durable medical equipment on the mainland, but it was their USVI addresses that were showing up on DME claims.

It turned out that the mobility of elite, temporary island residents – often called 'snowbirds' because they winter in the territory's tropical islands – was blocking the ability of the Medicare bureaucracy to see the realities faced by full-time USVI residents. The information listed on the durable medical equipment claims – which did not enable the distinction between snowbird and full-time island resident – was the only bureaucratic lens through which representatives from this branch of Medicare could see DME accessibility and distribution. This lens obscured the DME crisis from their view, foreclosing possibilities for them to pay attention to it.

'The only way to be heard': Inaudibility and absent complaints

The final example that I will discuss of a mechanism of disregard is one not of illegibility, but of inaudibility. One of the branches of the Medicare bureaucracy with which the task force worked most regularly was what can most simply be called the 'customer service' branch. This branch was in charge of receiving and documenting complaints from Medicare beneficiaries (patients) themselves. Throughout my participation with the task force, the perspective and role of their 'customer service' representatives was made very clear: they were there to try to support an increase in patient complaints, and to monitor and relay progress in the numbers of patient complaints to the task force. While in some ways it might seem odd that a company in charge of customer service would be trying to rustle up more patient complaints, it was clear to them that the only way to have documentation of the DME crisis was for patients to make official complaints through the Medicare helpline. As far as they were concerned, if there were not enough documented complaints, then there was no evidence that there was actually a problem.

This branch of Medicare passed this logic on to the task force, who enthusiastically took up the project of trying to increase patient complaints. Flyers were produced and handed out at every meeting, and health-care providers were encouraged repeatedly to direct their patients to call the helpline and file an official complaint. This was a project that discursively aligned with pre-existing tropes of voicelessness among older adults in the local health-care sphere. Indeed, it was very common to hear among health-care providers or administrators, or local leaders, that St Croix's seniors 'suffer in silence', or that they 'do not have a voice' (Flaherty 2018b). This discourse was echoed in the reminders from the representatives of this Medicare branch to the task force about the importance of educating patients about their right to complain to Medicare: 'It's the only way to be heard,' they would say.

However, despite the blanketing of the helpline message to health-care providers, the number of complaint calls remained extremely low. On one task force conference call, a representative of the 'customer service' branch reported on the recent numbers. She said that there had been a definite 'upswing' in calls to the helpline, with four calls in the last month, compared to six calls in the previous 18 months. She made it clear, however, that four calls did not make a crisis, and that a lot more complaints would be needed from patients in order for them to be 'heard'.

Unlike the other bureaucratic mechanisms of illegibility that I have discussed here, this constructed inaudibility places the blame for not being heard directly on older USVI residents themselves. The Medicare bureaucracy itself is entirely naturalised here: in this logic, it is not that the bureaucracy has muted the interests of USVI residents, but rather that USVI residents are making *themselves* inaudible by not registering their complaints in the correct fashion (Flaherty 2018b). The perduring disregard maintained by this stance of unhearing is positioned as the fault of the disregarded themselves.

I have presented these three engagements between the DME task force and branches of the Medicare bureaucracy in order to demonstrate some of the ways in which disregard for the USVI is built into Medicare's contemporary bureaucratic operations, and thus into federal governance. In each of these examples, the task force's claims to deservingness, made on behalf of those in the territory in need of medical equipment, met a different aspect of bureaucratic disregard. Through this systematised disregard, older adults with chronic illness in St Croix end up in circumstances of de facto undeservingness, with unequal access to state-sponsored care, such as affordable medical equipment, which would help support the continuing temporal expanse of their lives.

It is this continuance, this enduring survival, that is the precondition for chronicity. What happens to the chronicity of 'chronic' ailments when the normative supportive care for their continuance is absent? In this next section, I return to Ms Donovan. I present her case as one response to this question, and as an exploration of interpersonal disregard and claims to deservingness in a context in which hospice represents the only chance at long-term ('chronic') care.

Ms Donovan

Of all the older adults in my study who signed up for hospice care in St Croix, none of them did so out of a readiness to die, an acceptance of death or a desire to halt curative treatment. This included Ms Donovan, a focal older adult in my study.

Ms Donovan was an Afro-Crucian woman who had lived most of her life in St Croix. While she had a large family that was spread out throughout the USVI and the rest of the country, she was relatively estranged from most of them (including her only child), and she did not have any regular family visitors during her illness. Ms Donovan had held several jobs in the territorial government,[7] primarily as the assistant principal at a public school. This meant that in her retirement, she received regular payments through the Government Employees' Retirement System (GERS), income supplemented by her monthly Social Security cheques. While Ms Donovan was in a better financial position than many other participants in my research, she did not have any savings, and she was living from pay cheque to pay cheque. She lived by herself in the house in which she had grown up (which was currently owned by one of her siblings). The house was not fully furnished, it was breaking down in some areas, and Ms Donovan did not keep it up.

As for many older adults in St Croix, Ms Donovan's trajectory was shaped by St Croix's deeply deficient health-care landscape. The absence of Medicare-certified durable medical equipment suppliers, on which I have focused here, is one very important example of these deficits, but there are several others. At the time of my fieldwork, there was no home-nursing service on the island, only one very small nursing home and extremely restricted opportunities for 'assisted living'. For Ms Donovan, as for many other older adults with chronic conditions, hospice was her only option for daily professional care.

While Ms Donovan had a number of 'chronic' ailments, as a hospice patient she was, like all hospice patients, treated as if her condition were terminal. While her care included efforts to help stabilise her condition, such as the provision of pharmaceutical drugs to lower her blood pressure, and continual encouragement from her nurses to check her blood sugar regularly, she was not seen as someone who needed to be healthy enough to keep on living, or who deserved the kind of heroic care that biomedicine famously employs to save lives (see Chapple 2010; Kaufman 2005). Once she became a hospice patient, the health-care landscape whose deficiencies drew her to that form of care was disregarded by her caregivers.

For her part, Ms Donovan staked many claims to her deservingness of care that would support her continuing to live with her chronic conditions. In addition to Medicare, she maintained her membership with two other health insurance plans (one which she paid for out of her pocket, and one which was included as part of her government retirement package). She did this so that whatever care she wanted or needed – whether or not it was covered by Medicare – would be accessible to her.[8] As a hospice patient, she often insisted upon extra nursing visits, beyond the number of visits inscribed in her care plan – beyond the number of visits that her hospice caregivers had decided was appropriate, given her level of need. If something felt wrong, or if she was worried about one of her symptoms, she never wanted to wait until her next scheduled visit, instead calling on a nurse to come to her house as soon as possible to do a checkup. She also frequently asserted her need for more medical supplies than the hospice was providing her, telling her hospice nurses that they needed to bring more than it had been determined she needed. This happened especially with 'bed pads', the large absorbent pads that Ms Donovan placed across every surface she might sit or lie down on in her house, as a way of managing her chronic urinary incontinence. In these ways, Ms Donovan made claims to care that surpassed what hospice was offering her. She was, through these actions, claiming her deservingness of more care – care that was actively supporting her life – instead of simply keeping her comfortable until death.[9]

These active claims to 'extra' care became, for Ms Donovan's hospice caregivers, paradigmatic of who Ms Donovan was as a patient. It was well known among the small hospice staff that Ms Donovan was, as was at times noted in hospice visit logs, 'demanding'. They saw her as asking for more than was owed her, more than hospice was supposed to be providing. And because it was their job to respond, in some way or another, to her claims to more care, it wore on them, making them often annoyed and sometimes even fed up. These attitudes are the result, I suggest, of the way her hospice caregivers' attention toward their patients was organised: because they saw Ms Donovan as a dying woman who had chosen hospice care, her 'demands' felt excessive, even ridiculous. This was the view of her that was reinforced by daily engagements with, and responsibility to, the Medicare bureaucracy. Medicare hospice guidelines regulate every aspect of patient visits, and caregivers document care according to Medicare procedures using hospice-specific software. This view was also reinforced by the shared discourse between hospice team members, and the informal training and socialisation they received from the more experienced members of the care team. The scope of their attention was co-constituted through their everyday engagements in these and other practices; together, their habitual attention and everyday practices reinforced each other in affirming the boundaries of hospice care and the boundaries of what, as a patient who had 'chosen' hospice, Ms Donovan deserved. What this left out – what their attention was not drawn toward – was the deficient landscape of care that had brought Ms Donovan to hospice in the first place. Their attention was not drawn to the aspects of Ms Donovan's situation that showed her to be a woman attempting to live with chronic conditions, but rather to those that showed her to be a woman whose chronicity was quickly coming to a close.

Conclusion

This chapter has focused on three distinct, but ethnographically interwoven, arguments about (un)deservingness. The first is that deservingness, as a politics, a discourse and a conceptual tool, is not restricted to those without claims to rights. While 'deservingness' has generally been used, among anthropologists, to explore the politics of inclusion of those in some way outside hegemonic modes of citizenship, rights or belonging (such as undocumented migrants), I have argued that evaluations of, and claims to, deservingness can occur within the sphere of those with legal rights to the services or care in question (see Montesi and Calestani, this volume). The second argument is based in a characterisation of deservingness as a relation constituted by forms of attention. With this as a conceptual starting point, I have suggested that situations of de facto undeservingness – in which deservingness is neither granted nor denied, but, rather, ignored, recreating the situation of the undeserving – are constituted through disregard. Finally, I have argued that the de facto undeservingness characterising the health-care landscape in St Croix, constituted through modes of disregard on the part of the federal government (specifically the bureaucracy of the Centers for Medicare and Medicaid Services) shapes the experiences, possibilities and trajectories of older adults with chronic illness on the island.

As a product of social life, chronicity can be created, and it can also be cut short (see Montesi and Calestani, this volume; see also Manderson and Smith-Morris 2010). For those on the geopolitical periphery of the nation, the de facto undeservingness constituted through disregard not only denies equal access to care and services, but also to chronicity itself.

Notes

1. Medicare is an extremely complex programme whose intricacies are outside the scope of this chapter. What is important here is that Medicare is close to universally available to US citizens who are 65 years old and above residing in the USVI.
2. It is important to point out that there are specific eligibility criteria that must be met in order to receive hospice care. These criteria relate to the severity of illness and overall ill health. However, in my experience, older adults in St Croix with chronic conditions, who had reached a point where they needed daily professional care, almost always qualified.
3. For an extended version of the argument presented in this section and in 'Claims to deservingness and bureaucratic mechanisms of disregard', see Flaherty 2018b; see also Flaherty 2021.
4. In what follows, I often use the somewhat less precise 'Medicare' instead of 'CMS' or 'the Centers for Medicare and Medicaid Services' for purposes of readability.
5. See Flaherty 2021 and Flaherty 2018b for more detailed explanations of how and why all durable medical equipment suppliers in the USVI went out of business at this time.
6. The genesis of this task force was complex: while composed mainly of local health-care professionals, it was organised and facilitated by the Quality Improvement branch of Medicare itself. This was a quality improvement company that Medicare had contracted to serve this role within the organisation. What I refer to as the 'branches' of Medicare that the task force engaged with were similarly companies that Medicare had contracted to fulfil specific organisational roles. A full discussion of this arrangement is outside the scope of this chapter (but see Flaherty 2018b).
7. At the time of my fieldwork (2014, 2015–16), the most recent data showed that approximately 28 per cent of employed residents of the USVI worked for the territorial government (US Virgin Islands Bureau of Economic Research 2015).
8. It is notable that even despite Ms Donovan's coverage by these multiple health insurance plans, she had no choice other than hospice for daily professional care (because nothing else was available in St Croix). As I mention earlier, for most older adults in St Croix, Medicare is their only option for affordable health care, forcing reliance on a programme that then fails to fully serve them.
9. It is worth noting that this kind of behaviour was very exceptional among hospice patients in St Croix. This is one of the reasons that it was so bothersome for hospice staff, as it was not what they had come to expect from their patients.

References

Agamben, Giorgio. 1998. *Homo Sacer: Sovereign power and bare life.* Stanford, CA: Stanford University Press.

Boyer, William W. 2010. *America's Virgin Islands: A history of human rights and wrongs.* Durham, NC: Carolina Academic Press.

Carney, Megan A. 2015. 'Eating and feeding at the margins of the state: Barriers to health care and undocumented women and the "clinical" aspects of food assistance', *Medical Anthropology Quarterly* 29 (2): 196–215. https://doi.org/10.1111/maq.12151.

Chapple, Helen Stanton. 2010. *No Place for Dying: Hospitals and the ideology of rescue*. Walnut Creek, CA: Left Coast Press.

Csordas, Thomas. 1993. 'Somatic modes of attention', *Cultural Anthropology* 8 (2): 135–56. https://doi.org/10.1525/can.1993.8.2.02a00010.

Duke, Michael R. 2017. 'Neocolonialism and health care access among Marshall Islanders in the United States', *Medical Anthropology Quarterly* 31 (3): 422–39. https://doi.org/10.1111/maq.12376.

Duranti, Alessandro. 2009. 'The relevance of Husserl's theory to language socialization', *Journal of Linguistic Anthropology* 19 (2): 205–26. https://doi.org/10.1111/j.1548-1395.2009.01031.x.

Flaherty, Devin. 2018a. 'Between living well and dying well: Existential ambivalence and keeping promises alive', *Death Studies* 42 (5): 314–21. https://doi.org/10.1080/07481187.2017.1396643.

Flaherty, Devin. 2018b. 'Growing old alone: Disregard, care and end of life in St Croix, US Virgin Islands'. PhD dissertation, Department of Anthropology, University of California, Los Angeles.

Flaherty, Devin. 2021. 'Extraterritoriality at the end of life: Disregard and the exceptional in St Croix, US Virgin Islands', *Culture, Theory and Critique*. https://doi.org/10.1080/14735784.2021.1918012.

Foucault, Michel. 2004. *The Birth of Biopolitics: Lectures at the Collège de France 1978–1979*, edited by Michel Senellart, translated by Graham Burchell. New York: Picador.

Goldstein, Aloysha. 2014. 'Introduction: Toward a genealogy of the US colonial present'. In *Formations of United States Colonialism*, edited by Alyosha Goldstein, 1–32. Durham, NC: Duke University Press.

Goodwin, Charles. 1994. 'Professional vision', *American Anthropologist* 96 (3): 606–33. https://doi.org/10.1525/aa.1994.96.3.02a00100.

Gupta, Akhil. 2012. *Red Tape: Bureaucracy, structural violence, and poverty in India*. Durham, NC: Duke University Press.

Hansen, Thomas Blom and Finn Stepputat. 2006. 'Sovereignty revisited', *Annual Review of Anthropology* 35: 295–315. https://doi.org/10.1146/annurev.anthro.35.081705.123317.

Holmes, Seth M. and Heide Castañeda. 2016. 'Representing the "European refugee crisis" in Germany and beyond: Deservingness and difference, life and death', *American Ethnologist* 43 (1): 12–24. https://doi.org/10.1111/amet.12259.

Horton, Sarah. 2004. 'Different subjects: The health care system's participation in the differential construction of the cultural citizenship of Cuban refugees and Mexican immigrants', *Medical Anthropology Quarterly* 18 (4): 472–89. https://doi.org/10.1525/maq.2004.18.4.472.

Husserl, Edmund. 2001. *Analysis Concerning the Active and Passive Synthesis*. Translated by Anthony J. Steinbock. Dordrecht: Kluwer.

James, William. 1954 [1890]. *The Principles of Psychology*. Edited by Robert Maynard Hutchins. Chicago: Encyclopaedia Britannica.

Kaufman, Sharon R. 2005. *… And a Time to Die: How American hospitals shape the end of life*. Chicago: University of Chicago Press.

Kleinman, Arthur, Veena Das and Margaret Lock, eds. 1997. *Social Suffering*. Berkeley: University of California Press.

Manderson, Lenore and Carolyn Smith-Morris. 2010. 'Introduction: Chronicity and the experience of illness'. In *Chronic Conditions, Fluid States: Chronicity and the anthropology of illness*, edited by Lenore Manderson and Carolyn Smith-Morris, 1–20. New Brunswick, NJ: Rutgers University Press.

Marrow, Helen B. 2012. 'Deserving to a point: Undocumented immigrants in San Francisco's universal access healthcare model', *Social Science and Medicine* 74 (6): 846–54. https://doi.org/10.1016/j.socscimed.2011.08.001.

Ochs, Elinor and Bambi Schieffelin. 1984. 'Language acquisition and socialization: Three developmental stories'. In *Culture Theory: Essays in mind, self, and emotion*, edited by Richard A. Shweder and Robert A. LeVine, 276–320. Cambridge: Cambridge University Press.

Ong, Aihwa. 1999. *Flexible Citizenship: The cultural logics of transnationality*. Durham, NC: Duke University Press.

Rivera Ramos, Efrén. 2001. 'Deconstructing colonialism: The "unincorporated territory" as a category of domination'. In *Foreign in a Domestic Sense: Puerto Rico, American expansion and the constitution*, edited by Christina Duffy Burnett and Burke Marshall, 104–17. Durham, NC: Duke University Press.

Stevenson, Lisa. 2014. *Life Beside Itself: Imagining care in the Canadian Arctic*. Berkeley: University of California Press.

Throop, C. Jason. 2003. 'Articulating experience', *Anthropological Theory* 3 (2): 219–41. https://doi.org/10.1177/1463499603003002006.

Throop, C. Jason. 2010. *Suffering and Sentiment: Exploring the vicissitudes of experience and pain in Yap*. Berkeley: University of California Press.

Throop, C. Jason and Alessandro Duranti. 2015. 'Attention, ritual glitches, and attentional pull: The president and the queen', *Phenomenology and the Cognitive Sciences* 14: 1055–82. https://doi.org/10.1007/s11097-014-9397-4.

US Virgin Islands Bureau of Economic Research. 2015. *The United States Virgin Islands 2015: Comprehensive economic development strategy*. Accessed 25 May 2021. http://www.usviber.org/wp-content/uploads/2017/03/CEDS-Plan-2015.pdf.

Willen, Sarah S. 2012a. 'How is health-related "deservingness" reckoned? Perspectives from unauthorized im/migrants in Tel Aviv', *Social Science and Medicine* 74 (6): 812–21. https://doi.org/10.1016/j.socscimed.2011.06.033.

Willen, Sarah S. 2012b. 'Special issue introduction: Migration, "illegality", and health: Mapping embodied vulnerability and debating health-related deservingness', *Social Science and Medicine* 74 (6): 805–948. https://doi.org/10.1016/j.socscimed.2011.10.041.

Willen, Sarah S. 2015. 'Lightning rods in the moral economy: Debating unauthorized migrants' deservingness in Israel', *International Migration* 53 (3): 70–86. https://doi.org/10.1111/imig.12173.

Willen, Sarah S. and Jennifer Cook. 2016. 'Migration and health-related deservingness'. In *Handbook of Migration and Health*, edited by Felicity Thomas, 95–119. Northampton, MA: Edward Elgar.

Yarris, Kristin and Heide Castañeda, eds. 2015. 'Special issue: Discourses of displacement and deservingness: Interrogating distinctions between "economic" and "forced" migration: Introduction', *International Migration* 53 (3): 64–123. https://doi.org/10.1111/imig.12170.

3

Publicly privatised: Relative care support and the neoliberal reform in Finland

Erika Takahashi

Introduction

Thinking about care brings up various inherent dichotomies, such as home versus institutional care (Shield 1988), informal versus professional care (Kemp et al. 2013) and private versus public care (Horton et al. 2014). While the precise framing of the care issue varies according to the context, public debate usually positions one type of care as superior to the opposed types because 'it [care] evokes the *goods* and *bads* that are at stake in care practices' (Mol et al. 2010, 11).

As extensively discussed in the introduction to this volume, the politics of deservingness often uses such dichotomisation to legitimise a certain category of people as designated caregivers. As Thelen and Coe (2017, 280) point out, 'all forms of care have the potential to create political belongings'. This 'boundary work' (Thelen et al. 2018, 11) aspect of care establishes divisions between people, organisations and institutions, as care is inevitably related to a political-economic structure, which introduces various political connotations into caregiving/care-receiving relationships. By activating these boundaries, the politics of deservingness 'determines whether a care relationship is morally acceptable or not' (Montesi and Calestani, this volume, 11).

Nonetheless, it is important to be aware that these normative dichotomies of care are not stable, especially when it comes to care systems in transition, because the boundary-drawing process is not consistent in practice. For example, a reform of a care system is generally thought to entail a shift in focus between two opposing ideologies, such as the construction of a welfare state versus the privatisation of the care system. If a government changes its policy to allow private firms to perform public care services, the care system is regarded as having been privatised. However, the ideologies behind public and private care are not always mutually exclusive. For example, scholars have shown that public morality becomes more pronounced when public health care is privatised (Abadía-Barrero 2015; Ellison 2014). Therefore, the neoliberal reforms of care systems should be described not as simple transitions within the care dichotomy from a citizenship-based ideology to consumerism, but as a redrawing of this ideological boundary.

Given that care systems in transition involve redrawing the boundaries of care dichotomies, the politics of care are more complex than simply swinging from one side of a dichotomy to the other. Even though policy reforms involve 'distributed intensities of worth', as Montesi and Calestani (this volume, 13), drawing on Moreno Figueroa (2010), contend, the line between citizens who are said to deserve public health care and those who supposedly do not is constantly redrawn based on changing ideologies. The inequalities caused by policy reforms need to be redressed at least to some extent, especially in strong welfare states. Therefore, the new boundary instituted by the politics of deservingness becomes even more intricate.

For example, the 'social-democratic welfare regime' (Esping-Andersen 1990), also known as the Nordic Welfare State, was supposed to guarantee the equality of citizens via public care services. In Finland, the state has been responsible for caring for senior citizens since the 1970s, which is typical of said regime. However, since the beginning of the twenty-first century, Finland's care system has undergone various changes, provoked by the fear of the financial impact that an ageing population would have on the social security system. Most interestingly, the Finnish state has started promoting informal care to ease the burden placed on the public care system by the ageing population. This policy is called 'relative care support' (*omaishoidontuki* in Finnish and *närståendevård* in Swedish).[1]

The promotion of relative care is neither a simple abdication of public responsibility by the welfare state nor an increase in senior citizens' inequality, as Finnish relative care support entails economic assistance and the right to respite for those certified as relative caregivers. This Finnish policy is particularly intriguing considering that anthropological studies on intergenerational relationships have generally characterised support within extended families as supplementing the deficiencies of the public care sector (Cruz-Saco and Zelenev 2010). According to these studies, informal care is distinct from state-sponsored care. However, in Finland, informal care takes place in collaboration with public eldercare services. So, to what extent is relative care a public matter? Which parts of informal care have remained private?

To answer these questions, I analyse the dichotomies associated with care, and explore the boundaries between the various dichotomous elements, by providing an ethnographic account of Finland's relative care practice for older adults. Since ageing is a chronic experience that requires constant 'tinkering' (Mol et al. 2010), eldercare would be an ideal example to observe how the chronicity of care interferes with the volatile boundary of dichotomies. By describing what kinds of practices set informal caregivers apart from ordinary relatives, and how the local governments decide who does and does not deserve to be a relative caregiver, I elucidate the newly established boundary of care.

The data are based on the ethnographic fieldwork that I have conducted from 2001 to the present in a municipality called 'Archipelago Town' in south-western Finland. As the pseudonym indicates, this municipality consists of thousands of small islands. Archipelago Town, with a population of approximately fifteen thousand, has provided sufficient institutional and home-based care to its citizens for decades. Its suburban-rural location and the close-knit nature of the community make Archipelago Town an ideal location for observing the emergence of informal care. Despite its geographical disadvantages, Archipelago Town's public care system has managed to provide care services even to remote areas. In a privatised care regime, people with geographical disadvantages can easily be dismissed as unprofitable. For example, in Chapter 2 of this volume, Flaherty describes a bureaucratic process that systematically ignored the fact that the ageing population of the US Virgin Islands was denied fair access to eldercare services. In Archipelago Town, the rise of relative care is also connected to diminishing public care in remote areas. By describing how the meanings of kin and paying for their care intersect in the context of relative care support in a small municipality, this chapter shows that the various domains that are normally considered to be dichotomous, such as informal/formal, private/public and professional/amateur, do, in fact, crisscross and interconnect in actual care practices.

The ethnographic description is based on fieldwork data from Archipelago Town. During the initial 18 months of intensive fieldwork between 2001 and 2003, I focused on developing a comprehensive understanding of the local eldercare system and its links with the collective experiences of ageing. At the same time, the municipality was facing increasing pressure to cut its social services and health-care budget after Finland's social welfare policy took a neoliberal turn. During the subsequent research period, which has lasted until the present time, I have carried out short-term fieldwork every year, for a total of 16 months, and shifted my research focus towards the reform of social care organisations, including relative care support, to understand the changing practices of eldercare in Archipelago Town. I have conducted interviews with senior citizens, relative caregivers and municipal employees ranging from administrators to care workers. I have also attended relative care support groups organised by non-governmental organisations (NGOs), observed respite care visits and attended municipal meetings. During this long-term research, I have had the opportunity to observe how the various national eldercare policies have been implemented and used locally. In particular, the implementation of relative care in Archipelago Town has unequivocally changed the definition and function of personal relationships and relatives in the time of privatised care.

Two facets of privatisation in the care system

Since the beginning of the twenty-first century, the municipality of Archipelago Town has promoted informal care practices. This promotion is based on the Act on Support for Informal Care (937/2005 *Laki omaishoidon tuesta*)[2] of 2005, which urged Finnish municipalities to encourage relatives to take care of their family members by providing caregivers with municipal support. Before the enactment of this law, relative care was not a prominent practice in Finland, as the government had assumed the responsibility for looking after senior citizens.

The Finnish welfare state's active role in promoting relative care practices is associated with a certain household structure in which families play a passive role when it comes to eldercare. In this household structure, it is common for children to live separately from their parents, with more than half of the population aged over 65 years living alone (Official Statistics of Finland 2018). Single-person household-dwelling units comprised 41 per cent of the total units in 2016. According to a United Nations report, this was the highest percentage among the 124 participant countries (United Nations, Department of Economic and Social Affairs, Population Division 2017). Although most of those living in single-person household-dwelling units are middle-aged, one-third of all single-person household-dwelling units are occupied by people aged over

65 (Official Statistics of Finland 2018). Besides the abundance of single-person household-dwelling units, the high rates of cohabitation (23.3 per cent) and divorce (40 per cent of marriages end in divorce) also affect the diversification of Finnish families (Suomen Virallinen Tilasto 2016).

These statistics indicate that Finland has undergone the 'individual-isation of families' (Beck and Beck-Gernsheim 2002). This concept refers to the weakening cohesion of families and the social welfare system taking over certain traditional functions of the family, such as eldercare. In fact, as a social-democratic welfare state, Finland has provided sufficient care to those who have needed it since the 1960s, based on the principle of universalism (Kettunen 1997). In Archipelago Town, the municipality has been the primary provider of eldercare for decades.

So, why has there been an attempt to reappraise informal care in Finland in the twenty-first-century Nordic welfare state? The main force behind this movement is the growing concern over the country's ageing population. It has become common for people to see the ageing popula-tion 'as a threat to the future capacity of the Finnish welfare state to pro-duce public services' (Henriksson and Wrede 2008, 125). The pressure to cut eldercare service costs has been further justified by invoking care recipients' right to choose.

The 2012 Act on Supporting the Functional Capacity of the Older Population and on Social and Health Services for Older Persons (980/ 2012 *Laki ikääntyneen väestön toimintakyvyn tukemisesta sekä iäkkäiden sosiaali- ja terveyspalveluista*) of 2012, also known as the 'Senior Service Act', declared that an organisational reform of the public service sec-tor was required to establish customer-oriented care. This Act requires municipalities to investigate older persons' service needs and provide services to meet those needs. According to Henriksson and Wrede (2008, 123), the key goal of neoliberal reform in Finland was to intro-duce 'more open competition' within the structure of 'a welfare mix, in which the public sector has the dominating responsibility for financing and control, while both private and public producers supply services'. Since the introduction of the Senior Service Act, Finnish munici-palities have purchased more private sector services than ever before (Tynkkynen et al. 2013).

This focus on customer-oriented care has led to private enter-prises participating in the provision of care services and caused the dissolution of institutional care. The Finnish Ministry of Social Affairs and Health (2003, 101) explained their health-care and social-service policy as follows: 'Providing services at home is the most humane and cost-effective approach, achieving huge results of welfare by available resources.' Consequently, the number of beds in Finnish nursing homes for those over 75 years of age has decreased dramatically, dropping from 22,180 beds in 1990 to 8,203 in 2015 (Väyrynen and Kuronen 2017, 4). To provide care for senior citizens in fragile conditions who choose to stay at home, Finnish municipalities have reinforced public home-care services and utilised relative caregivers as human resources to supplement the increasing home-care needs of senior citizens.

Let us now turn to the particulars of relative care support. The Act on Support for Informal Care has ensured that relative caregivers receive financial compensation for, and respite from, their caregiving tasks. More specifically, relative caregivers receive a monthly salary and three days off per month. These conditions could be interpreted as the law ensuring support for relative caregivers and protecting the 'workers' rights' of relative caregivers. Another notable fact is that the law does not regulate how closely related caregivers and care recipients should be. On the contrary, the law defines relative care as 'taking care of elderly or handicapped people, or people with diseases, by relatives or someone who is close to the person in need of care' (my translation). Logically, the law broadens the scope of 'relative' to include almost anyone, regardless of consanguineal or conjugal ties.

As a result of the financial incentive and the expanded definition of relative, the number of relative caregivers has increased. For example, in Archipelago Town, which had only 82 relative caregivers recognised by the municipality in 2001, the number increased to 123 in 2012 and to 180 in 2020. Seeing that Archipelago Town has fifteen thousand inhabitants, this number of caregivers does not seem large enough to impact the local welfare scheme; in fact, the home-care service is still the primary means of support for senior citizens who live at home. Nonetheless, the significant increase in the number of relative caregivers suggests that the municipality is strongly promoting relative care. Also, at the national level, the number of carers for older people (65+) who received the relative care allowance increased by 30 per cent between 1990 and 2010 (Kröger and Leinonen 2012, 323). Kröger and Leinonen (2012, 323) interpreted this overall tendency as '"familialism by default" [that] has become the prevailing model in Finland concerning those older people who do not yet need intensive help'.

As described earlier, in Finland, the shift in the care system from the public to the private sphere has taken place along two axes, which could be summarised as the marketisation and familialisation of eldercare. Increasingly, municipalities have purchased private providers' services, while simultaneously outsourcing a part of their care service provision to relative care. If the market and relative care resources complement each other in the expanding private sphere, the current trend of social care provision cannot be summarised as a simple balance shift within the public/private dichotomy. If this is true, then other boundary shifts in the era of neoliberal care reform should also not be taken for granted. To examine the intricate process of boundary shifting triggered by the promotion of relative care, we must look at the actual context in which relative care support has been put into practice.

Relative caregivers in Archipelago Town and municipal support

In Archipelago Town, the entry of for-profit service providers into the public care sector has been relatively slow. Although local government has rapidly grown to outsource its eldercare service to private service providers (Karsio and Anttonen 2013), private care services are significantly more popular in urban areas (Puthenparambil and Kröger 2016). Archipelago Town is an especially tricky case because it is a bilingual municipality, with roughly half the population speaking Swedish and the rest Finnish, which makes fluency in both languages a prerequisite for care workers. This language requirement makes private care service providers reluctant to develop businesses in this area.[3] Consequently, the public home-care service in Archipelago Town has not attracted much support from private care businesses. Instead, the municipality and local NGOs have tried to support the informal care provided by relatives.

In addition to a financial allowance, guaranteed respite and a health evaluation, the municipality provides relative caregivers with social gatherings and free lectures on relative care. The Red Cross, Folkhälsan[4] and the Lutheran parish church also offer relative caregivers opportunities to associate with one another and ask for advice. As the Act on Support for Informal Care legislates these forms of support, all Finnish local governments are statutorily obliged to provide economic support and guaranteed respite to relative caregivers. The aforementioned NGOs are active nationally,[5] and each of their branches is engaged in providing support for relative caregivers. The relative caregivers in Archipelago Town receive similar kinds of support to those available in any other municipality in Finland.

Nonetheless, the size of the allowance that relative caregivers receive differs considerably between municipalities. For example,

Helsinki, the Finnish capital, has its own system for setting allowances. Relative caregivers in Helsinki are categorised into three classes based on their tasks. The monthly allowance for each class is: 1,699 euros for Class 1, 784 euros for Class 2 and 432 euros for Class 3. By contrast, in Archipelago Town (where there are four classes), as of February 2020, caregivers in Class 1 receive 803.84 euros per month, those in Class 2 receive 681.64 euros per month, those in Class 3 receive 546.98 euros per month and those in Class 4 receive 410.78 euros per month. The allowances for relative caregivers are generally higher in bigger cities, such as Helsinki, while in Archipelago Town, the maximum size of the allowance is significantly lower than what Helsinki offers.[6] Currently, no relative caregivers are granted the Class 1 allowance in Archipelago Town.

Many factors, such as the financial conditions of municipalities and municipal prioritisation of social care policies, affect this urban–rural gap in relative care allowances, as well as municipalities' different levels of eagerness to promote relative care. Differences in allowances between municipalities are related to the difficulty of the burden that relative caregivers are expected to bear. Each municipality has its own official criteria for certifying relative caregivers. Archipelago Town grants relative caregiver status to applicants more flexibly than Helsinki. For example, Helsinki's guidelines state that caregiving tasks, such as dining assistance, movement assistance, medication, dressing, toilet assistance and other forms of health-care and nursing tasks, must be carefully considered when assessing relative caregivers. If a caregiver performs three tasks on the list, they would be classified as Class 3, while a caregiver needs to perform all six tasks to be classified as Class 1. Helsinki also has a rule that relative caregivers need to live in the same house as their care recipient(s).

The municipality of Archipelago Town uses much more flexible criteria. For example, Class 4 relative caregivers look after a care recipient 'who needs daily and regular help for their routines to such an extent that the caregiver is bound to them'.[7] The criteria are not based on a specific list of tasks, and care recipients can live alone. The differences in criteria across municipalities suggest that becoming a relative caregiver is easier in rural areas, although the allowance is generally lower in rural areas than in urban areas.

In urban areas, such as Helsinki, relative caregivers need to fulfil certain requirements to attain the status of a relative caregiver, as if they were applying for a regular job. In urban areas, there are enough for-profit service providers to ensure the provision of public care services, which means that there is no necessity to lower the standards for certifying relative caregivers. In the rural part of Archipelago Town, neither public care services nor services provided by for-profit providers are readily available because the town consists of thousands of small islands. Although bridges connect several islands, many islands can be reached only by public ferries or private boats.

Hanna Stenlund,[8] an administrator in her mid-forties who has worked for Archipelago Town's municipal relative care support office for eight years, told me:

> No one could look after the elderly persons in need of care in the peripheral areas. In the town centre, some of the current caregivers might be considered too old (and consequently too fragile) to receive caregiver status, but in a real archipelago area, they are the only choice.

Indeed, in the rural areas of Archipelago Town, the criteria for certifying relative caregivers are less demanding than in other places. For example, quite often, relative caregivers live separately from the person they look after. Most relative caregivers undertake only minimal caregiving tasks (Class 4), such as watching over their older kin, cooking and helping with grocery shopping. These tasks are not burdensome enough to be regarded as relative caregiving in the centre of Archipelago Town or in big cities.

Sometimes, according to Hanna, people do not apply for a relative caregiver position themselves; instead, the municipality asks them to become relative caregivers. Relative care support offers a financial incentive to people who may not have subjective reasons to care for those who require it. Applying different minimum criteria for relative caregivers in different localities can be understood as a strategic move by Archipelago Town to compensate for the shortage of public services in peripheral areas. To compensate for the scarcity of human resources in remote areas, the state and the municipalities rely on relative caregivers to ensure health-care provision while working with a limited budget.

Families, relatives and caregiving practices in Archipelago Town

There is another feature of relative caregivers that is particular to Archipelago Town. In remote areas of the municipality, the relationships between relative caregivers and care recipients are more varied than those in the central area. The registered caregivers are not only the spouses and children of those in need of care, but also their siblings, relatives and neighbours. For example, according to Hanna, in September 2015, five of the relative caregivers were not immediate family members of the care recipients. In these five cases, the care recipients were people living on comparatively remote islands in the archipelago. One caregiver owned a summer cottage near the care recipient's house, but the owner/caregiver usually resided in another city. However, the care recipient refused to receive any care services, except those provided by this particular caregiver. The second caregiver who was not an immediate relative was the sister-in-law of the care recipient's daughter-in-law. This recipient's house was on an island so remote that even the meals-on-wheels service could not reach it (due to legal restrictions on driving distance). Again, there was no one else who could take care of this person. The third caregiver was the wife of the care recipient's grandson. Both the caregiver and the care receiver lived on an island visited by ferries only twice a week. The fourth caregiver was the care recipient's daughter-in-law,[9] and the fifth was the care recipient's niece. This wide range of 'relatives' indicates that, at least in the peripheral part of Archipelago Town, the relative caregiving practice can extend beyond the circle of the nuclear family and, in some cases, beyond consanguineal ties. Does this situation indicate that families in rural areas are less individualised than families in urban areas?

Statistics do not indicate that the decreasing size of Finnish households is a recent phenomenon. Even before the construction of the welfare state, household-dwelling units were small in south-western Finland. In its coastal parishes, the mean household size was between 2.9 and 3.7 in 1930 (Moring 1993, 402). Already by the end of the nineteenth century, the proportion of extended families within the total number of households had dropped to 20.6 per cent, from 51.3 per cent in 1770 (Moring 1993, 405–6). In Finland, the nuclearisation of families had already started before the construction of the welfare state.

Moreover, these five exceptional relative caregivers are not the only examples of relative caregivers outside the nuclear family. There are divorced spouses and cohabiting couples who are also certified relative caregivers. With divorce and cohabitation being relatively modern phenomena, it is not plausible to interpret relative caregiving as a revitalisation of traditional family values. Thus, it is necessary to regard 'traditional' kinship as just one of several types of relationship ties that link relative caregivers to care recipients.

We should also not ignore the fact that relative caregivers are not simply relatives looking after their kin. To some degree, they are being paid for their caregiving tasks. Although it is quite common for relative caregivers to interpret the economic assistance from the municipalities as support rather than a salary, the fact that relative caregivers are receiving money often brings conflict into the practice of relative care.

Struggling with closed doors

When I started my research on relative caregivers, Hanna, the administrator from Archipelago Town, was sceptical about me getting consent to conduct interviews with relative caregivers. She told me that the relatives might deny my interview requests because they do not want other people to know that they are paid to care for their relatives – that is, they may worry that receiving payment makes them appear cold-hearted. I sent letters to all the registered relative caregivers in Archipelago Town anyway, and, to Hanna's surprise, a few people agreed to be interviewed. Still, all the acceptances came from caregivers who were spouses and children of the care recipients. None of the relative caregivers with the more unusual relationships agreed to be interviewed. Presumably, the remoteness of their relationship to the care receivers in terms of kinship makes the caregivers more cautious about outsiders because the caregiving relationship may seem less legitimate.

Of course, none of the relative caregivers I interviewed stated that the economic benefit played any part in their decision to take care of their relatives. For example, Erna Laaksonen, who is in her sixties and is taking care of her husband, explained the reasons as follows:

> It is very normal that people get divorced after the other gets ill. ... We had been together for 15 years. There is a saying: If you want to have a very good crew, you have to marry it. And we got married. He was very good crew. ... It is very normal in my family that you take care of your relatives. I cannot understand that people can abandon each other when somebody becomes ill.

Even if relative care is not a predominant practice in Finland, the reasons behind it are often moralised.

As the fieldwork proceeded, it turned out that the wariness of outsiders exhibited by many relative caregivers was a problem for municipal workers as well. According to Hanna, 'they [the caregivers] want to be left alone'. Hanna's statement was based on her constant struggles when offering help to relative caregivers. As the chief of Archipelago Town's relative care support section, she planned various gatherings for relative caregivers, such as parties, seminars and camps, in cooperation with NGOs and the surrounding municipalities. However, she always worried about not getting enough participants, and sometimes her worries were justified. In fact, some caregivers flatly refused to receive any respite care services. As Hanna once said: 'Our job is to make people think it's not so bad to accept help. [To convince] those who say, "We don't need outside help."'

Relative caregivers were often suspicious of municipal workers. This reluctance to cooperate became especially evident when relative caregivers decided to stop taking care of their family members and to apply for institutionalisation. Agnes Sjöman, who was in her late sixties when I interviewed her in 2014, had been taking care of her mother for some time. She found her caregiving task increasingly difficult to handle. However, she struggled to communicate her decision to the municipal officials. Her daughter urged her to contact the municipality, but Agnes was reluctant:

> When you have a meeting [with the municipal officials to apply for the institutionalisation of a family member], you have to say you can't cope with her anymore. I cannot manage anymore. But I couldn't say it. You must say it: otherwise there is no chance [for the municipal authority] to understand you.

In principle, it does not matter whether the relative caregivers truly need outside help or not. They are certified relative caregivers entitled to receive respite and allowances, and they can quit if they want to. Nonetheless, they may wish to stay private, or their family values may clash with the public nature of being a relative caregiver as a job, which causes problems with getting paid and accepting outside help. In this regard, the state-led politics of care challenges and tries to expand the notions and practices of kinship, but encounters resistance.

The professionalism of relative care

In Archipelago Town, the municipal office must consider numerous factors when evaluating relative caregivers because the general criteria do not always apply to specific cases. Consequently, evaluating and supporting relative caregivers is a sensitive issue for municipal employees. The difficulty is especially prominent in childcare. For example, a single mother taking care of her disabled child requested that a respite care worker provide her with transportation so that she could buy clothes for her child. The municipal administrator decided that it would not be appropriate to provide transportation in this case because the child's disability was not relevant to the mother's difficulties in going shopping. Hanna told me that they never grant relative caregiver status to parents who take care of children with disabilities under 3 years of age because even a baby without physical or mental challenges needs a considerable amount of care from adult caregivers. 'Ordinary' parents also commit to feeding and bathing their children and changing diapers. Therefore, the parents of infants with disabilities must wait until their babies turn 3 before they can be registered as relative caregivers.

This ambiguity between registered caregiving and 'ordinary' domestic care practices can also be found in eldercare. There was an application for relative care support by a son who claimed to be taking care of his father because he prepared his father's food. The application was rejected because the preparation of food is a typical activity in every household. These requests were denied because the municipality found that the tasks that the applicants claimed to be performing as relative caregivers were no different from ordinary domestic chores. It is quite common for unregistered relatives to help their older relatives with daily tasks. For example, adult children often help their parents by going grocery shopping, cleaning, making phone calls, filling in application forms to coordinate public services and attending care meetings with municipal care workers. It is possible to ask for outside help with these tasks. There are grocery-shopping services provided by the municipality and supermarkets, private cleaning services and various kinds of voluntary help from the Red Cross and the parish deacons. Still, these tasks are usually regarded as domestic chores, which indicates that there is a boundary between ordinary domestic chores and relative care.

As shown by these examples, municipal officers need to distinguish the specific difficulties faced by relative caregivers from the general difficulties faced by all families. What sets relative caregivers apart from ordinary family members and care workers is the skill required and the burdensome nature of the tasks. In other words, the tasks performed by care workers and relative caregivers entail a certain degree of professionalism, and it is this professionalism that municipal workers consider when distinguishing relative caregivers from ordinary family members and other actors. However, in certain conditions, the professionalism of relative caregivers, or lack thereof, is sometimes overlooked by municipal workers. To illustrate this, I will describe a case in which a relative caregiver's qualifications became an issue.

In this case, Maria Froberg, a female in her early nineties, was the relative caregiver for her husband, Ben Froberg, a male in his early nineties. They lived in an apartment in the city centre of Archipelago Town. They also relied on the home-care service to carry out physically burdensome tasks for Ben. During these visits, the municipal officials noticed that Maria had a memory problem that was getting worse. For example, when the home-care worker visited the couple on one occasion, Maria said she was going to prepare them their morning coffee, even though it was actually evening. After the care worker had changed Ben into his pyjamas, Maria and Ben started drinking their evening tea. Because they had consumed a substantial amount of caffeine in the evening, the two probably stayed up until quite late, or so the leader of the home-care team surmised. The care worker reported that it was difficult to wake them up in the morning.

I asked Hanna about Maria's case. She answered: 'You have to respect them even if their choice is not the best one. But it is tough.' Then, addressing whether Maria could continue to be a relative caregiver, she said:

> I always try to think about what would happen to this person if I made them quit being a relative caregiver. Maria will surely take care of Ben. If so, it is better to have some support. Probably we would stop the allowance and keep the [respite care] service. There was such a case before.

Even though Maria and Ben lived in an apartment building in the city centre, rather than on a remote island, where sometimes simple domestic chores can be classified as relative caregiving because of the scarcity of public/private services, Hanna was considerate towards Maria as the relative caregiver. She took into account not only the wellbeing of the care recipient, but also the chronic condition of the caregiver. In fact, the availability of human resources, the intimate nature of the caregiving relationship and the caregiver's objective skills were all weighed up.

As we have seen, the politics of deservingness often come into play when a municipality has to evaluate relative care practices. In sparsely populated regions, availability is what counts the most, whereas for older couples, a caregiver's welfare and the relationship between a caregiver and a care receiver matter more than the deservingness of the caregiver. Therefore, during the process of providing municipal support for relative caregivers, the boundary between professional care work and relative caregiving is chronically redrawn based on the complex relationship between a relative caregiver's professionalism and other values, such as the geographical location of care recipients or caregivers' personal welfare, which need to be considered in care situations.

The difference between relative caregivers and care workers

Another boundary of care has been brought into question by the promotion of relative care. How can relative care be distinguished from other kinds of care work? In other words, how has the boundary between informal/formal care been redrawn by relative care support in practice? The introduction of relative care support means that relative caregivers need to be distinguished from ordinary family members and from professional care workers.

According to the Act on Support for Informal Care, relative caregivers are entitled to three days of respite per month from their caregiving tasks. In Archipelago Town, two[10] municipal care workers, who are qualified 'practical nurses',[11] provide respite care services.[12] Becoming a practical nurse requires three years of vocational education, including a one-year specialised course in home-care services. These care workers are trained professionals with specialised education, skills and knowledge, although care work generally suffers from low wages due to its gendered nature (England et al. 2002). However, the tasks involved in respite care are quite different from those of home care, even though the care workers performing these two types of care have the same qualifications.

The case of Helena Enlund and her relative caregiver demonstrates the cooperation between relative caregivers, respite care workers and home-care workers. Helena, who was in her late eighties, was living in an apartment in the city centre. Being a large lady, she used a wheelchair, and she required a mechanical lift to get her out of bed and into her wheelchair. Her registered relative caregiver, Emil Abrahamson, was in his early nineties. He was her friend, and he lived more than a hundred kilometres from Archipelago Town. He would spend three weeks a month at her apartment before returning to his hometown for a week. The respite care and home service providers had to cover the week when Emil was absent by visiting Helena four times a day.

When I paid a visit to Helena with a respite care worker, we spent two and a half hours in the morning moving her out of bed, preparing her food and chatting with her. In the afternoon, it was the home-care worker's turn to visit her, although they spent less time with her than we had in the morning because they had to attend to other clients as well. In this situation, relative care, respite care and home care are logically interchangeable, even though the three types of caregivers spend their time at Helena's in somewhat different ways.

The division of labour between relative caregivers, respite care workers and home-care workers is neither static nor straightforward. In principle, the objective of respite care is to substitute for a relative care-giver, while respite care workers are certified practical nurses who specialise in home care. In theory, the three kinds of caregivers can provide similar types of care to recipients. However, as Helena and Emil's case indicates, there is a division of labour between the three kinds of actors based on the unique individual situation. Helena's life was supported by a patchwork of care offered by three types of caregivers, who were spending their time in distinctly different ways.

Care workers and relative caregivers sometimes have conflicting opinions regarding the other party's skills and knowledge. For example, the home-care team found Emil's attitude towards Helena to be problematic for a caregiver. Dorothea Sandel, the leader of the home-care team, told me how appalled she was when she found out that Emil had been showering Helena by seating her in her regular wheelchair. When she visited Helena to prepare a home-care service plan and asked about her hygiene, Emil demonstrated how he did it. Emil did not find his caring technique to be problematic in the slightest. However, because of the showering method, dirt was stuck to the wheels of the wheelchair, which impeded smooth mobility. Another problem was Emil's refusal to use a nursing bed, which had been recommended by an ergotherapist. This bed would have prevented Helena from falling and would have made it easier for the care workers to lift her. However, Emil had returned the rented nursing bed to the municipal stockroom without explanation. A week later, Helena fell out of bed and had to be hospitalised.

As Helena's case demonstrates, relative caregivers are not always responsible, logical or consistent. They make seemingly wrong choices or withdraw from their tasks. As Dorothea once commented: 'Sometimes, relatives do not understand the condition of the customers [the relatives that they care for]. They do not want to. Because the truth is very sad, depressing and hard.' Still, Dorothea and her home service team could not override the decisions of the relatives. Unless there are immediate physical risks to the care recipient, relative caregivers are allowed to make the wrong decisions because they are not strictly professional care workers. Moreover, due to the aforementioned Senior Service Act, it has become even more challenging to address relative caregivers' potentially problematic decisions. Dorothea explained that the Act has given 'customers a right to choose. [They can] decide as long as they do not harm themselves. But we know what will happen in the near future. But we can only wait for it [to happen].' Home-care workers distanced themselves from relative caregivers when they encountered problems when providing services to relative care recipients. The tasks performed by both the professional and the relative caregivers were typically not different, but the professionals' knowledge and judgement were usually better, or so they thought. Therefore, the boundary between formal and informal care is in a constant state of tension, and it needs to be renegotiated almost on a case-by-case basis depending on the arrangements between the care services and the relative caregivers.

Conclusion

This chapter has described the attempt by a Finnish municipality to incorporate relative caregivers into the public domain of care by offering them municipal support. Although a change in the care system is often regarded as a shift of focus within a certain dichotomy, it is more accurate to interpret the neoliberal reform of Finland's social democratic care regime as a process of redrawing the boundary between public and private care. By promoting relative care, the public domain of care has been expanded, while the informal domain has narrowed in scope.

This does not mean that the state has wholly incorporated informal care practices into the public domain. There are always care practices, such as shopping, cooking and cleaning, that, in principle, do not qualify as tasks for certified relative caregivers. Especially in urban areas, these practices are deemed to be outside of relative care. However, as I demonstrate in the ethnographic part of this chapter, care workers in a smaller municipality evaluate relative caregivers' individual situations based on the relative caregivers' skills, residence location and the caregiving–receiving relationship. Even when it comes to the same policy, the boundary between public and private care is not stable.

Furthermore, relative caregivers are not entirely equal to professional care workers. When relative caregivers and municipal care workers collaborate, conflicts of opinion can occur. On these occasions, municipal workers have to deal with the fact that relative caregivers are 'customers' instead of fellow caregivers. The boundary between professional care workers and relative caregivers is constantly examined by the municipal workers, upon whom it falls to decide whether a relative caregiver is a dependable partner or a problematic customer.

Based on these ethnographic descriptions, we can now pose the following question: How exactly has the promotion of relative care impacted the actual practices of eldercare in Finnish society? First and foremost, the issue of family and kinship has gained public attention. There has always been informal support between relatives. However, after the introduction of relative care support, municipalities have had to 're-acknowledge' relatives as a potential resource. Simultaneously, as diverse persons have been encouraged to take care of someone close to them, the definition of 'relative' has expanded. Now, it is the 'relatedness' (Carsten 1995) created by the practice of care that 'performatively' (Butler 2010) binds a caregiver and care recipient together as relatives.

Nonetheless, the relatives recognised by the government as caregivers are fundamentally different from the kinship organisation traditionally studied by anthropology. Since it is always an individual who receives support from the municipality, relative care giving/receiving is a one-to-one transaction at the policy level. As I discussed earlier, in Finland, the rise of relative care and the individualisation of families are related phenomena. If we consider weakening cohesion and the outsourcing of its function to be symptoms of individualisation, then we can say that not just families but relatives too have been individualised, in the sense that being a relative depends on individual choices and public policies.

This chapter has also revealed that there is a fundamental ambiguity within relative care practice. By not recognising the deservingness of their status as relative caregivers, some caregivers want to keep their practice away from the public arena of care policy. Their attitude is possibly related to the ambiguous implications of the monthly allowance for relative caregivers. Relative caregivers may interpret their monthly allowance as public support for their hard work; however, their reluctance to open up to outsiders may indicate that some interpret this monthly allowance as profiteering. Although there is established criticism of domestic labour as 'unpaid work' (see Shelton 2006) in feminist literature, getting paid to care and being a relative contradict each other in principle. By assigning a publicly recognised role to informal caregivers, the relative care support system exposes individualised relatives to this fundamental contradiction. Therefore, the introduction of relative care support has opened up the possibility of observing how families and relatives deal with the constant pressure of individualisation.

Although this study has described the process of changing boundaries in relation to care, the policy promoting informal care is not, in and of itself, inherently problematic. Municipal support can provide assistance to informal caregivers who are struggling alone or encourage someone to feel responsible about their kin. Nonetheless, this chapter has shown that the unequal opportunities in receiving care brought about by the neoliberal reform are too complex to be effectively addressed by simple solutions. As eldercare involves long-lasting, ever-changing interactions between people, achieving equality in the practice of care is always a precarious undertaking. Such constantly shifting boundaries induced by the chronicity of care are fundamentally a part of the neoliberal 'carescape' (Milligan and Wiles 2010) that underpins the new reality of the Finnish care sector ushered in by the neoliberal reforms.

Notes

1. This Finnish/Swedish word is usually translated as 'informal care'. However, considering the basic meaning of the words *omainen* in Finnish ('someone of your own') and *närstående* in Swedish ('someone standing nearby'), I believe 'relative care' is closer to the original meaning. When I refer to this specific policy service, I use 'relative care' to emphasise the local national context.
2. For the English version of the law published by the Finnish Ministry of Justice, see Finlex (2005).
3. There is a private medical clinic and private serviced housing with 24-hour assistance in Archipelago Town. However, home care is still operated by the municipality.
4. Folkhälsan (Swedish for 'public health') is an NGO advocating for the social welfare and health care of Swedish-speaking minorities in Finland.
5. This excludes Folkhälsan, which operates mainly on Finland's eastern and southern coasts and in the metropolitan area, where Swedish-speaking municipalities are prominent.
6. These data are based on the official document 'Omaishoidon tuen myöntämisperusteet, hoitoisuusryhmät ja hoitopalkkiot Helsingissä 1.1.2018 alkaen' ('The Criteria, the Groups and the Fees of the Informal Care Support') (Helsingin Kaupunki 2018).
7. This quotation comes from an administrative document of Archipelago Town, which was provided by the municipal relative care support division.
8. All proper names used in this chapter are pseudonyms.
9. It is worth noting that daughters-in-law are common relative caregivers in countries with conservative welfare regimes. However, in Finland, this case was rare enough to be mentioned by the administrator.
10. While this number may seem too low to provide respite for hundreds of relative caregivers, care recipients can also stay in municipal and non-profit care facilities for short periods. Relative caregivers request respite care services when they need to go out for a few hours and someone has to look after their care recipients while they are away.
11. In Finland, 'practical nurse' (*lähihoitaja* in Finnish) is a basic qualification for workers in the social and medical field. This qualification covers 10 specialised professions, including home care for seniors and day care for children.
12. In Finnish, a respite care worker is called *lomittaja*, meaning someone who interweaves in between, while in Swedish, the word is *avlastare*, meaning someone who helps to unburden. Both terms adequately connote what this job entails.

References

Abadía-Barrero, Cesar. 2015. 'Neoliberal justice and the transformation of the moral: The privatisation of the right to health care in Colombia', *Medical Anthropology Quarterly* 30 (1): 62–79. https://doi.org/10.1111/maq.12161.

Beck, Ulrich and Elisabeth Beck-Gernsheim. 2002. *Individualisation, Institutionalised Individualism and Its Social and Political Consequences*. London: Sage.

Butler, Judith. 2010. 'Performative agency', *Journal of Cultural Economy* 3 (2): 147–61. https://doi.org/10.1080/17530350.2010.494117.

Carsten, Janet. 1995. 'The substance of kinship and the heat of the hearth: Feeding, personhood, and relatedness among Malays in Pulau Langkawi', *American Ethnologist* 22 (2): 223–41. https://doi.org/10.1525/ae.1995.22.2.02a00010.

Cruz-Saco, Maria Amparo and Sergei Zelenev, eds. 2010. *Intergenerational Solidarity: Strengthening economic and social ties*. New York: Palgrave Macmillan.

Ellison, James. 2014. 'First-class health: Amenity wards, health insurance and normalizing health care inequalities in Tanzania', *Medical Anthropology Quarterly* 28 (2): 162–81. https://doi.org/10.1111/maq.12086.

England, Paula, Michelle Budig and Nancy Folbre. 2002. 'Wages of virtue: The relative pay of care work', *Social Problems* 49 (4): 455–73. https://doi.org/10.1525/sp.2002.49.4.455.

Esping-Andersen, Gøsta. 1990. *The Three Worlds of Welfare Capitalism*. Cambridge: Polity Press.

Finlex. 2005. 'Act on Support for Informal Care'. Accessed 31 May 2021. https://www.finlex.fi/en/laki/kaannokset/2005/en20050937.

Helsingin Kaupunki. 2018. 'Omaishoidon tuen myöntämisperusteet, hoitoisuusryhmät ja hoito-palkkiot Helsingissä 1.1.2018 alkaen' [The Criteria, the Groups and the Fees of the Informal Care Support]. Accessed 27 September 2019. https://www.hel.fi/static/sote/omaishoito/tiedotteet/omaishoidon-tuki-171107.pdf.

Henriksson, Lea and Sirpa Wrede. 2008. 'Care work in the context of a transforming welfare state'. In *Care Work in Crisis: Reclaiming the Nordic ethos of care*, edited by Sirpa Wrede, Lea Henriksson, Håkon Høst, Stina Johansson and Betina Dybbroe, 121–30. Lund: Studentlitteratur.

Horton, Sarah, Cesar Abadía, Jessica Mulligan and Jennifer J. Thompson. 2014. 'Critical anthropology of global health "takes a stand" statement: A critical approach to the US's Affordable Care Act', *Medical Anthropology Quarterly* 28 (2): 1–22. https://doi.org/10.1111/maq.12065.

Karsio, Olli and Anneli Anttonen. 2013. 'Marketisation of eldercare in Finland: Legal frames, outsourcing practices and the rapid growth of for-profit services'. In *Marketisation in Nordic Eldercare: A research report on legislation, oversight, extent and consequences*, edited by Gabrielle Meagher and Marta Szebehely, 85–125. Stockholm: Stockholm University.

Kemp, Candace L., Mary M. Balla and Molly M. Perkins. 2013. 'Convoys of care: Theorizing intersections of formal and informal care', *Journal of Aging Studies* 27 (1): 15–29. https://doi.org/10.1016/j.jaging.2012.10.002.

Kettunen, Pauli. 1997. 'The Nordic welfare state in Finland', *Scandinavian Journal of History* 26: 225–47. https://doi.org/10.1080/034687501750303864.

Kröger, Teppo and Anu Leinonen. 2012. 'Transformation by stealth: The retargeting of home care services in Finland', *Health and Social Care in the Community* 20 (3): 319–27. https://doi.org/10.1111/j.1365-2524.2011.01047.x.

Milligan, Christine and Janine Wiles. 2010. 'Landscapes of care', *Progress in Human Geography* 34 (6): 736–54. https://doi.org/10.1177/0309132510364556.

Ministry of Social Affairs and Health. 2003. *Trends in Social Protection in Finland 2003*. Helsinki: Ministry of Social Affairs and Health.

Mol, Annemarie, Ingunn Moser and Jeannette Pols. 2010. 'Care: Putting practice into theory'. In *Care in Practice: On tinkering in clinics, homes and farms*, edited by Annemarie Mol, Ingunn Moser and Jeannette Pols, 7–26. Bielefeld: Transcript.

Moreno Figueroa, Mónica. 2010. 'Distributed intensities: Whiteness, mestizaje and the logics of Mexican racism', *Ethnicities* 10 (3): 387–401. https://doi.org/10.1177/1468796810372305.

Moring, Beatrice. 1993. 'Household and family in Finnish coastal societies, 1635–1895', *Journal of Family History* 18 (4): 395–414. https://doi.org/10.1177/036319909301800407.

Official Statistics of Finland. 2018. *Dwellings and Housing Conditions*. Helsinki: Statistics Finland. Accessed 28 September 2019. http://www.stat.fi/til/asas/index_en.html.

Puthenparambil, Jiby M. and Teppo Kröger. 2016. 'Using private social care services in Finland: Free or forced choices for older people?', *Journal of Social Service Research* 42 (2): 167–79. https://doi.org/10.1080/01488376.2015.1137534.

Shelton, Beth A. 2006. 'Gender and unpaid work'. In *Handbook of the Sociology of Gender*, edited by Janet Saltzman Chafetz, 375–90. Boston, MA: Springer.

Shield, Renee R. 1988. *Uneasy Endings: Daily life in an American nursing home*. Ithaca, NY: Cornell University Press.

Suomen Virallinen Tilasto. 2016. *Perheet tyypeittäin 1950–2016*. [Families by Type, 1950–2016]. Helsinki: Tilastokeskus. Accessed 27 September 2019. https://www.stat.fi/til/perh/2016/perh_2016_2017-05-26_tau_001_fi.html.

Thelen, Tatjana and Cati Coe. 2017. 'Political belonging through elderly care: Temporalities, representations and mutuality', *Anthropological Theory* 19 (2): 279–99. https://doi.org/10.1177/1463499617742833.

Thelen, Tatjana, Larissa Vetters and Keecet von Benda-Beckmann. 2018. 'Stategraphy: Relational modes, boundary work, and embeddedness'. In *Stategraphy: Toward a relational anthropology of state*, edited by Tatjana Thelen, Larissa Vetters and Keebet von Benda-Beckmann, 1–19. New York: Berghahn Books.

Tynkkynen, Liina-Kaisa, Ilmo Keskimäki and Juhani Lehto. 2013. 'Purchaser–provider splits in health care: The case of Finland', *Health Policy* 111: 221–5. https://doi.org/10.1177/10.1016/j.healthpol.2013.05.012.

United Nations, Department of Economic and Social Affairs, Population Division. 2017. *Household Size and Composition Around the World: Data booklet*. Accessed 31 May 2021. https://www.un.org/en/development/desa/population/publications/pdf/ageing/household_size_and_composition_around_the_world_2017_data_booklet.pdf.

Väyrynen Riikka and Raija Kuronen 2017. *Sosiaalihuollon Laitos- ja Asumispalvelut 2015*. Institutional Care and Housing Services in Social Care 2015]. Helsinki: Terveyden ja Hyvinvoinnin Laitos. Accessed 1 July 2020. http://urn.fi/URN:NBN:fi-fe201702141564

4

The 'hassle' of 'good' care in dementia: Negotiating relatedness in the navigation of bureaucratic systems of support

Lilian Kennedy

Introduction

Dementia – living with it, or alongside it as a familial carer – is a marathon. It is a chronic illness that demands care in the immediate everyday, but also into the future as behavioural, physical and cognitive symptoms emerge and deepen. Between 2014 and 2015, I spent 17 months in a range of activities run by Alzheimer's Society staff members in south London, such as 'Caring Cafés', 'Supper Clubs', 'Singing for the Brain' sessions, support groups for carers, and support groups for people with dementia. The Alzheimer's Society is a not-for-profit UK charity, which works to provide information and support to people living with dementia and their familial carers, while also pushing for, and funding, greater research of dementia pathology, treatment and cure. Community-based Alzheimer's Society activities are typically funded through one- to two-year grants from local city councils to provide services and support for members of their community affected by dementia, as well as through a form of charitable outreach from local businesses. The nature of Alzheimer's Society activities is often informed by funders' decisions about best practice. For example, a Caring Café I regularly attended had to change from social meetings focused on 'support and respite' for carers to more formalised 'advice and information' sessions, due to a shift in the funding agenda of its private funder. This disrupted the routines and expectations of attendees who had been coming for years, mirroring the confusion that carers and people with dementia felt navigating other upstream factors which impacted their local experience. Through a focus on conversations in support groups for unpaid carers and support groups for people with dementia, this chapter unpacks the common and pressing issues they raised, which often related to the navigation of confusing processes to gain access to future support promised by national policies.

Support groups are private spaces of conviviality and, as such, fertile ground for the difficult work of discussing the future. People come together to socialise and catch up with friends, as well as to share difficult stories of stress, exhaustion, frustration and sadness. What remained true, no matter the tone of a meeting on any day, is that support groups are sites of collaborative strategising, wherein people with dementia and carers craft expertise on how to 'live well with dementia', despite biomedical uncertainty about the disease and a lack of cure. This chapter details the 'hassle' of bureaucratic processes and paperwork with which my interlocutors contended in an effort to access state-funded support in the face of a future coloured by expectations of growing care needs and the cognitive decline of a person with dementia. Social isolation and carer burnout that often accompany life with dementia (Serrano-Aguilar et al. 2006) were common grounds in group discussions, and underscored the necessity of support. Group members' efforts to 'keep managing' were positioned against the backdrop of the 2009 National Dementia Strategy in England, and the Care Act 2014, which promised to address the needs of people with dementia and carers. However, the actualisation of these promises was uneven, and demanded that my interlocutors navigate large, abstract and often alienating bureaucratic structures if they 'wanted to see anything from it'. What emerges is that 'paperwork' became a site at which concepts of agency and independence, and affective kin relationships, were rebalanced and reshaped to try and achieve 'good care' and 'the good life'.

As in other chapters in this volume, the moralities of kinship and citizenship structure my interlocutors' care relationships, and the expectations of those relationships. In line with Adams et al.'s (2009, 1) theorising about the 'state of anticipation, of thinking and living toward the future', here I examine the ways in which my interlocutors navigate 'the moral responsibility of citizens to secure their "best possible futures"' (Adams et al. 2009, 2). London support group discussions could often be coloured by a tone of *preparedness* as living in "preparation for" potential trauma', as well as a tone of *possibility* as "ratcheting up" hopefulness, especially through technoscience' (Adams et al. 2009, 1). While Adams et al.'s focus is on hope through technoscience, my interlocutors' efforts show that the possibility of less painful futures is instead pursued through care work, rendered by family members – perhaps one of the oldest human technologies. In the context of my research, families apply the 'old' technology of care work to the unfamiliar, bewildering legal and bureaucratic landscape of 'sorting all the paperwork'. The particular 'traumas' of dementia become clear in looking at the working definitions and novel dynamics of 'good care' created by support group members: navigating the hassle of 'sorting' the future centred on a seeming paradox – acknowledging the growing dependence of a person with dementia, while maintaining their identity, autonomy and control. I argue that striking this balance is at the heart of my interlocutors' care and 'paperwork' strategies to keep the 'who' of a person with dementia 'still there' and present within relational dynamics – be they with family or with the state.

This chapter is a story of hassle in two acts: first, I present an illustration of Londoners affected by dementia attempting to understand and 'sort' power of attorney documents, and, second, I present them attempting to procure state-funded services promised by the Care Act 2014 by 'doing the Carer's Assessments right'. These documents and bureaucratic processes were murky terrain that was badly signposted and demanded enormous reserves of time and determination. Many people sought guidance from those 'who actually know what's what' – namely, their peers and trusted 'experts', such as Alzheimer's Society staff, attorneys and 'Carers Hub' hotlines – which challenged the intimate boundaries of dementia care. What becomes clear is that engaging in the winding hassle of planning for, and safeguarding, the future through bureaucratic processes often created significant tensions in people's relationships within and outside the home. Disagreements about care decisions, and who had the authority to make such decisions, emerged between family members. Additionally, my interlocutors' conception of the state as a reliable provider of care was often challenged, as people felt that the needs of people living with dementia, or their carers, went unrecognised or addressed, in contrast to what was expected after the Care Act 2014 was passed. Questions of deservingness run through both these sets of tensions. Who is most qualified to be a 'lead decision maker' in the life and care of a kinperson with dementia? How should the sacrifices and burdens inherent in being a 'carer' be recognised by family members and the state? What say and responsibilities do 'peripheral' family members have in the context of dementia care? Should the state be responsible for the care of people with dementia? Is the state indebted to familial carers who care for its citizens with dementia? Questions such as these highlight how notions of relatedness are implicated in familial and bureaucratic processes centred on care – at times, it was affirmed and strengthened, and at other times, it was made tenuous and painful. The questions also underline that care shows 'what is at stake' for people (Kleinman 1999), but also unveils 'how' it matters and 'who' really matters.

Discussion of the 'hassle' of these processes also contributes to theorisation about the temporalities of waiting created by prolonged efforts to secure governmental services that are seen as inadequate, uneven (Auyero 2012; Mathur 2014) and unable to deliver personalised care (Day et al. 2017). I suggest that my interlocutors' experiences make room for a critique of the state as a 'bad relative' that does not recognise carers and people with dementia as 'deserving' of such care. What becomes clear is that my interlocutors' bureaucratic efforts often challenge notions of what 'counts as care', and, I argue, reveal a hidden aspect of dementia care – 'getting it all sorted' requires considerable exertion that 'doesn't necessarily come to much'. As such, when my interlocutors navigated bureaucratic systems that were meant to safeguard a future made uncertain by the unpredictability of dementia, these processes often lent futures a greater sense of precarity instead.

'Official' paperwork

At Alzheimer's Society support groups, staff members often distributed handouts that were headlined with statements such as 'Planning for the future'. They included explanations about different categories of 'paperwork', such as lasting power of attorney (LPA), enduring power of attorney (EPA), advance decision, and advance statement, mirroring Alzheimer's Society webpages (Alzheimer's Society 2017). The explanations in handouts often served as the cornerstone of group consensus about what different types of bureaucratic processes were 'about'. They explained that power of attorney, often officially referred to as 'lasting power of attorney', is:

> a legal tool that gives another adult the legal authority to make certain decisions for someone if they become unable to make them themselves. The person who is given LPA is known as an 'attorney'. They can manage finances, or make decisions relating to a person's health and welfare. (Alzheimer's Society 2017)

In discussions about the future and 'what should be sorted first', carers, people with dementia and Alzheimer's Society staff members brought up power of attorney documents frequently, and they often became a catch-all term to refer to a variety of this kind of 'official paperwork'. Under this umbrella, medical directives, or advance directives also arose, which Edith, an Alzheimer's Society staff member, explained as 'hav[ing] to do with decisions about what the doctors would have to do to keep you alive, really, like if you wanted to go on life support or want extra measures'.

Notably, much of the information in handouts, web pages and staff members' explanations was neatly laid out with ample use of acronyms, capitalisation and references to rights and powers. While these handouts were targeted at support group attendees, the style and presentation of 'all this paperwork' textually signified these documents, and working knowledge of how to complete them, as being apart from the everyday and under the jurisdiction of governing bodies or those with legal expertise, in line with Bourdieu's (1994) examination of written sources created and kept by the state. Indeed, during support group meetings, experienced carers often explained to new members that 'getting this all sorted' would help ensure that arrangements would be safeguarded by the state, as opposed to by casual conversations or agreements between kin 'that might not hold up if you have to go to court'. Perla, a carer in her sixties, told me that she and her sibling disagreed about how to handle the finances of their father with dementia, and her sibling threatened to 'try and get power of attorney themselves'. Maggie, a carer from a different support group, explained to me she and her husband with dementia had:

> waited too long to set up the power of attorney, and even though we'd talked about how to spend his pension before his dementia got worse, we didn't put me on his account at the bank, so now whenever I need to pay for his carer, or something, from his account, I have to go to court to get it approved.

The 'official-ness' imbued in a document sanctioned by the state often piqued people's interest. They asked each other direct questions such as 'Do you have your will sorted yet?', and asked whether they had their 'power of attorney done', or had 'thought about a medical directive'. People expressed frustrated confusion about 'what exactly needs doing' in terms of 'paperwork', and this was a frequent topic in support groups. This consistent attention to 'paperwork' is also grounded in my interlocutors' acceptance, however uneven and uneasy, of the inevitability of 'needing the power of attorney', because, as Terrance, a man with dementia, explained in his support group, 'Herr Alzheimer's going to come sooner or later.' He went on to warn that:

You know – some banks, when they find out you have dementia – I don't know how they find out – they'll freeze your account! And won't let you into it without someone else, like my daughter [his named relative with power of attorney], signing off.

The Alzheimer's Society website explains that people with dementia 'reach a point where they are no longer able to make decisions for themselves – this is known as lacking "mental capacity"' (Alzheimer's Society 2017).

Power of attorney documents created an official bridge between the private arrangements within families, and public, official spheres outside of family life. People with dementia skirted the topic of capacity more carefully than carers did, but, nonetheless, the likely impending event in which a person with dementia would no longer have 'capacity' was spoken about more clearly and directly in discussions about power of attorney than in any other discussions to which I was privy. Group members proposed hypothetical scenarios to test their understanding of these documents. People with dementia usually focused on 'when it would be triggered' or how, and carers were most concerned with the extent of their decision-making power as the attorney in an LPA. For example, Melanie, a woman who had been living with dementia for about two years, put a question to Barbara, an Alzheimer's Society staff member:

Melanie: If I make my daughter my power of attorney …

Barbara: [interrupting] She would be called just your 'attorney'.

Melanie: Right, my attorney, what kinds of things does she decide? Money and medical things … you can't know exactly why you'd be in hospital, would you? So, what are you meant to decide about what you want done? Or does the decision just go to her then [when the LPA is completed]?

Alzheimer's Society staff were consistent and adamant that these documents 'don't give away your right to make decisions', especially when speaking with people with dementia. For example, Barbara explained to Melanie that LPA documents housed one's decision about an attorney *for the future*, if that was what was wished, mirroring explanations I witnessed in other groups. During an interview with Karen, another Alzheimer's Society facilitator, she explained that she makes sure:

they [carers and people with dementia] know that drawing up your power of attorney and activating your power of attorney are two different things that can happen 20 years apart … so you can fill out an LPA, send it off and then actually wait a few years until you actually hand it over …

When it was highlighted in dementia support groups that paperwork was 'there to make sure [their] wishes' were safeguarded and 'followed through on', this was often met with audible positive acknowledgment: 'Oh, I see', or 'Well, good thing!' Carers responded similarly with nods, and comments such as, 'Now that I finally have it sorted – it's good to know what he wants done is decided and written down.' My interlocutors' consistent attention to decision making – who held the power to make decisions, under which circumstances, and the boundaries of a person's decision making – point to the cultural value of being able to make decisions.

Such explanations also helped to position these documents as representations of future events. In explaining that they did not give away 'rights' *now*, an implicit *yet* that pointed to an approaching future was evoked. Peers and staff members assured one another that LPAs could only be activated without a person's wish if that person was deemed to have lost capacity to make sound decisions. Interestingly, however, *how* a person's capacity would be tested in such an event was rarely discussed. People with dementia often skirted around asking this question, and staff members did not voluntarily go into any details. Explanations were often left to implications that a clinician would make such a determination, but how the results of a clinician's assessment of lost capacity would then be carried over to other realms of one's life – such as one's bank – was left undiscussed. Thus, while LPAs were cast as 'something that has to be done' to safeguard one's future, the specifics of how they accomplished this task was often left murky, with implications that it would involve people in positions of authority making decisions about capacity, and sanctioning a carer's new role as 'attorney'.

Medical directives usually only specified a few decisions about what should *not* be done, and LPAs generally did not lay out any details about 'what would be done'. As such, I argue that these documents were predicated on an anticipated loss of mental capacity, and positioned 'safeguarding' as deciding just one very important decision – *to whom* the power of making future decisions would fall. In this way, these documents not only legalised procedures having to do with autonomy, but stipulated the future nature of a kinship relationship – specifically, the future decisions of a kinsperson so as to uphold both the right of a person with dementia to assert autonomy in these matters now, and their decisions in the future.

Considering the significance of decision making to the making and maintenance of personhood (Lamb 2014), we can see how official documents become a place within which this capacity is housed and transferred to keep it alive. Indeed, advance directives were also, at times, referred to as 'living wills'. Because the choices made by an autonomous person are laid down in official documents that must be enacted at a later date by someone else, usually their carer or family member, the concept of independence becomes both temporally suspended and relationally bound. In operating as attorneys, carers enact independence for their person with dementia when this person is seen as unable to reliably make sound choices to ensure the safety of their bodies, possessions and finances. Thus, I argue that the independence that is seemingly lost in later stages of dementia is resurrected in different and novel ways. Legally recognised documents in the context of dementia care are a medium through which the intimate workings of family life are made 'official'. And often, the process of 'sorting' them – or having others recognise their validity – forced people to lay bare, and remould, family dynamics. In what follows, it also becomes clear that reckonings of relatedness become implicated in moral calculations of the deservingness of a particular kinsperson to hold the power to make decisions for and about someone with dementia.

The fuss and trust of relatedness

Riona, an energetic and animated woman in her forties, sat across from me in a private room in the same building where the carers' group that she attended normally met. In the previous group meeting, she had told her fellow carers that her father (with dementia) had recently wandered away from home, only to be found miles away in the early hours of the following morning. I opened our conversation gently, asking her, 'How have things been?' The quiet of the room was immediately broken by a hurried monologue:

> It's been awful, Lilian, really it has – Dad named me power of attorney over all the money things ages ago, before my Mum died, and now that he can't really do it for himself, I've got full run of his accounts to pay all his bills and for the house, and the carer that

comes four days a week. But my brother and sister are always on about how they want his money spent on other things – that I'm spending too much on his carer, they know they could find cheaper ones – but Lilian, I've tried the cheaper ones, and Dad hated it, always stuck at home, and now we've got Wallace, a sweet, young black man, who gets on really well with Dad. He takes him out to his favourite places – they play billiards; it works so well with him. And I say to them, 'Look, it's Dad's money and he deserves to have the carer that he gets on with, and who I know I can trust; you know Dad wanted to stay at home,' and they come back saying that I'm probably using some of Dad's money for my own things, and that I've got no right to just spend it without checking with them first. And it's terrible, really, it's been bad enough that I can't sleep sometimes, and so I ask our accountant, who we've had for ages, and I ask him, 'Am I doing this right? Should I be talking with them about what I think needs doing?' And he goes to me, 'Riona, *yes*, you are doing this right, we have it all written down here, we can see that every bit of your Dad's money is going to his things, I've got it all down and, Riona, *it's down to your decision – you're the attorney.*'

Riona looked up with a long inhale and shrugged her shoulders, suggesting that this issue – these official, legal paperwork processes, these conversations with experts and siblings, her father and his professional carer – were far from resolved, but instead part of the ongoing duties of a carer of a family member with dementia. The decision housed in a power of attorney document, for example, needed to be 'sorted' via official channels, and then acted upon by third parties such as accountants for the powers they bestowed to be validated and actionable. This document is one example of the many 'bits of paperwork that need sorting' in the lives of carers and people with dementia. They matter in conversations with other officials, such as an accountant, and they allow for carers to 'do what needs doing' for a person with dementia. However, the validity of these documents is not understood in the same ways across all spheres of the lives of carers and people with dementia.

Riona's story also illustrates that official processes often impact the dynamics in families affected by dementia. In previous group discussions, Riona described exhaustion at having to manage relationships with her extended family, 'not just Dad', and that she 'didn't ask for this [to be named attorney]'. While in the abstract, a document giving power of attorney is 'official', and legally stipulates who holds which kinds of responsibilities at the moment, or will in the future, this did not always play out the same way in familial life. Indeed, the family tensions that these processes instigate often make them 'debatable' long after they would be considered legally official, or settled. The LPA that Riona's father put together created resentment in her family, as her authority appeared to be out of step with her siblings' perceptions of prior family dynamics, reflected in part by their frequent questions about the rationale of her choices. Other people's experiences mirrored this. Another carer in Riona's group, who held power of attorney over her mother's finances, explained that her sister demanded to know 'where every bit of money was going'. In another support group in a different borough, a woman named Claire warned others that 'once that kind of relationship is started, it's hard to close it down', in reference to contentious discussions with her brother about which care decisions were 'best'. While it was unclear whether Claire's mother's LPA had been 'sorted', Claire explained that an LPA would not 'change our [her and her mother's] disagreements all that much'. These experiences illustrate that the meaning of power of attorney in carers' groups, among carers, does not evenly translate to the understandings of other people in carers' lives beyond these groups.

The public, 'official', 'one-size-fits-all' documents associated with future planning did not reflect the unique terrains of responsibility and power within families. Some carers felt that they were treated as though they had 'stolen something from Dad' and their wider families. Carers with familial tensions such as Riona's often felt that their families undermined their status as attorney by questioning whether the carer-attorney was 'really doing things the way he [the person with dementia] would have wanted'. Different family members held differing ideas about the importance of ensuring that the decisions of people with dementia were supported or enacted. Carers, who often saw themselves as 'closest' to their relative with dementia, explained that they best 'knew what he would have wanted', and felt compelled and deserving of the position to make decisions based on the desires of a person with dementia, not based on the opinions of other family members who sometimes 'only see her once a year!' and 'don't know what's really going on'. For many carers, the responsibility of 'being power of attorney' encompassed determining *which decisions* to make that were 'right' and 'what he would have wanted'. At times, this has to be done against the backdrop of familial worries and complaints that 'there goes everyone's inheritance' when expensive in-home or residential care was selected. In the midst of, and often because of, these familial debates, carers often felt great doubt about holding the position of attorney. Riona and other carers often wavered about the validity of their position as 'decision maker', or wondered if they were 'doing what he really would have wanted'. The persistent uncertainty that carers face about what LPAs mean legally, as well as relationally, contextualises the effort that Alzheimer's Society staff and carers put into collective conversations and education about powers of attorney to create a coalesced understanding of the boundaries of these documents.

In an examination of both families' and carers' uncertainty about the deservingness of main carers to hold rights such as 'attorney', we see how this deservingness was often linked to having a history and close bond with the person with dementia. Relatedness to a person with dementia, evidenced by 'knowing them well', was key to being able to make decisions as their person with dementia would have, if they were cognitively well, as well as the grounds for having the moral 'right' and authority to be 'attorney'. An underlying goal was to carry forth the decisions of a person with dementia, by proxy, past a time in which mental capacity had been lost. This became most clear when people with dementia explained who they had *not* named as power of attorney, and why. For example, a woman named Flora discussed her worries about her son's interest in her moving into a care home, noting that they 'hadn't spent as much time together'. Flora had been widowed some decades before, and while she spoke of her late husband with clear grief, she was also proud of her independence, her many interests and the home she had made after her husband's passing. Like many other people with dementia and elders, she felt strongly about remaining in her own home (Buch 2015), or at least 'knowing where I'm going to'. She explained that she had been putting off 'getting this [LPA] sorted', and that she was eventually counselled by an Alzheimer's Society staff member not to give her son power of attorney, 'because you have to trust the person you choose'. Other stories also underlined choosing one's attorney based on a close, trusting relationship with the person named. Maria, an elegant older woman with Alzheimer's, told her group that 'I've named my son [as attorney of my finances] – we're very close, and he works in the bank, so I know my money is going to be in good hands [laughs].' Meredith, in the same group, named her daughter 'because she's over all the time, helping all the time anyway – knows how things should be done'. People soothed their doubts about decisions being made well in the future because of trust between people, and a history of relational knowledge about how they 'like things done now'. In these renditions, against the backdrop of an ambiguous and unknowable future, and confusing and murky bureaucratic processes, one's closest kin could be a reliable mainstay. The 'good life' for people with dementia – now and in the future – is about relationships and trust.

'Getting it all sorted': (Mis)adventures in bureaucratic hassle

So far, I have focused on legal documents, and the relational consequences of this official paperwork. However, attention must also be paid to the bureaucratic processes by which these safeguards were 'sorted' to understand how the future is defined – or not – in the face of chronic illness. Sorting paperwork often involved tasks such as registering as a carer within the borough, qualifying for carers' allowance and council tax waivers, requesting carers' assessments and continuing care, or procuring a disability sticker if mobility became an issue. From interviews and group conversations, I learnt that only a few couples had their power of attorney arrangements in place previous to a diagnosis of dementia being made. In most cases, these were couples that did not have children, and were financially well off. For most, however, tackling paperwork of this nature seemed to be the first time that families and carers were aware that laying down wishes and choices for the future could be done in these terms. Many made comments such as, 'I had no idea there was all this to do!'

In support groups, carers compared and contrasted methods to figure out what 'actually works', because many felt persistent exasperation that 'everything is confusing'. There was rarely consensus, typified by comments such as, 'Well, who knows what's best, really?', and 'It is a bit of a mystery, isn't it! What worked for Edith didn't work for me!' They were irritated that 'social services, NHS [National Health Service], GP offices, etc. … each just offer parts of what's needed!', but that they could not be consolidated to form a complete and reliable care plan that approaches health holistically, in the present or in the future, a finding well substantiated in research on UK health and social care systems (Pickard et al. 2016).

Carers, in particular, pursued these confusing and 'mind-numbing' processes because they were strongly encouraged to do so by their peers and staff. Carers emphatically reminded one another about the importance of breaks or respite, 'to be able to manage in the long term', and that the only way 'to make it through' is to 'take breaks when you can', underlining that their futures would be dominated by care. Many new carers had to be convinced by more seasoned carers that respite was necessary, 'because if you're sick on your back, how are you going to look after him?' – casting respite as morally 'OK' because self-care in this manner was ultimately in the service of their person with dementia. Thus, respite was understood as a necessity to be organised, and it would need to be self-funded or made possible through contributions of time, and possibly money, from kin – in both cases, an impossibility for many.

People explained that funds for respite 'could be awarded from the council – sometimes, but you have to ask for it'. This was cast as a somewhat daunting enterprise, and arranging for 'help' to take respite required help from others, such as Alzheimer's Society staff, to 'sort' the paperwork to 'get away for a bit'.

The Care Act 2014 promised support to unpaid carers based on a carer needs assessment performed by a trained staff member from the local authority. There was great initial anticipation and optimism about the plethora of services, funding and help for carers that it would provide, but assessments were slow to be scheduled and the questionnaire proved to be confusing and awkward for many carers. Many carers were never able to reach the point of assessment because of prolonged waiting times due to understaffed council offices, and the frustrating 'back-and-forth' of bureaucratic paperwork. Many asked 'What am I supposed to do in the meantime?', and the Care Act 2014 was often described with exasperation, and as a broken promise and 'failure to launch' initiative. Many carers fell back on the expertise of the group to 'figure out how to manage'. For those that were able to have carers' assessments scheduled, staff and some carers warned about the difficulty of rendering their daily lives in terms of quantifiable levels of burden and caring hours that would secure 'help'.

Carers described the significance of experts, particularly Alzheimer's Society staff and social service workers recommended by word of mouth, in helping to translate their lives into 'what counted as care' in assessments. For example, a carer commented:

> I had no idea how much I was actually doing! I was thinking, OK, I spend a few hours a day helping him wash and eat, and taking him to the day centre on Wednesdays, but then she asks me – 'OK, are you also staying with him at home to make sure he's not getting into trouble?' (Which I am.) And 'Are you doing all the cooking and cleaning for him as well? Staying up nights?' She had me tally all that up, and it's more than full-time hours! I hadn't thought that those other things counted, for the assessment.

In sharing stories about this 'ongoing hassle' and 'what I've managed', people with dementia and carers often constructed narratives of success tied to help and advice received from charity professionals. These professionals were seen to have expertise about social services paperwork processes, and a willingness to help with the repeated calls to council offices, GPs, mobility services and so on, on behalf of their clients, which were required to 'get something sorted'. Indeed, members frequently recommended particular charity staffers, with explanations such as:

> You have to call Nicky – she's the one who knows all about the carer's assessment – it's too hard to figure all out on your own, so you've got to have her to help you … she helped with calling them [the council] to make sure they actually sent someone out [to the home to do the assessment].

In enlisting and recommending 'experts', carers and people with dementia were effectively asking for help with interpreting their circumstances in terms of governmental 'services' language, frameworks and bureaucratic processes. Parallels can be drawn with Giordano's (2014, i) work on ethno-psychologists working with foreigners in northern Italy, which explores the work of *translation* – beyond that of the linguistic variety – in which the 'difference' in people's situations 'poses the issue of alternative forms of life, of radically heterogeneous worlds that the state must reduce to recognizable categories'. While the context of Giordano's interlocutors differs from that of mine, both illustrate the persistence of state-sanctioned 'categories', as well as the need for others' help in fitting one's story into those categories to qualify for care – or cure – from the state. For the carers that I worked with, seeking out these 'experts' stood in contrast to support group discussions about members' expertise and command over other, intimate aspects of their lives. This redefined realms of expertise: expert knowledge about processes and content of legal and social service bureaucracy was held by Alzheimer's Society and governmental staff; expertise and success were crafted by carers (and, to a less pronounced degree, by people with dementia) by building knowledge and a network of people from whom to ask for help. Importantly, my interlocutors' accounts also show that they were very particular about which 'experts' they sought out and recommended to one another. Carers made clear delineations between 'experts' who could recognise the complexities and nuances of dementia care and family life, and were able to appreciate that respite was not a 'cure' for long-term caring, but instead a necessary part of ongoing care to allow carers to 'keep going'. For example, Nicky often came highly recommended because she 'knows how the assessment works … how to make sure you really put in all you're doing in each section' – underlining both this woman's expertise in state-sanctioned categories and an attuned cognisance that 'what it means to be a carer' 'is different for everyone'.

Bureaucratic hassle was not accounted for in official assessments, but, I argue, can be cast as 'hidden care work'. Carers did not consider that the considerable time and effort that they put in to understand, track down, organise and complete the extensive legal and social services paperwork was care work. In support groups, it was rarely compared to the daily at-home, intimate work that many carers found themselves doing for their person with dementia, such as cooking, feeding, washing and supervising. These activities were what 'counted' as care work in their reckoning of the term, and they were what carers' assessments and needs assessments focused on most. This connects to discourses on 'deservingness', because to qualify as 'deserving' of state care and support, carers had to expend extraordinary efforts to 'speak in the language' of the state. However, these efforts remained unrecognised because there was no 'category' to tally this work. Many carers commented that their kin with dementia 'has no idea how much time I spend trying to get it all sorted' – a doubled invisibility.

Lack of appreciation is part of what made paperwork so maddening and draining, and why these efforts were not perceived as care work. This links with discussions about the significance of acknowledgement and reciprocity of care in perceptions of, and constructions of, relatedness and kinship in dementia contexts (Taylor 2008). Here, I push Taylor's discussion further to suggest that the reciprocity and acknowledgement of care is what makes certain actions 'count as care', to use the language of my interlocutors. This lack of acknowledgement is perhaps complicated by the fact that 'hassle' pertains to public domains, and is undertaken by carers away from the private spaces shared with kin. Its visibility is thus obscured by both its lack of intimacy and the fact that the scope and processes of bureaucracy are only truly understood once one 'actually tries to get it sorted'. Tellingly, carers became worried that they were being a 'bad' daughter, wife, son and so on when they spent 'too much time chasing this [bureaucratic hassle] down, and not enough time with him [person with dementia]', particularly since these efforts were at times dedicated to securing 'respite – away from him'. Doing work that did not seem to be care work appeared to threaten bonds of relatedness between family members. At the same time, doing this bureaucratic work or, rather, trying very hard 'to get anywhere with it' also jeopardised people's trust and expectations of the state.

The state as a bad relative

In line with other anthropological research on the topic, relationships between people in my fieldsite, as citizens, and the state are informed by the temporality of bureaucratic processes, and, specifically, the temporality of waiting (Auyero 2012; Day 2016; Mathur 2014). These temporalities of waiting enervated, and thus illustrated, my informants' relationship to the state, which, I suggest, is one predicated on moral framings of care that seemed to reverberate with traces of kinship.

It is significant that my research was among a group of people, mostly British English by birth or current nationality, who strongly associated their identity with a nationalised system that boasts the NHS and socialised social care services. In her work on waiting for health care in UK contexts, Day (2016, 180) argues that the 'recognition of the care claimed and given ... defines a public to which you belong'. In strongly identifying with socialised services, my interlocutors positioned themselves as belonging to, identified by, and deserving of care by these systems. I make the leap from expectations of care from the NHS and related services to suggesting a moral relationship to the state, as envisioned by my interlocutors, through a consideration of their commentary about the role and responsibilities of the NHS and state to provide care over the course of their lives. 'Early' carers often spoke with confidence about how 'services will help sort things', that is, the increasing needs of a person with dementia, alongside proud comments that 'I've had the NHS all my life.' Carers at all points in their journey often made comments that 'the government really does have a duty to take care of them [people with dementia]', and 'dementia is an illness – it's part of the NHS's remit – everyone's health is important ... has to be looked after'. These expectations of care were further underlined when 'new' carers, over time, began to express confusion that 'nothing was happening', and exasperation: 'but we have the NHS!' Their disappointment mirrored more seasoned carers' more subdued resignation that 'dementia has shown' that 'they don't even care about us!'

In considering my interlocutors' comments that they and people with dementia were 'owed' by the NHS through the concept of the moral obligation of care (Faubion 2001), it is possible that carers' beliefs in the aims and promises of the NHS were derived partly through a nationalised identity as British. Some commented that the unpaid care that they were performing for their person with dementia was care they were 'doing for the government', which they had 'paid into my whole life', and that they should be given support for doing this care 'for free'. While the comments of carers and, to a lesser degree, people with dementia that they 'had paid in my whole life – working, taxes', and hopes for payments from the government, might seem to undermine this moral underpinning of care, this can be read otherwise. Kinship relations and economic relations are not necessarily oppositional in straightforward ways. If we consider that reciprocation of care is an important element underpinning kinship (Faubion 2001; Pettersen 2011), then my interlocutors' lifelong investment in the economic health of the state can be seen as akin to an act of care that prompts reciprocal support in return. This point is strengthened if one considers other findings, albeit based on work in Botswana, exploring how care also encompasses financial and material resources (not only labour and sentiment), which can contribute to wellbeing or ill-health in others (Livingston 2003, 2005). As discussed by Reece (2015, 119, 121), the ambiguous position which 'contributions' occupy between gift and commodity in Tswana families 'beget[s] further contributions in their turn … giving them a cyclic, continuous temporality and generative potential' that 'adapt the moral framework of exchange to incorporate … collectivity'. Here we see that 'contributions' to and from the state have a potential constitutive power to create bonds that define an inclusive group. Further, some carers' comments that much of the work that they were doing 'should be done' by the state likens the care they provided to that which the state could and should provide. Noting the importance they placed upon maintaining the embeddedness of their relative within family and society, this signals a nod to NHS and state support as more akin to the moral charge of kinship care than only the moral fulfilment of obligations and debts. Indeed, carers worked to establish their family member with dementia as a continuing citizen of, and participant in, the state, and an individual who was 'owed' something, and not only as a cared-for appendage to the family unit.

The expectation of reciprocation became most clear in my informants' discussions about extended waits for NHS and social care support. Feelings of betrayal and bitterness often marked carers' discussions about the kinds of care and support that they felt they were due. They traded tips on how to navigate the confusing bureaucratic hassle of powers of attorney and medical directives to 'be able to arrange things', 'because they [the state or NHS staff] don't explain anything'. These processes were also frequently altered by new 'promises' (such as those offered by the Care Act 2014), alongside the slow implementation of these new policies due to understaffing in local and national teams. At a large forum about the Care Act 2014, hosted by a university in central London in March 2015, many people in the audience who identified themselves as carers used the microphone to ask panel members 'when will we actually see any of this?', referring to provisions for stipends and respite for support carers, and whether 'everyone gets this, or is it up to your local authority?' They highlighted that 'much of this is too little, too late – I'm lucky that I could even come here today – so many carers can't even get out. We deserve better than this.' Some of the more frustrated and disbelieving carers who I recognised from support groups, as well as new contacts that I made on the day, commented to me privately that 'I'll believe it when I see it,' and 'The NHS, all of it, really is going downhill.' Tellingly, one woman likened the help she had received from the state thus far to family that just wanted to 'pay lip service'. These carers' frustrations also mirrored how they felt when family members found them 'undeserving' of the position of attorney over the affairs of the person with dementia – at a Carers Conference I attended, one carer told me that 'if they [the state] really wanted to help, they would'. Carers' frustrated comments signal a debt unpaid and recognition withheld, as well as dissatisfaction that the support promised 'won't reach everyone', but instead would differ between local authorities.

Auyero's (2012, 157) work illustrates the ways in which waiting for health and social care among the urban poor in Argentina 'appears to be "in the order of things" – as something normal, expected, inevitable'. Day (2016, 180) points out that waiting as an activity in the UK and other Western settings, with 'connotations of a delay endured, and an expectation unfulfilled' is relatively recent, and that before the early part of this century, it was not associated with queuing. Auyero (2012, 157, emphasis in original) argues that through waiting, 'the *everyday recon-struction of political domination*' is created. He casts waiting as a state tool to regulate the poor that turns citizens into patients and binds them to the state. However, my interlocutors' experiences of waiting for bureaucratic processes and state services to be implemented actually worked to unbind and distance citizens' perception of being cared for by the state and their embeddedness in socialised health systems. The disjointed, complicated governmental processes and responses to the specific needs of my informants created room for their sharp critique of the state. Among my informants, this critique centred on the state's default on promises of care earned. This analysis also reinforces findings on research with cancer patients using UK health services, wherein patient pathways became increasingly complicated by initiatives to introduce 'stratified medicine' approaches, aimed at personalisation and precision (Day et al. 2017). Day et al. (2017) show that the hassle created actually resulted in less personal care. Like their informants, instead of being drawn into a closer, more personal caring relationship with the NHS and support services, my interlocutors seemed to regard the relationship as estranged, often in bitter terms.

The aggrieved nature of these critiques signals an affront committed that was personally felt, pointing to an unravelling of a sense of relatedness with the state and a diminishment of membership of the very 'public' created through such services. As such, my material corroborates tensions between care and waiting in Day's (2016, 180) findings, which show 'the tensions within such a public, since participants consider that the NHS belongs to them while, at the same time, they are defined, contained, and put on hold by "the system"'. This state of affairs played out against a backdrop of warnings in the media that the 'NHS is in trouble', and providing less care support to the elderly (Triggle 2017), and an influx of privatisation that 'continues to threaten' the NHS – both in terms of viability and ethos (*The Guardian* 2019). Thus, we can see that in contemplating their futures, my informants reworked their relationships with the state as they redrafted their perception of the state as willing to recognise their needs, and as a capable provider of security against uncertain futures.

Conclusion

The bureaucratic hassles of familial carers' lives demonstrate the value of particular 'collectivities' (Mol 2008) in my interlocutors' lives: charities such as the Alzheimer's Society, and the power of peer support through support groups. They also reveal the profound impact that national policy projects such as the Care Act 2014 can have on the local and intimate details of people's lives. Perhaps most importantly, they reveal the significant creativity that people wield in finding their 'way through'. Looking at these people's willingness to continually wade through the 'hassle' also illuminates *for what and why* my interlocutors made this significant effort: the importance of the autonomy of a person with dementia, their decision-making capacity, and their deservingness of care emerges. My informants safeguard the wishes of a person with dementia in legal paperwork, in effect preserving their autonomy and 'right to choose' beyond their cognitive ability to do so. The 'what' and 'when' of genuine decision making are made more complex, and come to include the possibility of autonomous choice by proxy of close kin. As people with dementia become more dependent on the care and decisions of others, many people waded through the discomfort of confusing paperwork with 'strangers' to put plans in place to 'sort' the future, and also to 'sort' a delayed activation of 'what he wanted'. Further, carers and people with dementia sought consistent return to considerations of people's personal decisions and views, now and in the future, through paperwork – and tense arguments with extended kin about what authorities this paperwork grants.

Considering the importance of choice and autonomy in Western constructions of personhood (Mol 2008; Lamb 2014), my interlocutors' determination to navigate and mould legal and bureaucratic frameworks works to construct a personhood that can be extended into a future of marked, inevitable cognitive decline. Further, the deeply relational projects of using legal, official frameworks to preserve the choices and autonomy of people with dementia speak to debates about the importance of relationality in constructions of Western personhood (Carsten 2004). Carers' family discussions about the legal power and authority to 'decide what he would have wanted' pivot on questions of who is deserving of the power to make decisions in the future, based on who 'knows him the best now', at the time of the drafting of paperwork. Carrying forward the present frameworks of care of a person's life past the point they could autonomously do so themselves was paramount. Likewise, my interlocutors felt deep betrayal when promises of care from the state went unfilled and they were 'just put on a waiting list' – events they did not anticipate based on their previous conceptions of the state's nationalised health and social care, and therefore could not prepare for 'before it was too late'.

While relational, the work involved in safeguarding the choices of people with dementia into the future was often a deeply lonely and frustrating experience. Taking a bureaucratic lens on dementia care uncovers the disturbing realisation that carers' significant time and effort, and the very real emotional burden of 'hassle' to protect their family's wellbeing is not 'counted' as care – in their own reckoning, in acknowledgement from kin, or in the 'official' frameworks of the state. Indeed, this is what makes 'all this hassle' truly a hassle – it is hidden and unappreciated, and seems to produce little certainty. Thus, the enduring necessity of pursuing it to assemble some form of future security points to the chronic precarity of UK dementia care.

References

Adams, Vincanne, Michelle Murphy and Adele E. Clarke. 2009. 'Anticipation: Technoscience, life, affect, temporality', *Subjectivity* 28 (1): 246–65. https://doi.org/10.1057/sub.2009.18.

Alzheimer's Society. 2017. 'How a lasting power of attorney can help if you have dementia'. Accessed 10 October 2017. https://www.alzheimers.org.uk/get-support/legal-financial/lasting-power-attorney.

Ayuero, Javier. 2012. *Patients of the State: The politics of waiting in Argentina*. Durham, NC: Duke University Press.

Bourdieu, Pierre. 1994. 'Rethinking the state: Genesis and structure of the bureaucratic field', *Sociological Theory* 12 (1): 1–18. https://doi.org/10.2307/202032.

Buch, Elana D. 2015. 'Postponing passage: Doorways, distinctions, and the thresholds of personhood among older Chicagoans', *Journal of the Society for Psychological Anthropology* 43 (1): 40–58. https://doi.org/10.1111/etho.12071.

Carsten, Janet. 2004. *After Kinship*. New York: Cambridge University Press.

Day, Sophie. 2016. 'Waiting and the architecture of care'. In *Living and Dying in the Contemporary World: A compendium*, edited by Veena Das and Clara Han, 167–84. Oakland: University of California Press.

Day, Sophie, R. Charles Coombes, Louise McGrath-Lone, Claudia Schoenborn and Helen Ward. 2017. 'Stratified, precision or personalised medicine? Cancer services in the "real world" of a London hospital', *Sociology of Health & Illness* 39 (1): 143–58. https://doi.org/10.1111/1467-9566.12457.

Faubion, James D. 2001. 'Toward an anthropology of ethics: Foucault and the pedagogies of autopoiesis', *Representations* 74 (1): 83–104. https://doi.org/10.1525/rep.2001.74.1.83.

Giordano, Cristiana. 2014. *Migrants in Translation: Caring and the logics of difference in contemporary Italy*. Berkeley: University of California Press.

The Guardian. 2019. 'Letters: Privatisation continues to threaten our NHS', 8 December. Accessed 26 May 2021. https://www.theguardian.com/politics/2019/dec/08/privatisation-continues-to-threaten-our-nhs.

Kleinman, Arthur. 1999. 'Moral experience and ethical reflection: Can ethnography reconcile them? A quandary for "the new bioethics"', *Daedalus* 128 (4): 69–97.

Lamb, Sarah. 2014. 'Permanent personhood or meaningful decline: Toward a critical anthropology of successful aging', *Journal of Aging Studies* 29 (1): 41–52. https://doi.org/10.1016/j.jaging.2013.12.006.

Livingston, Julie. 2003. 'Reconfiguring old age: Elderly women and concerns over care in southeastern Botswana', *Medical Anthropology* 22 (3): 205–31. https://doi.org/10.1080/01459740306771.

Livingston, Julie. 2005. *Debility and the Moral Imagination in Botswana*. Bloomington: Indiana University Press.

Mathur, Nayanika. 2014. 'The reign of terror of the big cat: Bureaucracy and the mediation of social times in the Indian Himalaya', *Journal of the Royal Anthropological Institute* 20 (S1): 148–65. https://doi.org/10.1111/1467-9655.12098.

Mol, Annemarie. 2008. *The Logic of Care: Health and the problem of patient choice*. London: Routledge.

Pettersen, Tove. 2011. 'The ethics of care: Normative structures and empirical implications', *Health Care Analysis* 19 (1): 51–64. https://doi.org/10.1007/s10728-010-0163-7.

Pickard, Linda, Derek King and Martin Knapp. 2016. 'The "visibility" of unpaid care in England', *Journal of Social Work* 16 (3): 263–82. https://doi.org/10.1177/1468017315569645.

Reece, Koreen May. 2015. 'An ordinary crisis?: Kinship in Botswana's time of AIDS'. PhD thesis, University of Edinburgh. http://hdl.handle.net/1842/21083.

Serrano-Aguilar, P.G., J. Lopez-Bastida and V. Yanes-Lopez. 2006. 'Impact on health-related quality of life and perceived burden of informal caregivers of individuals with Alzheimer's disease', *Neuroepidemiology* 27 (3): 136–42. https://doi.org/10.1159/000095760.

Taylor, Janelle S. 2008. 'On recognition, caring, and dementia', *Medical Anthropology Quarterly* 22 (4): 313–35. https://doi.org/10.1111/j.1548-1387.2008.00036.x.

Triggle, N. (2017). '10 charts that show why the NHS is in trouble', *BBC News*, 8 February. Accessed 31 May 2021. https://www.bbc.co.uk/news/health-38887694.

5
Assemblages of care around albinism: Kin-based networks and (in)dependence in contemporary Tanzania

Giorgio Brocco

Introduction

From the early 2000s onward, international and Tanzanian media coverage has reported that groups of assailants guided by 'traditional healers' (*waganga wa kienyeji*) have orchestrated attacks on, and murders of, people with albinism in various regions of north-western Tanzania (Bryceson et al. 2010; Burke et al. 2014). The neoliberal context of the national fishing and mining industries triggered the rise of these violent events, fuelling the commodification of the limbs of persons with albinism throughout the country (Bryceson et al. 2010; Schühle 2013). Overlooking the social and political reasons behind the violence, most humanitarian agencies, such as the United Nations (UN), and numerous non-governmental organisations (NGOs) have assigned blame to 'witch doctors' (a depreciative term for traditional healers) and remarked on the importance of asserting human rights values for people with albinism throughout the African continent (Burke et al. 2014).

In biomedical terms, albinism refers to a group of related conditions resulting from a genetic mutation that causes a deficiency in melanin production in the hair, skin and eyes. Various health-related outcomes are associated with albinism: visual issues (for example, nystagmus, strabismus, photophobia, lack of both stereopsis and binocular vision) and high onset of skin cancer risk (Reimer-Kirkham et al. 2019, 748–9). According to previous research on albinism in Tanzania, people with the condition, generally living in contexts of economic precarity, can encounter community marginalisation and discrimination (Blankenberg 2000; Baker et al. 2010; Reimer-Kirkham et al. 2019). One reason for these social outcomes pertains to a set of ideas that consider albinism as an ambiguous condition. Machoko (2013) points out that in some African regions, people with albinism occupy an ontological place between humanity and the spirit realm. Other research has pointed out that moral discourses about albinism as a 'bad omen' resulting from previous moral misdeeds have underpinned the stigmatisation of people with the condition (Baker et al. 2010). Considered as unable individuals or people with cognitive impairments, Tanzanian people with albinism have to prove to society that their condition does not prevent them from realising their potential and contributing to neoliberal forms of development (*maendeleo*) of their communities. Nevertheless, in various African urban and rural contexts, effective enhancements of social inclusion depend on the presence of networks of support and care (Braathen and Ingstad 2006; Brocco 2016). The formation of self-help groups (Chelala 2007) and local activist organisations are two social factors that can further inclusion. Conversely, recent media appearances by musicians and fashion models with albinism contribute to the fetishisation of bodies with albinism in national and international public media platforms (Hohl and Krings 2019; Brocco 2020). While these political, media and humanitarian efforts focus on reframing albinism, these narratives have simultaneously contributed to the further victimisation of people with the condition in Tanzania. Individuals with albinism have been portrayed as subjects in need of protection from attack, (economic) help, and care because of the murders, high rates of skin cancer and widespread social stigma (Baker et al. 2010; Reimer-Kirkham et al. 2019; Brocco 2016).

In light of the killings and the subsequent media/humanitarian publicity, the present analysis has a double goal. First, it sheds light on how my interlocutors with albinism navigated and interacted with various forms of care and dependence, enacted within and shaped by their kin-based networks, neighbours, religious congregations, national and international organisations, and the Tanzanian nation state. The second goal is to reveal how notions of care over the last decades have shifted from being characterised as communitarian practices to individualised endeavours enmeshed within narratives of national development (*maendeleo*) and a spirit of (individual) empowerment (*kuwezesha*). By introducing the recent post-colonial history of Tanzania, I point out that institutional, political and economic changes have modified individual and social trajectories and practices of care. Despite this shift, people with albinism have shown that their practices of care are defined by efforts of mutual help and communitarian networks. To call attention to the interacting networks of care and support around them, I invoke the analytical perspective of 'assemblages of care', a concept that explains the intertwinements of heterogeneous discourses and divergent practices of care in various temporalities and (urban/rural) contexts.

The stories of Florentina[1] and Daudi, two research participants from the Ilula ward (Kilolo district, Iringa region) and Dar es Salaam, provide the ethnographic data on which my analysis is based. Their stories illustrate that people with the condition do not represent themselves as exclusively objects of care, as highlighted by humanitarian and media narratives. Rather, they see themselves as caring subjects able to forge various networks of mutual help and support. I collected Florentina's and Daudi's stories, and other life trajectories, over 18 months of fieldwork in Tanzania (2012–15) carried out during various research stays, first as an NGO staff member, and then as a PhD student. Florentina's and Daudi's cases exemplify similar vicissitudes experienced by other people with albinism in Tanzania in terms of creating various mutual networks of care and support. However, their stories also shed light on personal attitudes and diverging relationships of care in relation to various social contexts (for example, employment, social status and geographical areas) and gender differences. During these research stints, I conducted participant observations, semi-structured interviews and group discussions with people with albinism, their relatives, community members, NGO staff members, traditional healers, political representatives and religious (Muslim and Christian) local leaders. Hence, I spent the longest period of research in the villages of the Ilula ward (Kilolo district), inside the Iringa region in south-western Tanzania. This area is characterised by agricultural businesses of hybrid maize, onions and potatoes, and a regional market for tomatoes (considered to be a dominant crop). One Lutheran-Protestant hospital and several health dispensaries were the main health facilities in the area. Low-priced hotels and guest houses for seasonal migrants and truck-drivers (mainly from Dar es Salaam and headed to eastern Tanzania) represented specific characteristics of the Kilolo district. Two Christian (Catholic and Protestant) missions, two Muslim mosques and six Pentecostal churches underline the multiple and disparate religious presence in the Ilula ward. In addition to my fieldwork inside the Ilula ward, I also conducted research in Dar es Salaam, the most economically important city in Tanzania, where many NGOs and government officials are located.

Multiple assemblages of care around people with albinism

The concept of assemblages of care indicates the diverse connections, articulations and materiality of practices and ideas that constitute territorialised forms of care in specific temporalities and social contexts (Lamb 2020, 324; Van Eeuwijk 2020). In line with its analytical sense (Deleuze and Guattari 1987; for a critique of its use in sociocultural anthropology, see Bialecki 2018), I consider assemblages as conglomerations of contingent, diverse social attitudes that are, therefore, not stable, but structured around multiple criticisms, ethical discourses, contestations and moral practices (Ong and Collier 2004, 4–5; Zigon 2011, 31; Marcus and Saka 2006; Rabinow 2003). For people with albinism, for instance, assemblages of care materialise in the intricate networks of families, communities, the state and NGOs. To illustrate how assemblages of care are formed, I describe Florentina's and Daudi's attitudes of (in)dependence, which are specular, but intrinsically interrelated, and a counterpart to caring practices in Tanzania.

Care is 'a shifting and unstable concept' that is 'moral, relational, historically specific, and embedded within forms of governance and global political economic transformation' (Buch 2015, 287). Everyday practices, daily engagements with various social domains, and networks constitute important focuses in which relations 'to do with the good' manifest in their multiple 'practical tinkering' and 'active experimentation' (Mol et al. 2010, 13; Mol 2008, 2010). The analysis of care for/ about and by people with albinism/disability takes into account the contingent and fluid processes of creating relatedness and forging social bonds among people living in similar precarious conditions (for example, Carsten 2000; Manderson and Block 2016). Intended as a set of relational and enacted practices (Warren and Sakellariou 2020), care involves both affective dimensions (caring about) and real practices (caring for) (Buch 2015, 279).

Forms of hierarchical subordination and patronage between the population and state/supra-national entities such as humanitarian agencies and NGOs (variously interpreted as forms of modern sovereignty (Ecks 2004)) represent an important perspective to comprehend various notions of care generating multiple 'politics of deservingness' (see Montesi and Calestani's introduction in this volume). Social relationships based on 'declarations of dependence' (Ferguson 2013) within economic landscapes of 'distributive labour' (Ferguson 2015) lead to the understanding of how various forms of care are enacted in, and shape the life experiences of, people with albinism in Tanzania. On the one hand, an analysis of assemblages of care and dependence reveals how individuals with albinism in economic situations of precarity endeavour to assert their rights and social claims towards actors with a greater socio-economic capacity to provide (such as NGOs, political parties and the state). In this way, these people establish symbolic and material relations of hierarchy and dependence as vehicles for social and economic mobility; these are the means for securing and sustaining life in circumstances of relative deprivation, where the state cannot be counted on, or fails to provide, support (Ferguson 2015; see also Kennedy's contribution in this volume). On the other hand, this perspective underlines that people with albinism are enmeshed in mutual relationships of care and dependence with other people living in similar or divergent socioeconomic contexts (Ferguson 2013, 231). The latter also defines how social networks are sustained and enacted.

The non-normative bodily difference of people with albinism in Tanzania is another relevant element to understanding assemblages of care. Anthropological studies on forms of care and dependence around people with disabilities, debility (Livingston 2005) and other chronic conditions in the Global South and African regions are fundamental. The analysis of modes of citizenship (Ingstad and Whyte 2007, 21–2; Das and Addlakha 2007), understandings of economic and political activities of people with mobility disabilities (Kohrman 2005; Devlieger 2018), comprehension of deaf social worlds and activism (Nakamura 2006; Friedner 2015) and studies of agency, politics of appearance and belonging among people with various forms of human difference (Staples and Mehrotra 2016) highlight the centrality of modes of care and belonging enacted within kin-based relationships and social networks around rights claims. For people with albinism and other disabilities/chronic conditions in Tanzania, for instance, manifold actions of caring depend on economic and political situations. In this regard, Dilger (2010) observes that practices of caring and nursing for people with HIV/AIDS rely on kinship networks and religious congregations in the context of international funding strategies and implementations of structural adjustment programmes in the country.

In present-day Tanzania, my interlocutors with albinism used various terms to refer to their assemblages of care. While *kutunza* entails acts of care for sick or disabled people, *kujitunza* is related to the care for oneself and one's kin-based relatives. *Kujali* translates the action of taking care of, or looking after, someone with a vulnerable condition within specific kin-based networks. *Kusaidia*, instead, concerns practices of providing help in more general terms. These words not only illustrate practical actions and affective dimensions in inter-subjective relationships in Tanzanian society; they also address the meaningful emergence of interventions by humanitarian and health organisations implementing multiple regimes of care (Fassin 2011) which are the expression of ambivalent 'politics of deservingness' (see Montesi and Calestani's introduction in this volume). These words are the practical terms that translate the assemblages of care within which my research participants were immersed. To unpack the semantic complexity of these terms, the following section explores notions of care that have emerged in the post-colonial history of Tanzania.

The reduction of institutional care and the 'NGOisation' of the nation state

In the 1970s, the socialist government of Tanzania under President Julius Nyerere (1964–85) suffered from growing external debt and exploding costs in its heavily subsidised economy and over-funded external systems. The international oil crisis and global economic depression further exacerbated this situation. With the end of the Nyerere era and the election of President Ali Hassan Mwinyi in 1985, the Tanzanian state accepted the World Bank and International Monetary Fund's structural adjustment policies. This political decision marked the start of the country's neoliberal phase, and the implementation of various types of economic reforms concerning the implementation of cash economy, trade liberalisation, deregulation of foreign investments, and para-statal and civil services. The adoption of these economic and political measures caused a steep reduction in governmental expenditures for health care, education and housing programmes. As a consequence, the Tanzanian state started to greatly rely on external socioeconomic support from international institutions and NGOs for services, and international private companies for industrial development (Dilger 2010, 103–4).

The years from the 1970s to the 1990s, however, constituted an important period for the legal and political recognition of people with albinism and disabilities in Tanzania. Under the Nyerere government, the Tanzania 1977 Constitution prohibited discrimination against people with disability (Aldersey and Turnbull 2011, 161–2). Through a series of subsequent legal acts, people with albinism and other disabilities (deafness and blindness, for example) succeeded in constituting their first organisations. Under the Nyerere government's motto of self-reliance (*kujitegemea*), freedom (*uhuru*) and national unity (*umoja*), people with non-normative bodies were considered to belong to the Tanzanian national community at large (Nyerere 1966). The Tanzania Albinism Society (TAS) was one of three state-funded organisations. Founded in 1978, TAS was categorised by the state authorities as a Disabled People's Organisation (DPO). My interlocutors with albinism did not agree with this classification, as they believed that the label 'disability' could add even more social burden and stigma to their daily experiences. Between the 1980s and the early 2000s, a series of international documents, declarations and legal acts for the enhancement of human rights for people with disability were promulgated (Ingstad and Whyte 2007, 4–5). Post-Nyerere governments in Tanzania later ratified these official documents (Aldersey and Turnbull 2011, 160). The Disability Act of 2010 is the most recent legislation that attests to the right of people with a disability to make human rights claims and demand protection.

Despite the promulgation of these legal acts, the Tanzanian state continued to reduce funding for the welfare, health care and education systems, and awareness activities by many national DPOs. Instead of being administered through public funds allocated by networks of state-supported health facilities and the former Ministry of Health and Social Welfare (*Wizara ya Afya na Ustawi wa Jamii*), the material forms of care and economic relief for disabled individuals and people with albinism and/or other chronic conditions began to depend solely on their families, religious congregations, international NGOs and informal networks of community solidarity and mutual help. In various postcolonial countries in Africa, these assemblages of care, although flexible and unstable, sustained the sociality of people with non-normative bodies, and provided them with material means for their daily survival (Livingston 2005; Whyte 2014; Dilger 2008; de Klerk and Moyer 2017; MacGregor 2018). In addition to practices of caring for and caring about, acts of care for oneself (*kujitunza*) in neoliberal times also became relevant. *Kujitunza* constituted the material means through which disabled people could react 'to the demands of their positions as parents, as children of elderly parents, as partners, as patients' (de Klerk and Moyer 2017, 315–16).

During the two decades before the outbreak of news about the killings of people with albinism in about 2006/7, TAS was the first Tanzanian organisation supporting people with the condition, mainly those living in Dar es Salaam. Despite the organisation's claim of having many regional and district offices throughout Tanzania, only a few local branches existed in the past and were still active during my fieldwork in 2014/15. From the early 2000s onward, there was political pressure from various international institutions (for example, the United Nations and the European Union) and NGOs on the Tanzanian government to mobilise after the spread of news about the murders of people with albinism. Various international NGOs and the Tanzanian government started to conduct privately and publicly funded awareness campaigns and humanitarian interventions using booklets and educational activities in rural and urban areas (Engstrand-Neacsu and Wynter 2009). To protect children with albinism, the Tanzanian state instituted special camps. Under the Same Sun (UTSS), a Christian-Protestant NGO from Canada, was founded in 2008 by Peter Ash, a wealthy Canadian entrepreneur with albinism. Starting from 2009, the organisation conducted public awareness campaigns in both rural and urban north-western regions such as Mwanza and Shinyanga. Subsequently, UTSS provided students with albinism with approximately 320 scholarships countrywide, and compiled a research database with information on albinism in Tanzania and other African states. Although TAS had been under-resourced, the members continued organising the state-funded National Albinism Day. In 2015, this celebration day became the UN-recognised International Albinism Awareness Day. From the early 2000s onward, TAS also received economic support from other international NGOs and private donors for conducting awareness and health-related campaigns in Tanzanian hospitals, mainly in Dar es Salaam and Morogoro. Another important NGO for people with albinism is Standing Voice, a UK-based organisation founded in 2013 by Harry Freeland, director of the documentary *In the Shadow of the Sun* (2012). Standing Voice addresses advocacy and health issues for people with the condition. The main interventions include collaboration with the Kilimanjaro Christian Medical Centre (KCMC) in Moshi, aimed at implementing various mobile programmes on low-vision care and skin cancer prevention.

However, these humanitarian activities have concentrated mainly in the north-western regions and Dar es Salaam, and they have not reached other parts of the country. During my fieldwork, few humanitarian and state-funded projects were located in the Iringa region. One of these interventions (supported by the Tanzanian state, the United Nations Children's Fund (UNICEF) and UTSS), intended to distribute sunscreen lotions to the population with albinism. In 2015, the KCMC provided the Iringa Regional Hospital with hydrogen therapeutic instruments for curing skin cancer lesions. Additionally, the health facility in Moshi (Kilimanjaro region) started compiling national lists of people with the condition who could undergo surgical operations for removing skin cancers. The Tanzanian state, headed by the then President, Jakaya Kikwete (2005–15), allowed free ophthalmological and dermatological check-ups once a month in every public hospital, and the free distribution of second-hand sunscreen and hats to the population with albinism. In 2010 and 2013, the Iringa regional government, in collaboration with the Kilolo district office, organised meetings with local TAS members and other people with albinism living in the area. Their scope was to deliver sunscreen and hats to people with albinism, and to provide them with safety guidelines against possible attacks, as well as information on how to prevent the onset of skin cancer. In addition to the few humanitarian and state projects, the Christian-Catholic mission and the Ilula Orphan Project (a Norwegian–Tanzanian NGO) included disadvantaged children with albinism in their support programmes.

From the post-independence history of Tanzania, it emerges that the negative outcomes of the liberalisation measures have affected the life experiences of many people with non-normative bodies. Welfare services, social benefits and activities for people with albinism by NGOs were mainly based in specific regions. Although there have been a few national measures taken by the Tanzanian government (for example, the creation of a governmental task force for preventing murders and promoting the presence of politicians with albinism in the Tanzanian Parliament), unequal and temporary distribution of humanitarian care remains across the Iringa region. Additionally, some interlocutors with albinism from Dar es Salaam have refused to become involved in the NGOs' activities because they were critical of the provisional dimensions of their humanitarian interventions and services. Within this scenario, religious (Christian and Muslim) congregations, kin-based and communitarian forms of care assume a relevant status. Individual modes of caring for oneself and one's family also become important, especially in big cities such as Dar es Salaam. The two cases of Florentina and Daudi epitomise the materialisation of all multiple and unstable assemblages of care in the wake of neoliberal measures and the correlated 'NGOisation' of carescapes in Tanzania.

Kin-based care and humanitarian discourses in Ilula: Florentina's experiences

In 2015, Florentina, a 30-year-old woman with albinism, shared a house with her mother, in her sixties, in the Ilula ward of the Iringa region. Florentina's father had passed away 10 years earlier. While two of Florentina's brothers had migrated to Iringa city and Dar es Salaam looking for more suitable job opportunities, one sister and two other brothers chose to settle in the area. After her second marriage failed, Florentina and her three children returned to Ilula. Despite her vulnerable social conditions and economic uncertainty, Florentina has experienced love and care from her relatives since birth. Her mother described this event in the following terms:

> When Florentina was born, we all were very surprised [*tulishangaa sana*] to have had a child *zeruzeru* [albino]. Some villagers brought more presents than they used to bring for the birth of normal children. They gave us soaps, cloths or money as presents [*sabuni, vitenge au hela kama zawadi*] and our neighbours [*wajirani wetu*] were keeping saying '*amepata mzungu jamani, amepata mzungu* [we have an albino, people, we have an albino]!' ... When Florentina grew up, anyway, I came to think that she was a normal child [*mtoto wa kawaida*], and also my husband, who was really sceptical [*mwenye shaka*], began to consider her as normal. ... At the beginning, actually, my husband suffered a bit because we were all black, but afterward he was relieved when we discovered that *binti mwenye ukoo wetu alikuwa zeruzeru tu* [a daughter within our lineage had had albinism too]. ... By asking within our family group [*familia*], we also got to know that *mama yetu na ndugu zetu* [our grandmother and our family members] had 11 children with albinism as well. ... We saw many persons *zeruzeru* but, of course, there were other neighbours [*watu wengine wa jirani*] who asked me why Florentina was this way, and I always replied saying that skin colour is not important ... According to the choice of God [*uchaguo wa Mungu*] she was a normal woman!

At first, the birth of a child with albinism was considered an unusual event. However, Florentina's parents succeeded in identifying the presence of other relatives with the condition and associated it with God's will. In the meantime, neighbours and other community members behaved in an ambiguous way. On the one hand, they brought presents for Florentina's birth, as usually happens. On other hand, they emphasised Florentina's bodily difference and related her corporeality to a white person, as signalled by Florentina's mother. The material and symbolic forms of care enacted by Florentina's parents were concerned with finding an explanation for the birth of a child with albinism. In this way, they aimed to explain Florentina's condition to the entire community, and asserted the normalcy (*kitu cha kawaida*) of albinism. Overall, their attitude intended to dismiss the ambiguity in the words and actions of some of Florentina's neighbours. This form of kin-based care facilitated the introduction of the child with albinism into the community's social life, and the reassertion of her family's moral position. As underlined by other interlocutors with albinism, the birth of a child with the condition could also provoke a fracture in kin-based networks, especially on the father's side. The appearance of a child with albinism could be understood as a curse (*laana*), a sign of the child's mother's amoral conduct towards her relatives and ancestors. As many interlocutors mentioned, children with albinism were usually hidden by their parents. Thus, Florentina epitomises a positive example in which her parents' moral integrity was re-affirmed by the presence of previous family members with albinism. Therefore, the stigmatisation and marginalisation of people with albinism within their nuclear and larger family circles do not represent fixed affective and behavioural states. On the contrary, these attitudes are mobile, vague and variable across a wide spectrum of feelings and affects.

In her younger life, Florentina helped her mother as a housekeeper, and later worked as a hired hand cultivating fields around the Ilula ward. Once married, she traded vegetables in Ilula and neighbouring villages. The majority of her family income was provided by her two, consecutive, husbands. Once her last marital union ended, she was employed by her sister, who had a tiny restaurant along the paved highway from Dar es Salaam to Iringa. In our discussions, Florentina explained that she usually spent time with her female neighbours talking about various subjects, such as unexpected events in Ilula, the lives of other villagers, their children, or rumours about the priest of the nearby Christian-Catholic mission. These networks of relatedness were built up on a reciprocity of words, but also on mutual care in the case of an unexpected disease, on economic support and affective relations. Relevant elements in the assemblages of care around Florentina were also constituted by her membership of the Christian-Catholic religious congregation of Ilula, and her relationships with other people with albinism in the Kilolo district. Her relationships of care within the Catholic community, and with some of her neighbours, materialised in 2014, when they donated food and money to help Florentina and her children overcome a separation from her second husband. On another occasion, they also financed her journey to Moshi for a surgical operation to remove a skin cancer. For these reasons, Florentina asserted that she felt protected by her parents (*wazazi*) and friends (*marafiki*) against possible attacks and stigma by unknown people.

After the organisation of the first state-funded meetings for people with albinism in 2010/11, Florentina got in touch with other people with albinism from neighbouring villages. She met them in the sporadic gatherings organised by TAS and the Kilolo district office during the time when people with albinism were being murdered. Afterwards, in 2014/15, she regularly saw some women with albinism every three months for sunscreen lotion distribution organised by the KCMC in the Kilolo district. During this period, Florentina hosted two of these women who came to Ilula to buy and sell their crops and other items in the local markets. Thus, she underlined that she considered them as her friends. Thanks to her contact with the national humanitarian world, Florentina started to envision albinism not only as the will of God, but also as a disability. She expressed her thoughts in this way:

> Albinism [*uzeruzeru*] is a disability! Of course, this condition [*hali hii*] is! Everything is more difficult for us ... You cannot carry out duties in the field if you have a skin like mine. Your skin burns and you aren't able to see nothing. ... My disability of the skin [*ulemavu wangu wa ngozi*] is different from the one of deaf people, cripples or blind persons! I feel to have a distinct disability [*ulemavu tofauti tofauti*] because I have both my physical strength [*nguvu zangu za kimwili*] and cognitive capacities [*akili*]! ... I didn't do anything wrong and I am a creature of God!

Being a single woman with albinism generated difficulties for Florentina and did not facilitate the construction of new networks of relatedness outside her circle of kin-members and friends. Therefore, her words and practices highlight how she tried to create networks of solidarity and support with other people with albinism, and relied on discourses brought forward by NGOs and humanitarian agencies. Her definition of albinism as a distinct disability allowed her to prove her capacities and skills to other community members, while highlighting her humanity and desire to be part of society in a material way. Her body acquired another meaning, understood as a difference that did not diminish her physical and cognitive capacities. Florentina's parallel between albinism and representations of the condition as a disability pointed out how she intended to stress the needs for special care for people with albinism. In her opinion, she felt part of the national community of people with albinism in Tanzania, especially during the waves of killings and violence. Between the lines, she also stated that albinism was not due to her or her parents' moral misdeeds. For this reason, her consideration of albinism as a distinct kind of disability marked her as belonging to all human beings created by God.

While Florentina worked in her brother-in-law's restaurant in 2015, she continued farming the small piece of land held by her mother and two of her brothers. One day, she remembered that her previous farming as hired hand represented 'hard work' (*kazi ngumu*):

> I cannot work as others do because under the sun my skin becomes *nyekundu* [red] and develops *vidonda sana* [many wounds]. ... Like today, the only way to cultivate the field is to go there at dawn. ... Before, my husband didn't work and I needed money, so I was going there every day no matter what! ... Thanks to God, I am with my sister working in the restaurant!

Florentina's words underline two important elements in her life trajectory. On the one hand, her socioeconomic condition is characterised by precariousness and economic vulnerability. Her agricultural activities further exacerbate her worsening health, and have produced two cancerous lesions on the back of her neck. The onset of her wounds provoked a reprocessing by the KCMC health worker, who signed her up for a free surgical operation at the KCMC hospital in Moshi. Despite the harshness of her life, the direct and indirect socioeconomic support provided by her closer relatives (mother and sister) constitute the materialisation of forms of care that manifested within her networks of family and friends. However, the precariousness of her socioeconomic conditions did not allow her to autonomously care for her three children and give back the material care provided by her relatives as economic support.

Florentina's assemblages of care are constituted by her parents' behaviours, social networks of relatedness, religious affiliation, new acquaintances with other people with albinism, and the various humanitarian organisations. Although the NGOs and the Tanzanian state applied their institutionalised regimes of care as guidelines for protection against the killings and the onset of skin cancer, people with albinism such as Florentina continue to be sustained by established and new, unstable but strong, wider assemblages of care. On the one hand, national activist organisations and international NGOs influence life experiences and subjectivities of people with albinism by creating relationships of (in)dependence based on the financial and material support they claim to provide. On the other hand, humanitarian narratives such as the equation of albinism with a disability represent tangible ways for people with albinism to claim equal social and political rights to health, education and job opportunities.

(In)dependence in Dar es Salaam: Daudi's self-care, care for and care about others

During the time of my fieldwork in Dar es Salaam, I met Daudi, a 45-year-old *bajaji* (auto rickshaw) driver with albinism. Having spent his youth in his hometown Tanga (a city in north-eastern Tanzania) trading vegetables and farming, he moved to the economic capital of Tanzania in the mid-1990s. Thanks to a contact of a friend from Tanga, he started to work as a *bajaji* driver. In the early 2000s, Daudi decided to buy a small wagon with economic support from one of his sisters living in Zanzibar. By transporting goods and vegetables from various coastal cities to Dar es Salaam, Daudi saved enough money to purchase an electric millstone – an enterprise in which his sister and a *bajaji* renter participated. Some years later, he also bought a *bajaji* for one of his brothers to start a business in Tanga. In the meantime, Daudi was able to set up a small restaurant in Morogoro, managed by his wife, his two older sons and two nephews. In addition to Daudi using his personal earnings, two of his brothers living in Dar es Salaam contributed to the construction of the restaurant. In 2008, however, Daudi lost almost all his savings. In an attempt to enlarge his net worth, he set up a society with a man from Kenya who defrauded him. Due to these circumstances, he sold the millstone and the *bajaji* to repay his accumulated debts. To keep his restaurant, he resolved to ask for money from two of his friends, who were in the *bajaji* business in Dar es Salaam. With this economic support, he succeeded in renting an auto rickshaw and started working again as a *bajaji* driver. He once said to me: '35,000 TZS per day for normal rickshaw or 50,000 TZS for bigger vehicles. It is a bit expensive, but I can get by!'

When I asked Daudi to describe his life trajectory and the way he had created various business opportunities in both Tanga and Dar es Salaam, he used two terms related to neoliberal vocabulary: development (*maendeleo*) and empowerment (*kuwezesha*). However, rather than being considered as a triumph of individualism, these two terms referred to his ability to establish networks of care and dependence in contemporary Tanzania. *Kuwezesha* derives from the recent 'NGOisation' of the Tanzanian state, and the importance of the humanitarian sector in improving the life experiences of Tanzanians, and ameliorating the functions and services provided by the national state. Development is a concept dating back to Nyerere's times, and entails community or national improvement through the participation of all the state's citizens. For Daudi, the assemblages of care materialised in the support and help provided by his networks of family members and friends from both Tanga and Dar es Salaam. These relationships of care consequently demanded interdependence, established through mutual exchanges of economic and moral obligations towards the extended family (*familia*) and migration community (*jamii*), considered as social contexts for the realisation and sustainment of an individual. As proof of such networks of mutual help, people employed in either Daudi's restaurant or his millstone business were younger members of his extended family, and people belonging to his urban network. In his story, the only person who jeopardised his plans was a man from Kenya with whom he wanted to build a business relationship.

The production of new, and the maintenance of old, networks are also ways by which people with albinism are able to prove to society and other family members that they can empower others and contribute to their socioeconomic 'development'. For instance, Daudi encountered several issues of acceptance by his wife's relatives. He recounted:

> I started to know my wife in Dar es Salaam, and I wanted to marry her. At that time I was also thinking of going back to Tanga as I wanted to buy a *bajaji*. I had the money and I had already bought a *machine ya kusaga mahindi* [a millwheel to grind maize]. I remember that I had lots of troubles, as her relatives did not allow their daughter to marry an albino. They said, in particular her mother, that they were afraid to have a grandson albino, and that I would not have been able to provide for my family … It was not nice, but my wife wanted to marry me, and I had the money to marry her at that time, so at the end we got married. … Afterward, even her parents understood our will.

In addition to the economic status of his paternal family, Daudi had to show his wife's relatives that he had multiple sources of income to pay his wife's bride-wealth and create a stable future for her and their children. Therefore, his albinism became for his wife's family just a non-normative bodily difference that did not entail any disability and/or physical impairment.

Although every person with albinism born in Tanzania automatically becomes a member of the TAS, Daudi did not feel part of the national organisation. Unlike Florentina, who saw her membership as a chance for personal improvement, he confessed: 'I do not have the time to go there! It is not useful at all, and they are not even able to collect sunscreens! … I had to work!' Even though Daudi was aware that he could become a victim of murder or target of stigma in Dar es Salaam due to his appearance, he believed that through the 'will of God' and hard work (*kufanya kazi ngumu*), every person with or without albinism could succeed in life and provide help to (*kutoa msaada*) his own networks.

While NGOs, humanitarian institutions and broadcast media generally portray people with albinism as victims who deserve care and humanitarian support, Daudi's story underlines the individual agency and subjective dispositions of many people with the condition. His life trajectory underlines the individual capacities of people with albinism, and the network of relatives and friends that sustain their efforts. In the creation of Daudi's networks of friends and kin-based relatives, notions of masculinity also played an important role. While Florentina was abandoned by the fathers of her three children, Daudi succeeded in marrying his wife and having other occasional sexual partners in Dar es Salaam. My male interlocutors with albinism were married to wives with or without albinism, while many female research participants did not have stable partners, or experienced troubled relationships. Gender differences for people with albinism are further underlined by the fact that, unlike Florentina, Daudi did not look for active participation in the humanitarian world. Nor did he emphasise his membership in a Pentecostal congregation in Dar es Salaam.

Daudi's ethnographic case underlines that care for others is strongly connected with the economic capacities of the people providing support. While Daudi's assemblages of care seem to only epitomise values of self-reliance and independence, these relationships highlight the importance of networks of care and dependence towards others. Nevertheless, his insistence on notions of care as caring for himself and his relatives/friends imply a resemantisation of current political and NGO narratives of empowerment (*kuwezesha*) and development (*maendeleo*). These material forms of care therefore point out that the socioeconomic improvement of Daudi depends on the related amelioration of life conditions of other persons within his own networks of relatedness and community (*jamii*). Such constellations of care semantically refer to the values set up during the Nyerere government's socialist period. Finally, masculinity constitutes a further substantial element in this articulation of care that can subvert the corporeality of the subject of care through relationships of (in)dependence and labour. While in other social arrangements (such as the family, the state and international NGOs), articulations of care are directed to the person with albinism, Daudi's case underlines how the 'male' person with the condition has to, and can, provide care and economic stability for himself and other members of his networks.

Conclusion

The two ethnographic cases of Daudi and Florentina highlight the multiple assemblages of care and dependence of people with albinism in Tanzania. Florentina drew a parallel between albinism and representations of the condition as a disability to stress the need for special protection against the killings and claiming human rights for people with albinism. However, her strategic definition of the condition as a physical impairment also refers to the humanitarian categorisation of albinism as a disability that is not an inability to be productive and work. Therefore, Florentina's equation of albinism with a physical disability represents a symbolic and regimented form of care that NGOs, on behalf of people with albinism, use to claim rights to education, health and work, and access to various material resources. Florentina's conceptions of albinism indirectly derived from her networks of care that materialised in both her family's and her neighbours' reactions to her birth, and the support she has received from her neighbours and the members of her Catholic congregation in Ilula. In the neoliberal disabling Tanzanian society in which people with albinism can encounter various forms of stigma and discrimination, the informal material support provided by relatives, parents and other community groups constitute a way to cope with economic vulnerability, precariousness and social uncertainty.

Unlike Florentina, Daudi did not consider himself as a disabled person. On the contrary, he affirmed his able-bodied capacities to sort out his life by himself and contribute to the improvement of his family and friends. Despite his critiques of the humanitarian activities and the importance of social relationships in terms of social care, Daudi's practices illustrate the relevant role played by his kin-based and communitarian networks in Tanga and Dar es Salaam. While he was critical about the care and the lack of welfare benefits provided by the Tanzanian state and NGOs, Daudi's life experience epitomises a resemantised form of the neoliberal values of empowerment and development that he indirectly criticises. Instead of remarking on the values of individuality and self-reliance, his notion of empowerment and development underlined the relevance of assemblages of care in the affirmation of the 'male' subject in Tanzanian society. Daudi's ethnographic case shows this middle-aged man's efforts and difficulties when trying to economically support his family and gain recognised social status in Dar es Salaam. His life trajectory also highlights that care is entangled with relationships of dependence involving relatives, neighbours and friends in contexts of out-migration

(Dilger 2008, 2014). These are practices that can be performed by people with non-normative bodies such as Daudi's.

Assemblages of care around the life experiences of my interlocutors with albinism are therefore made up of multiple and diverging relationships and networks that change over time and across social contexts. The forced adoption of neoliberal reforms, the transformation of the Tanzanian economy, and the 'NGOisation' of its public services have provoked modifications in the institutional care provided to the most vulnerable members of the population. Despite these macro-transformations, and the presence of stigmatising attitudes towards people with albinism in society, the assemblages of care around them rely on multiple and conflicting networks and relationships with relatives, parents, community members, religious congregations, NGOs and the Tanzanian state. These unstable and vulnerable, but strong and effective, assemblages are symbolic and material arrangements of care that sustain the lives of my interlocutors with albinism against neoliberal abandonment.

Note

1. All the names used in this chapter are pseudonyms.

References

Aldersey, Heather Michelle and H. Rutherford Turnbull. 2011. 'The United Republic of Tanzania's national policy on disability: A policy analysis', *Journal of Disability Policy Studies* 22 (3): 160–9. https://doi.org/10.1177/1044207311397877.

Baker, Charlotte, Patricia Lund, Richard Nyanthi and Julie Taylor. 2010. 'The myths surrounding people with albinism in South Africa and Zimbabwe', *Journal of African Cultural Studies* 22 (2): 169–81. https://doi.org/10.1080/13696815.2010.491412

Bialecki, Jon. 2018. 'Deleuze'. In *The Cambridge Encyclopedia of Anthropology*, edited by Raquel Campos and Felix Stein. http://doi.org/10.29164/18deleuze.

Blankenberg, Ngaire. 2000. 'That rare and random tribe', *Critical Arts* 14 (2): 6–48. https://doi.org/10.1080/02560040085310081.

Braathen, Stine Hellum and Benedicte Ingstad. 2006. 'Albinism in Malawi: Knowledge and belief from an African setting', *Disability & Society* 21 (6): 599–611. https://doi.org/10.1080/09687590600918081.

Brocco, Giorgio. 2016. 'Albinism, stigma, subjectivity and global-local discourses in Tanzania', *Anthropology and Medicine* 23 (3): 229–43. https://doi.org/10.1080/13648470.2016.1184009.

Brocco, Giorgio. 2020. 'Notes of despair and consciousness: Performativity and visibility of albinism in musical practices', *Disability & Society* 35 (1): 67–88. https://doi.org/10.1080/09687599.2019.1609422.

Bryceson, Deborah Fahy, Jesper Bosse Jønsson, and Richard Sherrington. 2010. 'Miners' magic: Artisanal mining, the albino fetish and murder in Tanzania', *The Journal of Modern Africa Studies* 48 (3): 353–82. https://doi.org/10.1017/S0022278X10000303.

Buch, Elana D. 2015. 'Anthropology of aging and care', *Annual Review of Anthropology*. 44: 277–93. https://doi.org/10.1146/annurev-anthro-102214-014254.

Burke, Jean, Theresa J. Kaijage and Johannes John-Langba. 2014. 'Media analysis of albino kill-ings in Tanzania: A social work and human rights perspective', *Ethics and Social Welfare* 8 (2): 117–34. https://doi.org/10.1080/17496535.2014.895398.

Carsten, Janet, ed. 2000. *Cultures of Relatedness: New approaches to the study of kinship*. Cambridge: Cambridge University Press.

Chelala, Ninou. 2007. *L'Albinos en Afrique: La blancheur noire énigmatique*. Paris: L'Harmattan.

Das, Veena and Renu Addlakha. 2007. 'Disability and domestic citizenship: Voice, gender, and the making of the subject'. In *Disability in Local and Global Worlds*, edited by Benedicte Ingstad and Susan Reynolds Whyte, 128–48. Berkeley: University of California Press.

de Klerk, Josien and Eileen Moyer. 2017. '"A body like a baby": Social self-care among older peo-ple with chronic HIV in Mombasa', *Medical Anthropology* 36 (4): 305–18. https://doi.org/10.1080/01459740.2016.1235573.

Deleuze, Gilles and Felix Guattari. 1987. *A Thousand Plateaus: Capitalism and schizophrenia*, trans-lated by Brian Massumi. Minneapolis: University of Minnesota Press.

Devlieger, Clara. 2018. 'Contractual dependencies: Disability and the bureaucracy of begging in Kinshasa, Democratic Republic of Congo', *American Ethnologist* 45 (4): 455–69. https://doi.org/10.1111/amet.12701.

Dilger, Hansjörg. 2008. '"We are all going to die": Kinship, belonging, and the morality of HIV/AIDS-related illnesses and deaths in rural Tanzania', *Anthropological Quarterly* 81 (1): 207–32. https://www.jstor.org/stable/30052744.

Dilger, Hansjörg. 2010. '"My relatives are running away from me!" Kinship and care in the wake of structural adjustment, privatisation and HIV/AIDS in Tanzania'. In *Morality, Hope and Grief: Anthropologies of AIDS in Africa*, edited by Hansjörg Dilger and Ute Luig, 102–26. New York: Berghahn.

Dilger, Hansjörg. 2014. 'Claiming territory: Medical mission, interreligious revivalism, and the spa-tialization of health interventions in urban Tanzania', *Medical Anthropology* 33 (1): 52–67. https://doi.org/10.1080/01459740.2013.821987.

Ecks, Stefan. 2004. 'Bodily sovereignty as political sovereignty: "Self-care" in Kolkata, India', *Anthropology & Medicine* 11 (1): 75–89. https://doi.org/10.1080/1364847042000204906.

Engstrand-Neacsu, Andrei and Alex Wynter. 2009. *Through Albino Eyes: The plight of albino people in Africa's Great Lakes region and a Red Cross response*. International Federation of Red Cross and Red Crescent Societies. Accessed 30 May 2021. https://reliefweb.int/sites/reliefweb.int/files/resources/E492621871523879C12576730045A2F4-Full_Report.pdf.

Fassin, Didier. 2011. *Humanitarian Reason: A moral history of the present*. Berkeley: University of California Press.

Ferguson, James. 2013. 'Declarations of dependence: Labour, personhood, and welfare in southern Africa', *Journal of the Royal Anthropological Institute* 19: 223–42. https://doi.org/10.1111/1467-9655.12023.

Ferguson, James. 2015. *Give a Man a Fish: Reflections on the new politics of distribution*. Durham, NC: Duke University Press.

Friedner, Michele. 2015. *Valuing Deaf Worlds in Urban India*. New Brunswick, NJ: Rutgers University Press.

Hohl, Christopher and Matthias Krings. 2019. 'Extraordinarily white: The de/spectacularization of the abinotic body and the normalization of its audience'. In *Beauty and the Norm: Debating standardization in bodily appearance*, edited by Claudia Liebelt, Sarah Böllinger and Ulf Vierke, 75–103, Basingstoke: Palgrave Macmillan.

Ingstad, Benedicte and Susan Reynolds Whyte, eds. 2007. *Disability in Local and Global Worlds*. Berkeley: University of California Press.

Kohrman, Matthew. 2005. *Bodies of Difference: Experiences of disability and institutional advocacy in the making of modern China*. Berkeley: University California Press.

Lamb, Sarah. 2020. 'Assemblages of care and personhood: "Successful ageing" across India and North America'. In *Caring for Old Age: Perspectives from South Asia*, edited by Christiane Brosius and Roberta Mandoki, 321–38. Heidelberg: Heidelberg University Publishing.

Livingston, Julie. 2005. *Debility and the Moral Imagination in Botswana*. Bloomington: Indiana University Press.

MacGregor, Hayley. 2018. 'Mental health and the maintenance of kinship in South Africa', *Medical Anthropology* 37 (7): 597–610. https://doi.org/10.1080/01459740.2018.1508211.

Machoko, Collia Garikai. 2013. 'Albinism: A life of ambiguity – a Zimbabwean experience', *African Identities* 11 (3): 318–33. https://doi.org/10.1080/14725843.2013.838896.

Manderson, Lenore and Ellen Block. 2016. 'Relatedness and care in Southern Africa and beyond', *Social Dynamics* 42 (2): 205–17. https://doi.org/10.1080/02533952.2016.1218139.

Marcus, George E. and Erkan Saka. 2006. 'Assemblage', *Theory, Culture & Society* 23 (2–3): 101–6. https://doi.org/10.1177/0263276406062573.

Mol, Annemarie. 2008. *The Logic of Care: Health and the problem of patient choice*. London: Routledge.

Mol, Annemarie. 2010. 'Care and its values: Good food in the nursing home'. In *Care in Practice: On tinkering in clinics, homes and farms*, edited by Annemarie Mol, Ingunn Moser and Jeannette Pols, 21–34. Bielefeld: Transcript.

Mol, Annemarie, Ingunn Moser and Jeannette Pols, eds. 2010. *Care in Practice: On tinkering in clinics, homes and farms*. Bielefeld: Transcript.

Nakamura, Karen. 2006. *Deaf in Japan: Signing and the politics of identity*. Ithaca, NY: Cornell University Press.

Nyerere, Julius K. 1966. *Freedom and Unity: A selection from writings and speeches 1952–65*. Oxford: Oxford University Press.

Ong, Aihwa and Stephen J. Collier. 2004. *Global Assemblages: Technology, politics, and ethics as anthropological problems*. Malden, MA: Blackwell.

Rabinow, Paul. 2003. *Anthropos Today: Reflections on modern equipment*. Princeton, NJ: Princeton University Press.

Reimer-Kirkham, Sheryl, Barbara Astle, Ikponwosa Ero, Kristi Panchuk and Duncan Dixon. 2019. 'Albinism, spiritual and cultural practices, and implications for health, healthcare, and human rights: A scoping review', *Disability & Society* 34 (5): 747–74. https://doi.org/10.1080/09687599.2019.1566051.

Schühle, Judith. 2013. 'Medicine murder of people with albinism in Tanzania: How casino capitalism creates rumorscapes and occult economies'. CAS Working Paper 2, Center for Area Studies, Freie Universität Berlin. https://doi.org/10.17169/refubium-22785.

Staples, James and Nilika Mehrotra. 2016. 'Disability studies: Developments in anthropology'. In *Disability in the Global South: The critical handbook*, edited by Shaun Grech and Karen Soldatic, 35–49. Cham: Springer.

Van Eeuwijk, Peter. 2020. 'Precarity, assemblages, and Indonesian elder care', *Medical Anthropology* 39 (1): 41–54. https://doi.org/10.1080/01459740.2019.1640694.

Warren, Narelle and Dikaios Sakellariou. 2020. 'Neurodegeneration and the intersubjectivities of care', *Medical Anthropology* 39 (1): 1–15. https://doi.org/10.1080/01459740.2019.1570189.

Whyte, Susan Reynolds, ed. 2014. *Second Chances: Surviving AIDS in Uganda*. Durham, NC: Duke University Press.

Zigon, Jarrett. 2011. 'A moral and ethical assemblage in Russian Orthodox drug rehabilitation', *Ethos* 39 (1): 30–50. https://doi.org/10.1111/j.1548-1352.2010.01169.x.

6

Alcoholism and evangelical healing in Indigenous Mexico: Chronicity and care at the margins of the state

Chiara Bresciani

Broken men, severed relations and a polarised society: the repercussions of alcohol addiction require forms of care capable of reassembling the scattered pieces of broken subjectivities by reintegrating them into the social body. This holistic perspective on care contrasts with that of biomedicine, which detaches individuals from their social structure and dismembers their bodies into parts, cog-like malfunctioning organs, as mandated by its Cartesian legacy.

Religious care of addiction fills the gaps left by struggling, deficient public health systems, and thrives thanks to its focus on the salvation, agency and social inclusion of the deviant par excellence: the addict. By refusing to separate physical health from the functional integration in a social network of relations and obligations, religious care acts on the phenomena that produced addiction in the first place.

Responding to the invitation of critical medical anthropology to focus on the intersection of biography and history, I use the concept of alcoholisation to contextualise alcohol abuse and religious conversions in Indigenous Mexico within historically produced conditions of inequality and marginality. My analysis, grounded in ethnographic research conducted in San Dionisio del Mar, a Huave village in Southern Mexico, considers two options for the care of alcoholism: biomedical treatment and the religious healing performed by evangelical congregations. By retracing the exemplary life of a former addict who found solace and acceptance in religion, I interpret evangelical conversions as strategies of care at the margins of the state, and analyse them through the temporal lens of *chronicity*.

Heroin addicts of former Mexican settlements in New Mexico have been described as sharing a 'historical ethos of suffering', an identity based on melancholia and shaped by suffering, loss of land and dispossession at the hands of the United States. Their addiction is at the same time a product of their socioeconomic status and a way to escape nostalgia for their land, a reiterated, chronic expression of a perduring sense of loss (Garcia 2010). Similarly, alcohol abuse in Indigenous Mexico is the legacy of the colonial past, still alive and contributing to the impoverishment, marginality and helplessness of those living at the periphery of the state.

Evangelical healing and conversions may constitute a way out of the entrapment of chronicity, which I intend here both as recurrence (historical reiteration of different forms of dispossession) and permanence (persistence of colonial structures based on ethnic and class hierarchies). I argue that within unequal structures of relation, alcohol is a tool for the 'conquest of the body', by Spanish colonial power first, and by the neoliberal, capitalist economy today.

At the individual level, chronicity configures itself as the curse of the addict: by framing alcoholism as chronic illness, biomedicine defines and treats the alcoholic as a subject who is inherently vulnerable to addiction, hard to treat, prone to relapses and often undeserving of care. Religion responds to the exclusion of the poor from biomedical forms of care, caused by the disinvestment in public health, through the provision of accessible and inclusive care. Where medical treatment is absent, racially biased and culturally insensitive, religious healing configures itself as an effective strategy by virtue of its holistic character.

From comorbidity to syndemics of alcoholism and marginality

Alcohol use in the Americas is 30 per cent higher than the world average, and it represents one of the major health risks in low- and medium-income countries (OID and CICAD 2015).[1] Data collected in Mexico by the National Commission for Addictions report that 19.8 per cent of the general population (29.9 per cent of males) has consumed an excessive quantity of alcohol in the last month, and that 8.5 per cent (13.8 per cent of males) are habitual drinkers (consuming at least five units of alcohol once a week or more often).[2] Alcohol is the main cause of over 60 types of diseases and traumas, is closely related to violence, crime and family desertion (OID and CICAD 2015, 33–48), and is often present in comorbidity with noncommunicable diseases (mental disorders and diabetes in particular). In Mexico, alcohol-attributable deaths for males make up 64.4 per cent of fatalities from liver cirrhosis, 33.1 per cent of road traffic injuries and 4.5 per cent of cancer (WHO 2018).

However, an increasing number of authors have argued that mortality rates are not a reliable indicator of the impact of mental and addictive disorders, since they are rarely recorded as the official cause of death, and their statistical prevalence is then underestimated. The use of disability-adjusted life years (DALYs), the sum of the years of life lost to premature mortality and disability,[3] has therefore been proposed as a more valuable indicator of the impact of mental and substance-use disorders. When focusing on the number of years lived with disability, mental and addictive disorders emerge as the category with the highest disability burden, accounting for 18.7 per cent of the total. For men, alcohol-use disorders constitute the third cause of DALYs (335 point estimated per 100,000 in 2016) (Rehm and Schield 2019).

Particular attention should be paid to data from middle- and low-income countries. Public health scholars have focused on the correlation between the impact of mental illnesses and addiction on DALYs and income inequality (as per the Gini Index). The growth of economic inequality (measured through indicators such as low income, unemployment and quality of housing) has been linked to the increase of mental and addictive disorders, with gaps in prevention and treatment making their impact even more devastating (Rehm and Schield 2019). Characterised by a developing economy and high income divide, Mexico is experiencing a skyrocketing incidence of noncommunicable, comorbid diseases, particularly diabetes, obesity, hypertension and alcohol abuse.

Critical medical anthropology has elaborated a comprehensive concept to shed light on both the individual and the collective dimension of illness experience. *Syndemics* are clusterings of two or more diseases produced and intersecting with contextual social, biological and psychological factors, so that their synergistic interaction increases the disease burden beyond the simple concept of comorbidity (Weaver and Mendenhall 2014). In the case of alcohol, syndemic suffering is shaped by structural violence and co-produced by biosocial conditions such as diabetes, mental illnesses, violence, poverty and marginality.

Five centuries of alcoholisation

The entanglement of alcohol abuse with the impoverishment and marginality of Indigenous Mexicans dates back to the unequal society that came into being after the Spanish Conquest. Prior to conquest, alcoholic beverages in the Americas were fermented, and their use was generally limited to ceremonial events. We know from the sixteenth-century Florentine Codex that severe sanctions were in place in pre-colonial Mexico against those who broke the rules that regulated the consumption of alcohol (Olivier 2000).

With Christianisation, the process of dismantling the pre-Columbian social order began, which caused the end of ritual limits associated with intoxicating drinks and specifically *pulque*, a traditional drink made from the fermented sap of the agave plant (Ávila Palafox 2001, 171). After the conquest, distilled spirits (with a higher alcoholic gradation than fermented drinks) were introduced as commodities, to the benefit of the Spanish crown, which held a monopoly on alcohol production and sale. The commodification and widespread availability of alcohol resulted in the increase and generalisation of consumption. As elsewhere in European colonies, new categories of people, such as young men and women, started consuming alcohol (Dietler 2006, 241).

In the twentieth century, alcohol continued to play a role in the exploitation of natives and poor Ladinos by the dominant classes. Workers of plantations and industrial sites often had their salary paid in alcohol: in Chiapas, *aguardiente*, a distilled spirit produced from the fermented molasses of sugar cane, was used to keep workers tied to their patrons through addiction and indebtedness (*enganche laboral*) (De la Fuente Chicoséin 2009). Alcohol functioned as an antidote to organised forms of political action, as indebtedness and the induced state of semi-permanent intoxication contributed to keep a largely dispossessed workforce dependent on daily subsistence wages.

Despite the use of alcohol in cementing inequalities in the Republic, many ethnographers have stressed the functional value of drinking in social integration. The role of drinking in traditional medicine and to foster social cohesion has been described for distinct Mexican ethnic groups (Aguirre Beltrán 1994; Bunzel 1940; Eber 1995; Gross 2014; Lupo 1991), providing ethnographic insight into the concept of *constructive drinking* (Douglas 1987).

Concerned about the devastating impact of alcohol on Indigenous communities, some anthropologists have called for the acknowledgement of the dysfunctional traits of drinking (Spicer 1997), and of the consequences of alcoholism in contexts already plagued by poverty, marginality and violent forms of acculturation. Eduardo Menéndez, whose research on alcohol in Mexico spans over four decades, has argued for the need to consider the complex social worlds, values and ethics revolving around the ingestion of alcohol. Through the comprehensive definition of alcoholisation (*alcoholización*), he asserts the historical continuity in alcohol consumption from colonisation to the present day, highlighting its effects on physical and psychological health, family and societal structures. Alcoholisation contributes to the preservation of socioeconomic hierarchies by hindering upward mobility of lower classes through the impoverishment of households and intra-class violence. Alcoholisation emphasises the contradictory nature of alcohol consumption: it includes the positive cultural values associated with drinking (reinforcement of ethnic or class identity through festive exchange and sociality), as well as the pathological ones that biomedicine labels *alcoholism* (Menéndez Spina 1984, 1987, 1990, 1991; Menéndez Spina and Di Pardo 1996).

The multifaceted and processual character of alcoholisation draws attention to the limits of the biological, individualist clinical approach. While alcohol abuse is irrespective of social classes, careful consideration of its historical, socioeconomic, political and cultural aspects illuminates why its consequences are harsher for the weakest segments of society (Menéndez Spina 1984), where it is syndemic with poverty, marginality, violence and other diseases.

Drinking at the margins

The Southern state of Oaxaca is home to 17 of the 65 Indigenous and Afro-Mexican groups of Mexico. In 2018, 69 per cent of its inhabitants lived below the poverty line, 37.4 per cent in extreme poverty; 58.3 per cent lived in housing with inadequate access to basic services such as running water and drainage; 27.9 per cent experienced food insecurity; and 27.1 per cent did not complete secondary education (CONEVAL 2018). All socioeconomic indicators are markedly lower for the Indigenous population, which accounts for 32.2 per cent of the total – the highest percentage at national level (Dirección General de Población de Oaxaca 2018). San Dionisio del Mar is one of only four Huave villages. It is located on the shores of the Pacific Ocean in the Isthmus of Tehuantepec, and most Sandionisians work as fishermen and in agriculture. However, with 84.4 per cent of the inhabitants living below the poverty line, and

39.5 per cent in extreme poverty, most families are heavily dependent on remittances and public subsidies (CONEVAL 2015).

The beginning of mass consumption of alcohol in San Dionisio can be traced back to the mid-1970s. Its history is strikingly similar to the course of events described above at national level, and it exposes the continuity between old and new forms of colonisation and acculturation in structuring geographies of addiction (Bresciani 2012). Between 1973 and 1975, a governmental credit was granted to fishermen for the purchase of 20 motorboats. The abandonment of traditional *cayucos* (wooden dugouts) resulted in an increase in the amount of fish caught, and this surplus led to an increase in trade. Cash went directly into the pockets of the fishermen, thus subtracting an important part of family income from the control of the women. Fishermen began spending time in the *cantinas*,[4] whose number increased from 9 (before the motorboats) to 15 in 1985, and reached 32 between 1989 and 1992, when the granting of new permits was halted.

At the same time, significant improvements in infrastructure contributed to the circulation of industrial beverages in San Dionisio: in 1976, work started to improve the road that connected San Dionisio to the railroad, with the aim of linking it to the Pan-American Highway. Beer producers started trading beer directly with the cantinas shortly afterwards (1978), without intermediaries and paying a yearly entrance fee (*impuesto por pago de piso*) to the local authorities. The alcohol market in San Dionisio became controlled by global corporations, which since then have been commercialising two brands of industrial beer through agreements of exclusivity with local *cantineros* and successful marketing strategies such as the sponsorship of major festivities. As happened in the sixteenth and seventeenth centuries, alcohol in San Dionisio became a commodity within an economy increasingly based on cash and integrated in a national market readily accessible thanks to better infrastructure.

Consistently with colonial times, the commodification of alcohol implied a shift in consumption from ritual drinking of *mezcal* to frequent, recreative ingestion of beer in commercial establishments and fiestas. As in much of Latin America, the most important celebration in San Dionisio is the annual feast of the eponymous patron saint, the costs of which are now totally covered by the beer corporations. Some Sandionisians describe this as the degeneration of the religious meaning of the festivity, traditionally based on the economic sacrifice sustained by the *mayordomos* (the local hosts and sponsors of the fiesta) as a public display of their faith and devotion. In the eyes of the Protestant population, the worship of saints – a key element in Mexican Catholicism – thus came to be associated not only with idolatry, but also with the lavish ingestion of alcohol in the annual fiesta, disorderly conduct, waste of resources and an assorted variety of alcohol-induced 'sins'.

The introduction and diffusion of beer brought about a change in habits and contexts of drinking, but also in demographics, since the sponsorship of religious festivities extended consumption to broader strata of the population, such as women and young people – virtually all members of the Catholic majority. By the 1980s, alcohol abuse had quickly become a major social problem, requiring new and innovative strategies of care targeted to new, specific patterns of drinking (Bresciani 2012). To many, evangelicanism started to seem a feasible, culturally apt way out of both the cantinas and the festive cycle of prescribed alcohol consumption. Religious conversion thus emerged as the prime answer to this increased need of care.

Care for whom? Drinking patterns and the possibility of care

Different explanatory models orient the choice towards one or more modalities of care (Kleinman 1980, 1988). An understanding of the different options available for the care of alcohol problems (*therapeutic itineraries*) should start from the analysis of the ways in which coexisting disease models define health (*health ideology*) and treat illness. In San Dionisio, the choice of a strategy of care (and the choice to seek care at all) are made on the basis of accessibility (which options exist for care and how easy it is to access them) and qualitative criteria concerning the modalities and spaces of consumption, the social values and functions associated with drinking and the consequences of the ingestion.

In San Dionisio, a context marked by poverty, food insecurity and high rates of infectious and noncommunicable disease, health and illness are not defined in exclusively biological terms. Health is a measure of one's social functioning, and it is defined in relational terms: a healthy person is someone who complies with culturally expected behaviours, such as engaging in work in accordance to their gender and complying with age-appropriate life steps. A healthy masculinity is that of a man who works and is able to provide for his family and fulfil his obligations towards the community.

Local ethnophysiology is premised on the accordance of physical health, affective states and social relations; pain is measured through one's behaviours, and when social relations are negatively affected, the whole network is in pain (Kleinman 1988, 72). The quality of social relations is reflected in the body, and a healthy person is someone whose relations with others have not been compromised: illnesses, and typically diabetes, are in fact believed to be a consequence of strong emotions connected to interpersonal relations, such as fright (*espanto*), rage (*muina*) and public shame (*vergüenza*) (Montesi 2018a). To be effective, care must therefore take into account local conceptions of health and disease, and the entanglement of biological and social dimensions. Knowledge of the local health ideology, and of the options available to patients, can shed light on their therapeutic choices, be they biomedical or religious.

The main consequence with regard to Sandionisians' choice of care is that, differently than for biomedicine, this is not based on the quantity or frequency of alcohol ingestion, but rather on the modalities of consumption and values attached to them (Bresciani 2012). Binge drinking during fiestas and family gatherings is not considered problematic per se, despite the fact that it is a common trigger for violence, and heavy ingestion may last for days. On the contrary, social drinking is part of a local moral economy of sharing and reciprocity: participating and contributing to the organisation of fiestas, reciprocating invitations and drinking beer together reassert the networks of family, professional and social relations of which all Catholics are part, thus reaffirming and performing the group's identity and unity.

Conversely, males drinking beer or adulterated mezcal in the cantinas or in the streets are considered deviant and threatening, since they jeopardise the food security of women and children. This drinking pattern is unanimously considered in need of care, which sometimes means attending one of the two local Alcoholics Anonymous groups. More frequently though, the addict's family make use of the services of a *curandero* (traditional healer and sorcerer) or, if they can afford to do so, resort to the hospitalisation of their relatives into in-patient structures for detoxification known as *anexos*, in the district capital of Juchitán.

Anexos are notorious for humiliating and abusing patients, yet they are the most accessible mode of care for families in contexts plagued by poverty and endemic violence. Their capillary presence in the poorest Mexican neighbourhoods highlights the ways in which socioeconomic inequalities translate into differential access to the treatment of addiction (Garcia and Anderson 2016). The former patients I interviewed in San Dionisio have stressed the use of coercive measures such as deprivation of food and clothing, overcrowding and physical violence, describing confinement in anexos as 'prison-like'. The undeservingness of

Sandionisian deviant drinkers is constructed from the margins through isolation from family and society, and materialises through abusive practices of care. It is through such 'distributed intensities of worth' that care practices sustain inequalities and shape the undeserving subjectivity of alcoholics (Montesi and Calestani, this volume).

Medical (un)care: Governmental health providers

The context of the medical options for alcohol care in the Mexican public health system is characterised by the fragmentation into multiple institutes and structures of care, and practical limitations in the implementation of their goals. Of these, the most relevant actors are the National Commission for Addictions (CONADIC) and the Youth Integration Centres (CJI).[5] More recently, 341 Centres for Primary Care of Addictions (CAPA) were established, managed by CONADIC and part of the network of the Units of Medical Specialties (UNEME).[6]

However, these options for biomedical treatment of addiction are not accessible to the majority of the population, particularly in the poorer states of southern Mexico and in rural and Indigenous areas. The four million inhabitants of Oaxaca are served by only seven CAPAs, three out-patient CIJs and only one in-patient facility accredited by CONADIC, located in the capital. Oaxaca is the state with the highest number of municipalities in the country, and presents a pattern of geographically dispersed rural settlements throughout a vast, mostly mountainous territory. The cost of transportation often makes travelling impossible for the lowest socioeconomic sectors of the population, even when medical care is needed.

In most rural and Indigenous communities, primary medical care is provided through a network of public clinics, which are notoriously underfunded, understaffed and inefficient. In an effort to ensure low-cost primary care in the most disadvantaged areas, where it is difficult to retain medical personnel, 40 per cent of rural clinics are managed by one or more *pasantes*. Pasantes are final-year medical students at public universities; in exchange for the free education they have received from the state, they are required to work for one year in a clinic in a rural or urban disadvantaged area before graduating.

The San Dionisio clinic serves more than 5,000 inhabitants living in three main settlements, and is usually staffed by one pasante and two local nurses working in shifts. Sandionisians lament the low quality of the care administered in the clinic and the long waiting times; thus, those who can afford to pay for private health care usually choose to do so and travel to town.

The pasantes of San Dionisio have an urban, middle-class background and are students at the National Autonomous University of Mexico (UNAM), the largest Mexican higher education institution. The relations between them and the patients often reproduce structural inequalities based on race, economy and education. Many patients complain about not being listened to and respected during the clinical encounter, and criticise the inexperience and attitude of pasantes, who are often much younger than themselves.

Medical anthropologists have stressed the reproduction of relations of subordination along gender, class and ethnicity lines through the infantilisation of the users of health services, ultimately resulting in their distrust and self-exclusion from the health system (Muñoz Martínez et al. 2017). In San Dionisio, such distrust is explicitly referred to by some patients, who express the persistence of colonial legacy through their fear that the state uses the health system as a tool to eliminate the poor (Montesi 2018b, 14).

In the interviews and daily talks with four Sandionisian pasantes that I conducted between 2010 and 2015, they expressed dissatisfaction with the little time that they can dedicate to patients, as priority must be given to public health programmes (particularly those promoting family planning and hygiene). Young and unfamiliar with the social realities of rural Mexico, they lament the distrust of their patients, the long hours of service and the burden of being in charge of more than 5,000 people.

Primary care in Mexico has historically been developed around a hierarchical and assistentialist model of care that disregards the underlying socioeconomic and cultural structures, the needs of civil society and the necessity of collaboration between clinicians and patients in the design of treatment (Menéndez Spina and Di Pardo 1996, 25). A common complaint among Sandionisian pasantes is non-compliance with treatment, which they explain in terms of ignorance and stubbornness, even when non-adherence is due to structural issues such as a lack of access to adequate nutrition and clean water. In the context of a relation of care marked by the symbolic power of educated, urban, *mestizo* (non-Indigenous Mexican) pasantes over their Indigenous patients, non-compliance emerges as a moral term 'predicated on a professional view of the doctor–patient relationship that is paternalistic and one-sided' (Kleinman 1988, 136).

The mutual relation of distrust and the material limitations of the health care provided by the clinic seriously affect people's perception of biomedical care as a whole. The technical advancements of biomedicine remain out of the reach of most locals, and when it comes to alcohol, the structural limits of the health care provided in the local clinic become evident. Data on addiction and its impact on public health are not collected, and there is also a lack of data on chronic pathologies related to heavy alcohol consumption (with the exception of diabetes), at least until they have evolved into organ failure.

The self-medication hypothesis of alcohol addiction has emphasised the comorbidity of addiction and psychological issues, defining heavy substance abuse as a way to escape and cope with unresolved psychological conflicts and trauma. However, data are not available for mental illnesses either, although common psychiatric illnesses often occurring in comorbidity with addiction (typically schizophrenia, psychosis, paranoia, major depression or severe anxiety disorder) could be managed relatively easily with pharmacological treatment. This lack of data makes it impossible to design and implement strategies of intervention against addictions at community level.

In the absence of dual diagnosis and treatment for addicts suffering from mental illness, the pasantes tend to consider alcohol abuse as an individual choice with strong environmental influences. Current medical understandings of alcohol abuse include theories of genetic predisposition, according to which some individuals are intrinsically at risk to develop addiction. However, in San Dionisio, pasantes are instead inclined to give cultural explanations, placing the blame on a regional culture that they believe to be intrinsically tied to heavy drinking. In highlighting the central role of festive drinking, pasantes swap the biomedical paradigm of genetic predisposition with what we may call a theory of 'cultural predisposition' based on widespread, middle-class stereotypes of Indigenous groups. This happens despite the fact that, as argued above, alcohol abuse in San Dionisio was virtually non-existent until alcohol became a commodity in the 1980s. Moreover, data do not support higher alcohol consumption among Indigenous over non-Indigenous Mexicans: alcoholisation affects all social classes, although the consequences of alcohol abuse are perceived as stronger in the lower socioeconomic groups (Menéndez Spina 1984), because they are syndemic with marginalisation, poverty, malnutrition, psychological trauma and sociocultural disintegration in general.

Biomedicine has traditionally focused on mostly quantitative indicators to define problematic alcohol use: alcohol does not constitute a problem in itself, as long as it is not excessive in quantity, too frequent or constitutes a risk to the individual's health, behaviour or functioning.

Although nowadays medicine conceives problem drinking more holistically, taking into account psychological conditions, behaviour and social functioning, the biomedical health system remains primarily concerned with the impact of drinking on the body (what is considered an acceptable degree of bodily function).

The ideology of the biomedical model is, then, substantially distinct from that of the Huave health system, which assesses illness and health on the basis of the drinker's social integration and the quality of his interpersonal relations. Medical anthropology is premised on the fact that illness is not an individual experience, but is relational, embedded in the social world and 'inseparable from the structures and processes that constitute that world' (Kleinman 1988, 186; Weaver and Mendenhall 2014). In chronic illnesses, social suffering is central. However, the primacy of biology in the medical care of substance abuse (Hansen 2018, xiv) entails that care is limited to clinical settings, and does not deal with the social, political and historical determinants and characteristics of consumption, which are instead taken into account by the holistic concept of alcoholisation. Biomedical care is doomed to failure because it is built upon the medicalisation of the concept of 'alcoholism' (Singer et al. 1992), seeing it as a behavioural problem to address through individual treatment, without acting on its structural socioeconomic causes (Menéndez Spina 1984; Menéndez Spina and Di Pardo 1996).

A recurring element emerges from the interviews with pasantes: they are overworked and unfamiliar with local conceptualisations of body and personhood, and how illness is made meaningful. They do not detect alcohol abuse because they do not know which symptoms to look for; despite the fact that primary care is of pivotal importance to tackle problem drinking, public clinics only provide emergency care of alcohol-induced disease, accidents and violence (Menéndez Spina and Di Pardo 1996, 20, 33). In the clinical practice I observed, the comorbidity between alcohol and diabetes is overlooked by the pasantes, despite diabetes being one of the main diseases most attended to in the clinic, and although the interactions of diabetes and alcohol consumption have been demonstrated for Mexico and for San Dionisio itself (both as biological pathways, and as behavioural and socioeconomic associations and local aetiologies) (Montesi 2018b).

Regardless of the syndemic of alcoholism, poverty, violence and other illnesses, specific conditions and practices are prioritised by the Mexican health system and attended to in the clinic, particularly infectious diseases, diabetes, infantile malnutrition, pregnancy checks and pap smears. Despite its impact on health, poverty and domestic violence, prevention and treatment of alcohol addiction pay the price of the scarcity of resources allocated to rural clinics. This leads to a biased conceptualisation of alcohol abuse as a condition 'undeserving of attention' compared to other problems, eventually failing addicts and their families (see Menéndez Spina and Di Pardo 1996).

Having little awareness of the psycho-social determinants of alcoholism, and not adequately trained to treat addiction, clinicians often feel powerless and resent addicts, seeing them as difficult patients, comorbid and non-compliant. They doubt that they are deserving of care, as they are patients who 'don't want to be saved', whose relapses are to be expected due to lack of willpower (Garcia 2010; Hansen 2018, xiv, 16–18; Menéndez Spina and Di Pardo 1996). Both primary health care and private institutions (anexos) share this bias towards addiction as a self-inflicted condition, contributing to the construction of the addict body as undeserving, and to patients' mistrust in medical (un)care.

The failure of primary care in San Dionisio, and Mexico in general, to tackle alcoholism is due to the structural limits of the facilities and to the adoption of the biomedical approach with its medicalised focus on the individual, rather than on the syndemics of alcoholism and other conditions. The fieldwork data I collected through interviews and participant observation over the years also regularly highlight the distrust of the community towards medical care provided in the clinic. However, at the margins of the state, and in the cracks of the public health system, new forms of 'care from below' emerge.

Evangelicals and alcohol: Healing within the community

The development of new forms of care at the margins of the state has been described in post-colonial contexts as a consequence of neoliberal structural reforms and globalisation: the disengagement and failure of states in their duty of care towards citizens made them more dependent on international funding, particularly by faith-based groups such as charismatic Pentecostal congregations (Dilger 2009). The globalisation of health care was favoured by the 'social, economic, and spiritual uncertainties that have shaped people's lives in the context of neoliberal reform processes and growing inequalities' (Dilger 2009, 97), and this has also been the case for Mexico. From the periphery of the state, among the most marginalised groups, religious actors have come to assume state-like functions, coexisting with the health system of the nation and sometimes, as in San Dionisio, overshadowing and substituting it.

Moreover, when it comes to addiction, public health services work more as means of punitive containment than care, with the result of perpetuating, instead of breaking down, the cycle of addiction (Garcia 2010, 192). Responsibility for the care of the addicted poor is thus assumed by private actors such as families and communities. From the lack of services, new opportunities emerge precisely 'through experiences of loss, marginality and illegality' (Garcia 2010, 194).

The arrival of Protestant congregations in Mexico dates back to the second half of the nineteenth century, but it was not until the 1950s that numbers started increasing across the nation. The Protestant population in San Dionisio was 5.12 per cent of the total in 1990; it had increased to 20.6 per cent by 2010, and it is currently 34.9 per cent (according to the 2020 Census, INEGI 2020), although there is a remarkable difference between the main centre (24.9 per cent) and the smaller settlement of Huamuchil (53.3 per cent). Four Protestant denominations are present, but Pentecostals are by far the most numerous groups. Addressing alcoholism is not the reason why evangelism arrived in San Dionisio; nevertheless, it is one of the main reasons for its successful trajectory. The efficacy of care provided by the *hermanos* (literally, 'brothers' – evangelicals) lies in their capacity to effectively deal with alcohol problems, to the point that these, together with a number of diseases, are today the main reason why people choose to convert.

Avelino (not his real name) is a Sandionisian Pentecostal fisherman in his thirties, and a former alcoholic. My interview with him quickly took the form of a *testimonio*, a narrative style typical of evangelical conversions that the convert is expected to reiterate through public performance. A religious framework is superimposed on to the illness narrative, so that this specific discourse practice contributes to reorient the illness experience in a Christian sense (Hardin 2018, 54). Testimonios design an 'arc of addiction', from the mismatch to the alignment of the person with the Holy Spirit (Csordas 1994), highlighting the role of the divine intervention in their personal history. The years lost to addiction and suffering are not meaningless; instead, they led the person to conversion, and are therefore part of a grander divine design (Hansen 2018, 61–2).

Avelino's testimonio begins by recalling how he was introduced to alcohol at a young age, for which he blames the local gender expectations regarding the performance of manhood. Like most Sandionisian males, his drinking worsened after marriage, when he started spending the money he earned working as a fisherman in the cantinas. Shortly after that, Avelino was hanging out with other alcoholics in the bars of Juchitán; often intoxicated for several days, he eventually separated from his wife. At that point, he only worked to sustain his drinking habit, alternating weeks of work with days of binge drinking and visits to the city's red-light district.

Eventually, Avelino stopped fishing and visiting the village at all. Penniless, he joined one of the city's *escuadrones de la muerte* ('death squads'), gangs of homeless alcoholics, and started engaging in petty crime and risky sexual behaviours. Under the leadership of the most violent among them, the members of the *escuadrón* 'lived like brothers': forced to beg, sharing the little food they had, sleeping on the sidewalks of the market and drinking adulterated, cheap mezcal. Abandoned by his family, Avelino was looked at with disdain by the villagers who came to Juchitán to shop at the market, until a member of a Protestant congregation visited him to introduce him to the faith. Under the guidance of the congregation, he briefly reunited with his wife and stopped drinking.

Like hundreds of thousands of Indigenous Oaxacans before them, the couple decided to migrate to the industrial city of Ciudad Juárez, on the Mexico–US border. Avelino easily found a job; however, the experience of migration further exposed him, as an Indigenous person with no kinship or social support, to precariousness, racism and isolation. Work without protective equipment in a food processing plant in Ciudad Juárez left him partially deaf, and at the time of our interview, he still could not afford a hearing aid. In the 'North', his drinking habit worsened, and eventually led him to heavy drug use. Once again, he joined other addicts, begging and working irregular jobs to pay for alcohol and drugs. His family abandoned him and returned to San Dionisio. Sick and in pain, Avelino saw his friends die one after the other, and he was tormented by terrifying voices and visions.

He was again approached by evangelicals, and again he left drinking, returned to his family and tried to fit into a new life as a born-again Christian. However, the days of addiction and homelessness had caused lasting damage to his body, and Avelino was too weak and in pain to work. An hermano took him to fish on his boat, sharing with him the money they earned. Just as his faith grew stronger and his life seemed to be taking a turn for the better, his wife fell sick. A serious haemorrhage led to the discovery that she – and Avelino himself – were ill with AIDS. Their lack of money made it impossible for the couple to reach the hospital in Oaxaca, but Avelino kept praying, until divine help came in the form of a wealthy stranger who paid for an ambulance. In the hospital, the couple experienced first hand the structural violence of the national health-care system, inefficient and discriminatory against people such as them: poor, Indigenous and with AIDS. Avelino, unable to pay for the transfusions and the expensive machinery that his dying wife needed, recalls how medical personnel took away her oxygen tank and discharged her:

> The doctor said that they could not stop her haemorrhage, he said the virus had destroyed her defences. I was heartbroken and desperate, and then I received a revelation, something supernatural, in a dream. I was hopeless and wondered why we even got to Oaxaca, we were struggling and spending everything we had and there was nothing to do. That night I was spoken to, I was told that it would be the last night, that I would receive help. 'Cause I did not have any money left to buy platelets, I had nothing, nothing. I was told to go back to the blood bank tomorrow to get the last bag of platelets. Be strong, have faith, this will happen. I got up in the morning and told my wife that I had received a message, that she was going to get help, would have one last transfusion and would then be fine.

Motivated by this voice that urged him to have faith and to keep searching, Avelino eventually found people who donated their blood and offered him money for his wife's treatment, saving her life. When the couple returned to the village, Avelino's faith was stronger than ever. Thanks to the assistance and monetary donations of the hermanos, he was able to overcome his wife's sickness and physically recover. He definitively stopped drinking, and slowly went back to work to sustain his family, living a new life with 'a different conception, believing in God', and 'liv[ing] with faith, and this is how I could stop drinking forever'.

Like many HIV-infected migrants from rural areas, Avelino and his wife had been rejected by their families and had lost the support of their kinship networks. The congregation offered them monetary, but also moral, spiritual and psychological support. The couple forged new relations within the church, finding in the congregation a new 'spiritual family', a system of support that could take the place of kinship networks, care for their material and emotional needs and mobilise resources quickly and efficiently (Dilger 2009). Detoxification can be accomplished by creating new forms of sociality that do not expose the convert to risky situations such as the Catholic fiestas through which kinship is reaffirmed and performed. While overlooked by the pasantes, alcohol abuse is a central concern for Sandionisian evangelicals, who are deeply aware of the ways in which local forms of sociality enable and mandate heavy consumption. They respond by providing a holistic form of care that does not separate the biological, the social and the spiritual realms, consistently with the Huave health ideology.

However, and precisely because of the interdependence of these domains, the addict body is always vulnerable. The first failed detoxification-conversion of Avelino shows that health obtained through divine intervention can be definitive, but must be maintained through spiritual and bodily practices to perform within the congregation. Changes and obligations characterise the life of the former drinker: the convert would pay the tithe (*diezmo*), attend religious events (*cultos*), help spread the Gospel by organising public events (*campañas de evangelización*), take part in collective fasts and prayers, and provide material support to the hermanos in need through work, money or spiritual gifts. It is by submitting to God and the congregation that the individual regains agency and freedom, intended as a space and language to make new, non-conventional choices, such as removing oneself from the system of festive obligations and expenses. Also, the frequency of mandated communitarian duties and mutual surveillance permit the early detection and care of relapses of recovering alcoholics.

Conclusions

The lack of out-patient structures and support for recovering addicts has been recognised as one of the major obstacles to the long-term success of detoxification programmes (Garcia 2010). This difficulty, ingrained in the medical treatment of addiction, is greater in peripheral places such as San Dionisio, where primary medical care is deficient and premised on the perpetuation of racial hierarchies between the rural, Indigenous and impoverished population, and the urban, middle-class, educated medical staff. The failure of the state in its role of health provider leaves space for the successful realisation of forms of collective *care from below*. These alternative forms of care emerge when illness and suffering are syndemic with poverty and discrimination, 'rooted in the effects that globalisation and modernity are understood to have on local life-worlds' (Dilger 2007, 622).

The life of Avelino has been marked by a syndemic of alcoholism, poverty and marginalisation that led him to experience isolation, homelessness and migration. This clustering of diseases, disability and social problems has caused greater harm to his health and family than alcoholism alone could have produced were he to live under different socioeconomic circumstances. His story is also the story of the failure of the public health system: hard to reach, expensive to use, inefficient and brutal with the most vulnerable members of society. His case, emblematic of the life trajectories of the former addicts I interviewed, shows how the success of Pentecostal churches lies in their capacity for building a community of care and their preparedness to tackle a number of problems and conditions that are inextricably entangled, such as addictions and infectious diseases, but also poverty and other ills of the social groups most affected by unequal modernisation.

Religious healing provides lifelong support to those who share the same experience of vulnerability. Care takes the form of mutual responsibility, as the members of the congregation care for one another in moments of endangerment and isolation (Garcia 2010, 203). Their church offers them a form of collective care that gives meaning to suffering, in which everyone, and especially the addict, is deserving of care. Pentecostal healing configures itself as an ethics of care able to neutralise the alienation eminently linked with addiction (Garcia 2010, 182) through the creation of new, strong social networks and restoration of a sense of belonging. Since chronic illness is a symbolic bridge that connects body, self and society (Kleinman 1988, xiii), the efficacy of care depends on the adoption of a holistic approach that also takes into account the socioeconomic environment, inseparable from physical disease. This form of mutual care from below proposes a model of shared, collective responsibility in response to the hierarchical relations inherent to biomedicine, premised on the submission of the patient to the therapy prescribed by the clinician (compliance).

Intrinsic to Christianity is the faith in the possibility of salvation of all individuals upon conversion. While all humans are born into sin, their moral weakness does not make them less worthy of saving. Based on the acknowledgement of this shared human condition, evangelical healing of addiction is devoid of moral stigma, and care is offered to everyone. On the contrary, stigma towards alcoholics is perpetuated by a medical system that considers them difficult patients, undeserving of the little time and scant resources allocated to primary care in the rural milieu. Since the 1960s, medical understanding of addiction has been premised on the paradigm of a genetic and/or environmental predisposition and on chronicity: addiction could not be treated, but only controlled and stabilised through 'prostheses' such as pharmacological and psychological therapy (Garcia 2010, 16; Hansen 2018, 16). The addicts would thus be condemned to remain hopelessly trapped in the system of unjust relations that produced their addiction in the first place. The temporality of alcoholism is chronicity, not only as chronic disease, but also as embodiment of the suffering and social conditions of the drinker, and of a history of colonisation and alcoholisation (the endless recurrence of structural violence).

Examining evangelical healing of alcohol forces us to think in new terms about the entanglement of chronicity and care: through the lens of deservingness, it shows how chronicity can be shifted to healing itself. Religious conversion offers addicts a way out of the vicious cycle of chronicity, as by breaking the curse of the chronic disease, alcoholism is no longer an unescapable destiny. A shift is produced from chronic disease to chronic healing: the recovering alcoholic must actively engage in the religious activities of his congregation, or else he could experience terrible relapses. The addict can escape the ineluctability of his condition, as long as he is committed to a lifelong (chronic) healing process. No longer a victim of historical circumstances or genetic predisposition, he assumes an active role in shaping his own future.

Acknowledgements

I am deeply indebted to the men who shared their most intimate stories and sorrows with me. I treasure the memories of our conversations as the most meaningful moments of my fieldwork. I am particularly thankful to the late Professor Carlos Zolla Luque († 2019), who encouraged and supported my interest to pursue the anthropological study of alcohol. His presence and wisdom will be profoundly missed. I am also grateful to Verónica Claudia Cortés and Pedro Ocampo García, who helped illuminate my understanding of Mexican public anti-alcohol programmes.

Notes

1. The 2018 World Health Organization (WHO) Global Status Report on Alcohol and Health reports a per capita consumption of 11.1 litres of pure alcohol per year for males overall in Mexico, which rises to 19.7 litres among male drinkers. WHO figures sketch a multifaceted situation, with a minority (6.6 per cent) of Mexican men affected by alcohol use disorders or dependence, but also a high percentage (43.6 per cent) of men abstaining from consumption in the past 12 months (WHO 2018, 211).
2. Data from the National Commission for Addictions and from the WHO (2018) Report; both report data from 2016.
3. Disability is defined by the WHO (2021) as an umbrella term covering physical impairments, limitations on activity and restrictions in participation in life situations.
4. Originated in the nineteenth century, cantinas are the emblems of traditional Mexican drinking culture. With their rudimentary furnishing and sombre atmosphere, these rustic establishments are highly gendered spaces for the socialisation of working-class men.

5. CONADIC is a federal agency within the Ministry of Health in charge of coordinating the prevention and treatment of problems related to drugs, alcohol and tobacco. The CIJ network is a civil, semi-public association founded in 1969 and now managed by the Ministry of Health, constituted by a network of 106 out-patient centres for the prevention and treatment of addictions, plus 11 residential facilities across the nation. In 2016, 2,423 new patients accessed the services provided by the CIJs.
6. In 2016, 53,000 patients were treated at the UNEME-CAPA centres, 37.1 per cent of them for alcohol problems.

References

Aguirre Beltrán, Gonzalo. 1994. 'Pobreza, cáracter social y adicción'. In *Obra antropológica XIII. Antropología medica*, 171–216. Mexico City: FCE.

Ávila Palafox, Ricardo. 2001. 'Cantinas and drinkers in Mexico'. In *Drinking: Anthropological approaches*, edited by Igor De Garine and Valerie De Garine, 169–80. Oxford: Berghahn.

Bresciani, Chiara. 2012. 'Alcolismo, marginalizzazione e cambio culturale: una etnografia critica del consumo di alcol in una comunitá huave (Messico)', *Quaderni di Tule* (34): 343–56. Accessed 30 May 2021. https://www.academia.edu/8552004/Alcolismo_marginalizzazione_e_cambio_culturale_una_etnografia_critica_del_consumo_di_alcol_in_una_comunit%C3%A0_huave_Messico_.

Bunzel, Ruth. 1940. 'The role of alcoholism in two Central American cultures', *Psychiatry. Interpersonal and Biological Processes* 3 (3): 361–87. https://doi.org/10.1080/00332747.1940.11022291.

CONEVAL (Consejo Nacional de Evaluación de la Política de Desarrollo). 2015. 'Anéxo estadístico de pobreza a nivel municipio 2010 y 2015'. Accessed 14 July 2021. https://www.coneval.org.mx/Medicion/Paginas/AE_pobreza_municipal.aspx.

CONEVAL (Consejo Nacional de Evaluación de la Política de Desarrollo Social). 2018. 'Medición de pobreza 2018, Oaxaca'. Accessed 30 May 2021. https:// www.coneval.org.mx/coordinacion/entidades/Oaxaca/ PublishingImages/Pobreza_ 2018/Pobreza2018.jpg. .

Csordas, Thomas J. 1994. *The Sacred Self: A cultural phenomenology of charismatic healing*. Berkeley: University of California Press.

De la Fuente Chicoséin, Julio. 2009. *Monopolio de aguardiente y alcoholismo en los Altos de Chiapas: Un estudio 'incómodo' de Julio de la Fuente (1954–1955)*. Mexico City: CDI.

Dietler, Michael. 2006. 'Alcohol: Anthropological/archaeological perspectives', *Annual Review of Anthropology* 35: 229–49. https://doi.org/10.1146/annurev.anthro.35.081705.123120.

Dilger, Hansjörg. 2007. 'Healing the wounds of modernity: Salvation, community and care in a Neo-Pentecostal church in Dar es Salaam, Tanzania', *Journal of Religion in Africa* 37 (1): 59–83. https://doi.org/10.1163/157006607X166591.

Dilger, Hansjörg. 2009. 'Doing better? Religion, the virtue-ethics of development, and the fragmentation of health politics in Tanzania', *Africa Today* 56 (1): 88–110. https://doi.org/10.2979/AFT.2009.56.1.88.

Dirección General de Población de Oaxaca. 2018. *Población Indígena*. Accessed 30 May 2021. http://www.digepo.oaxaca.gob.mx/recursos/revistas/revista42.pdf.

Douglas, Mary. 1987. *Constructive Drinking: Perspectives on drink from anthropology*. Cambridge: Cambridge University Press.

Eber, Christine. 1995. *Women and Alcohol in a Highland Maya Town: Water of hope, water of sorrow*. Austin: University of Texas Press.

Garcia, Angela. 2010. *The Pastoral Clinic: Addiction and dispossession along the Rio Grande*. Berkeley: University of California Press.

Garcia, Angela and Brian Anderson. 2016. 'Violence, addiction, recovery: An anthropological study of Mexico's anexos', *Transcultural Psychiatry* 53 (4): 445–64. https://doi.org/10.1177/1363461516662539.

Gross, Toomas. 2014. 'Mezcal and Mexicanness: The symbolic and social connotations of drinking in Oaxaca', *Folklore: Electronic journal of folklore* 59, 7–28. https://doi.org/10.7592/FEJF2014.59.gross.

Hansen, Helena. 2018. *Addicted to Christ: Remaking men in Puerto Rican Pentecostal drug ministries*. Oakland: University of California Press.

Hardin, Jessica. 2018. *Faith and the Pursuit of Health: Cardiometabolic disorders in Samoa*. New Brunswick, NJ: Rutgers University Press.

INEGI (Instituto Nacional de Estadística, Geografía e Informática). 2020. 'Censo de Población e Vivienda'. Accessed 10 July 2021. https://censo2020.mx.

Kleinman, Arthur. 1980. *Patients and Healers in the Context of Culture: An exploration of the borderland between anthropology, medicine, and psychiatry*. Berkeley: University of California Press.

Kleinman, Arthur. 1988. *The Illness Narratives: Suffering, healing, and the human condition*. New York: Basic Books.

Lupo, Alessandro. 1991. 'Tatiochihualatzin, valores simbólicos del alcohol en las Sierra de Puebla', *Estudios de cultura Náhuatl* 21: 219–30. Accessed 30 May 2021. https://www.historicas.unam.mx/publicaciones/revistas/nahuatl/pdf/ecn21/364.pdf.

Menéndez Spina, Eduardo. 1984. 'El proceso de alcoholización en México', *Anales 1983* Mexico City: CIESAS, 426–47.

Menéndez Spina, Eduardo. 1987. *La alcoholización, un proceso olvidado: Patología, integración funcional o representación cultural*. Cuadernos de la Casa Chata. Mexico City: CIESAS.

Menéndez Spina, Eduardo. 1990. *Morir de alcohol: Saber y hegemonía médica*. Los Noventa, Mexico City: Alianza Editorial mexicana – Consejo Nacional para la Cultura y las Artes.

Menéndez Spina, Eduardo. 1991. *Antropología del alcoholismo en México: los límites culturales de la economía política (1930–1979)*. Mexico City: CIESAS.

Menéndez Spina, Eduardo and Di Pardo, René B. 1996. *De algunos alcoholismos y algunos saberes: Atención primaria y proceso de alcoholización*. Mexico City: CIESAS.

Montesi, Laura. 2018a. '"Como si nada": Enduring violence and diabetes among rural women in southern Mexico', *Medical Anthropology* 37 (3): 206–20. https://doi.org/10.1080/01459740.2017.1313253.

Montesi, Laura. 2018b. 'Diabetes, alcohol abuse, and inequality in southern Mexico: A synergistic interaction', *Medicine Anthropology Theory* 5 (1): 1–24. https://doi.org/10.17157/mat.5.1.541.

Muñoz Martínez, Rubén, Patricia Ponce and Matias Stival. 2017. 'VIH, culturas médicas y discriminaciones étnicas: El acceso al tratamiento antirretroviral y la atención médica de las poblaciones indígenas de Latinoamérica', *Actualizaciones en SIDA e Infectología* 25 (94): 22–31.

OID and CICAD (Observatorio Interamericano de Drogas and Comisión Interamericana para el Control del Abuso de Drogas) 2015. 'Informe del uso de drogas en las Américas'. Washington, DC: CICAD and OEA.

Olivier, Guilhem. 2000. 'Entre transgresión y renacimiento, el papel de la ebriedad en los mitos del México antiguo'. In *El héroe entre el mito y la historia*, edited by Federico Navarrete and Guilhem Olivier, 101–22. Mexico City: UNAMCEMCA.

Rehm, Jürgen and Kevin D. Schield. 2019. 'Global burden of disease and the impact of mental and addictive disorders', *Current Psychiatric Reports* 21 (10): 1–7. https://doi.org/10.1007/s11920-019-0997-0.

Singer, Merrill, F. Valentín, H. Baer and Z. Jia. 1992. 'Why does Juan Garcia have a drinking problem? The perspective of critical medical anthropology', *Medical Anthropology* 14 (1): 77–108. https://doi.org/10.1080/01459740.1992.9966067.

Spicer, Paul. 1997. 'Toward a (dys)functional anthropology of drinking: Ambivalence and the American Indian experience with alcohol', *Medical Anthropology Quarterly* 11 (3): 306–23. https://doi.org/10.1525/maq.1997.11.3.306.

Weaver, Lesley Jo and Emily Mendenhall. 2014. 'Applying syndemics and chronicity: Interpretations from studies of poverty, depression, and diabetes', *Medical Anthropology* 33 (2): 92–108. https://doi.org/10.1080/01459740.2013.808637.

WHO (World Health Organization). 2018. *Global Status Report on Alcohol and Health 2018*. Accessed 30 May 2021. https://www.who.int/substance_abuse/publications/global_alcohol_report/gsr_2018/en/.

WHO (World Health Organization). 2021. 'Disability'. Accessed 30 May 2021. https://www.who.int/topics/disabilities/en/.

7

When 'care' leads to 'chronicity': Exploring the changing contours of care of homeless people living on the streets in India

Sudarshan R. Kottai and Shubha Ranganathan

Recently, mental health policies and practices in India have increasingly focused on the issue of homelessness. One of the objectives of the National Mental Health Policy 2014 (Government of India 2014) is increasing access to mental health services for homeless persons through inter-sectoral collaborations between government and non-governmental organisations (NGOs). Section 18 (7) of the Mental Health Care Act (Ministry of Law and Justice 2017, 10) states that:

> Persons with mental illness living below the poverty line whether or not in possession of a below poverty line card, or who are destitute or homeless shall be entitled to mental health treatment and services free of any charge and at no financial cost at all mental health establishments run or funded by the appropriate Government and at other mental health establishments designated by it.

Many mental health NGOs in India have been focusing on homelessness since the 1990s. As these NGOs originated as mental health NGOs, their emphasis has been on homelessness as a mental health problem. The framing of social issues such as homelessness as mental health issues is part of a broader tendency to 'correct' social deviancy by 'treating' it. In looking at how broader structural issues are increasingly medicalised into mental health issues, Mills (2014) draws on examples from mental health NGOs working on complex issues such as homelessness and farmers' suicides. She describes how these come to be framed as psychiatric problems, where free medicine and its compliance are prioritised, rather than the structural bases of suffering. Mills also illustrates how this is part of a broader global mental health agenda, one that has invited widespread criticisms (Jacob 2016; Summerfield 2012). Importantly, scholars have argued that the approach of the Movement for Global Mental Health of paying exclusive attention to psychiatric categories shifts focus away from the structural determinants of health (Whitley 2015) that shape global health disparities. In this context, increased diagnosis of mental disorders in homeless people is being viewed with extreme concern (Christensen 2009; Dej 2016).

Homelessness, mental health care and chronicity

While the link between homelessness and mental illness cannot be denied, research has critiqued the representation of mental illness as the primary cause of homelessness (Johnson and Chamberlain 2011; see also Sullivan et al. 2000). Pointing to the dangers of psychocentrism, Dej (2016, 118) argues that the homeless industry in the contemporary neoliberal era frames homeless individuals as mentally ill and induces them to be responsible for their 'varied experiences of social inequality'. Ravenhill (2003) finds that a 'homeless culture' is often produced by a variety of pull factors, such as the need for friendship and acceptance, or a pseudo-family, or gaining approval for a drinking/drug habit, that draw people to see homelessness as the solution to their problems.

However, when homelessness is medicalised, it becomes framed as an individual's problem, rather than a social problem rooted in broader political-economic structure (Etter 2012). Cohen and Thompson (1992) exhort psychiatrists to collaborate with other social scientists in address-ing social problems related to homelessness. Marginalised people who deviate from the 'normal' always confront the 'obligation to recover' (Rose 2011). In this context, care interventions are closely tied up with the politics of deservingness.

In the biomedical model of psychosocial disability, care is mostly contingent on the course of illness – acute and chronic. Chronic ill-nesses require lifelong care and regular medicine compliance. However, 'chronicity' need not be linear or disease-driven, but is often shaped by chronic sociopolitical and structural conditions which mitigate or aggravate a 'chronic' medical condition (Manderson and Smith-Morris 2010; Manderson and Warren 2016; Whyte 2012). 'The associated representation of conditions as either/or, patterned predictably on "natural history of disease," denies the fluidity of life states that are simultaneously biological and social' (Manderson and Smith-Morris 2010, 3). Manderson and Warren's (2016) reference to syndemic suffering highlights how structural vulnerability and precarity predict the chronicity of non-communicable diseases and their recursivity. This creates new avenues to think about 'risk' away from the biomedical conceptualisation of chronicity that frames it in terms of temporality (life cycle). Writing on chronic identities in mental illness, von Peter (2013, 49) takes cues from Bruno Latour to 'think the world through connections' of the material and social world, rather than fitting people into distinct categories such as 'chronic', so that we see the ebb and flow of chronicity and identity. He cautions that biomedical 'classifications evolve into "master narratives", influencing patients' expectations and (self-)evaluations as well as those of their surroundings' (von Peter 2013, 49). As outlined in the introduction to this volume, for us 'chronicity' is thus as much related to chronic conditions of living, chronic social inequalities and structural violence as it is to biomedical factors.

The transactional nature of care also produces power relationships and inequalities (Bradley and Kennedy 2017). Kittay (1999) cautions that all of us are dependent on each other owing to the fragility of our bodies, a situation that she refers to as 'nested dependencies'. Visse (2017) writes about the negotiations between dependency and autonomy, and vulnerability and strength, involved in trusting relationships.

Drawing on these debates, and on fieldwork data, this chapter illustrates how the texture of care alters when particularities of deservingness are attached to an especially vulnerable category: people living on the streets. We explore how a complex social problem such as homelessness is managed by NGOs running a community mental health programme 'on the ground'. When care is articulated within a biopsychiatric paradigm that uses a decontextualised and reductionist approach, it results in increased vulnerabilities for the cared-for. Mainstream biomedical psychiatry almost always fails to 'recognise a physiological body which is inextricable from the imagined and lived body, the body which carries a person through space and time' (Mattingly 1998, 22). Following these contentions, we specifically look at how NGOs conceptualise the 'homeless mentally ill', and differentiate 'homeless mentally ill' persons from 'homeless' persons along the chronicity narrative. Yet narratives of street dwellers and social workers challenge strict biomedical definitions of chronicity. Leading from this, this chapter argues that care and chronicity get embroiled in complex ways when dealing with mental health care for the homeless.

Street beats: Differentiating the 'homeless' and the 'homeless mentally ill'

An ethnographic study of community mental health services run by two prominent mental health NGOs was conducted in 2017. Fieldwork was conducted at Shanthi in Kolkata city (West Bengal) and Mondip in Assam. These are pioneer NGOs set up expressly for the care of 'homeless mentally ill' persons, and they have won national awards for their work. We attended daily 'street beats' by social workers and weekly mobile street consultations by psychiatrists, observed the clinical interactions of mental health professionals and social workers with people living on the streets, and interviewed the shopkeepers designated as caregivers by the NGOs and police officers. To protect the identities of the NGOs and participants, we employ pseudonyms.

The care work of the NGO starts by differentiating the 'homeless mentally ill'[1] from the 'homeless' population, as the NGO workers put it. A typical day at Shanthi, Kolkata begins at around 10 a.m. on weekdays, when trained social workers[2] (many without a degree in psychology or social work) hailing from the city converge at the office. After reporting to the project head and completing documentation, by 11 a.m., the social workers are set for street beats in their designated areas. They make sure to carry medicines that are to be given to their 'patients', as well as food packets containing two *rotis*[3] each. During street beats, social workers traverse their designated area on foot on the busy city streets in search of 'homeless mentally ill' persons to be identified and inducted. A female social worker trained by Shanthi spoke about the process of identification of the 'homeless mentally ill': 'We can identify mental illness by just talking to them. They would be unkempt, untidy, irrelevant and incoherent in speech. Primary symptom of mental illness is wandering behaviour.' Shanthi collaborates closely with police in the training, identification and rehabilitation of homeless mentally ill persons. When we interviewed the officer in charge of the police station which houses the drop-in centre for homeless mentally ill persons – the first police station in India to do so – he confidently asserted that 'anyone can identify a mentally ill person'. He went on to elaborate:

> A person who is not in a position to take decisions on their own, and who does not talk normally is mentally ill. If we ask their names, they would respond with a different answer. Eating habit would not be normal. The way they have food is different from us. They will think a lot when they take food.

For the sub-inspector of police, identification of mental illness was even easier, as he remarked, 'We understand that a person is mentally ill when his speech and behaviour is different.' His remark can be read along the lines of commonsensical ways of equating homeless people in India with the deviant and the different – the errant, the mad, the wandering sack-cloth man or woman denounced as illegal and breaching the 'normal' life of the public spaces.[4] But in many cases, this quick identification is flawed, as the presentation of a self marked by untidiness and lack of self-care serves vital lifesaving/self-care functions for people living on the streets. 'Sexual and physical abuse are uncommon, as they are very untidy while on the streets,' a social worker remarked.

Social workers informed us that the assistance of the police is used if the person does not yield to their persuasive attempts at rescue. An excerpt from a case file highlights the point:

> [Dhanjit] was seen loitering around Paltan Bazaar area [Guwahati city] by our rescue team members. They immediately approached him and started talking to him. However, he couldn't be convinced to get inside the van. So one of our team members approached a policeman in the locality. When the police told him to get inside the vehicle, he immediately entered. Then rescue [team] brought him to the shelter and admitted him for further necessary psycho-social inputs.

Another excerpt from a case file describes a different rescue process: 'Rescue van stopped nearby [the street dweller] and observed his behaviour for some time and found that he has symptoms of mental illness, and he was brought to shelter home.' Such instantaneous diagnosis and identification of mental illness by the social workers reflect what Rose (1998) calls 'governing at a distance', which relates to risk-thinking in contemporary psychiatry. It is the new way of working in terms of risk assessment and risk management strategies,[5] which shapes the conduct and types of judgement in which mental health professionals engage. The NGOs and the state collaborate to provide the rescued person with Aadhar identity cards,[6] which fix the identity of the person in a 12-digit number. Acquiring government documents such as a ration card and a voter identity card entitles them to state-sponsored welfare benefits, but these are contingent upon the state 'knowing'[7] the person. This, in turn, also enables the state to control their identities and movement across time and space. The director of the NGO told us that their relationship with the government is symbiotic: 'We work closely with government, as all our programmes are housed in government buildings. They gave us an ambulance, and the cost of running it is borne by us.' Hence, the NGO acts as an extended arm of the state, partially fulfilling the state's pursuit of proof (Sriraman 2018) in keeping people under surveillance. Thus, self-identification as a homeless person, without a home that has been registered in a census, 'obliterate[s] constitutional identity' (Chandrachud 2018, 480), denying fundamental rights.[8]

The social workers are mostly drawn from non-mental health disciplinary backgrounds, often with minimum general education. After recruitment based on interviews, social workers are trained by psychiatrists and psychologists in basic psychopathology and identification of symptoms of mental illness, using psychiatric rating scales. Over time, psychiatric terms enter into their language repertoire, and their confidence in diagnosing mental illness increases, thanks to hands-on mentoring by mental health professionals: 'We can identify homeless mentally ill, as they are filthy, keep silent, mutter to self, don't talk to anyone and nod their head. We gather information about them from the surrounding community' (male social worker).[9]

Prachanda, a 53-year-old man, was 'rescued' from the street by the social workers at Mondip in Assam and brought to the shelter home for homeless mentally ill people. He was pleading with everyone to release him. Despite repeated attempts, his requests fell on stony ground. Finally, he chose to communicate with us to express his complaint, and his requests to the authorities, because the workers at the shelter neither paid attention to what he wanted to say nor met him as he wished. The shelter reminded us of the 'total institutions' that Goffman (1961) described: a closed system with rigid boundaries of communication between inmates and staff, where every aspect of a resident's life is controlled. The inmates are lodged inside a pavilion, a long building having a bed capacity of 40. The pavilion is fenced on the front side. Cots are spread out for the inmates inside, with beds similar to those in hospitals. In summer, the hot air simultaneously blows up from the concrete ground and descends from the tin roof. The plastic coating of the bed makes it even more uncomfortable without a bedspread and fan during summer. A foul smell pervades the pavilion due to bad maintenance of lavatories. The inmates are locked inside the pavilion for most of the day except during designated times for food, exercise, yoga and work. The shelter has a structured daily routine governing when to wake up, when to bathe and when to eat. Forbidden from any social interactions of their own will, residents undergo 'disciplining' of their bodies (forced haircut, uniform, restriction on movement).

Prachanda was dolorous when he spoke to us as we stood face to face leaning against the iron fence:

> We are poor people from Nepal. We don't have electricity in our home. I don't have a telephone in my home to inform my family that I am alive. I have a disabled son aged 25 years; another one of my sons expired at the age of 25. His wife and children are being looked after by me. My life has been a very difficult journey; I am the only support for my family.

When asked how and why he was found on the streets, he explained:

> I worked as a cleaner in a lorry for 15 days, and since I asked for my salary, I was deserted by the driver. I was searching for the railway station. I was hungry and thirsty. That is when these people came and took my photo. They told me that they would give me food, and so I consented to come along with them here. Now I am not being released. Why do they do this? I want to go home; my grandchildren would die of starvation without me. The authorities talked to me only once. Some say I will be freed in two or three days; some say it will take one month; others say one week. Someone said I would be released after the rains stop. And the residents here say that I will have to stay here life-long, just like them. I am not able to sleep properly due to worries about my home and my grandchildren – they are so small, 10 and 11 years old [cries inconsolably].

Prachanda ended up staying in the shelter home for more than three weeks, just because he was found roaming the street in a dishevelled state – a blatant violation of human rights. Rose (1998, 179) draws attention to the role of community psychiatry in governing 'risky' individuals:

> With the emergence of community as the new territory upon which psychiatry must work, asylum walls no longer mark a simple and fixed distinction between those within and without the psychiatric system. A complex institutional topography of community has emerged: out-patient clinics, open wards, day hospitals, sheltered housing, community psychiatric nurses, and so forth. The task for psychiatric professionals is now less therapeutic than administrative: administering problematic persons on this complex terrain in an attempt to control their future conduct. It is through the notion

of risk, and the techniques and practices to which it is linked, that care and control have become inextricably linked in the community.

The psychiatric gaze failed to acknowledge the struggles that Prachanda has endured throughout his life, including the most temporally valid one: a dispute with his employer. For the staff, inmates are simply 'mentally ill' people to be charitably treated. The programme officer told us that their main aim was to create awareness that people who are 'mentally ill' are not always violent, as they seem to be, for they are prone to physical abuse as a consequence of any transgressive/aggressive behavior. According to the shelter coordinator, 80 per cent of referrals come from the police; other referrals come from community members when people are seen in vulnerable states. The director termed it not only a mental health issue, but also a health risk (alluding to the high risk of HIV/AIDS, dehydration and tuberculosis) and a human rights issue; 'It is also a law and order issue, as there is a Vagrancy Act in force which empowers police to arrest and lodge them in a vagrants' home. These people don't have an identity too.' Thus, the NGO situates its work primarily within development logics of welfare and rehabilitation.

The caregiver who was part of the team who 'identified' Prachanda on the streets spoke about his experience of dealing with the 'homeless mentally ill' for the past four years:

> Some patients speak a lot; some don't speak at all, even if we persuade them. They are mentally ill. They have homes, but they roam on the streets; they don't know what they are doing; they even eat from the dustbin. Beggars don't eat from the dustbin, but mentally ill people do.

The caregiver's narrative brings to the fore how psychosocial disability is stigmatised more than poverty. Also, the spontaneity on the part of the mental health workers in identifying the 'mentally ill' reinforces the idea that mental health disciplines have a set of algorithms to identify/diagnose psychosocial disabilities,[10] analogous to diagnostic tests used in other medical disciplines. Lack of recognition of the fact that human experiences are diverse, and that psychiatry cannot be like cardiology, has enormous repercussions for care-receivers, as Prachanda's case illustrates. This case also evidences the absence of intersectoral collaboration in the Community Mental Health Programme for finding solutions to Prachanda's problems. Davar (2012) reminds us that social position, gender and mental distress are co-determined. Dhanda (2000) draws attention to the infringement of legal capacity of persons with psycho-social disability, as mental illness remains a medicalised field overdetermined by law.

Medicines and employment as the mainstays of 'care'

The initial contact and rapport built by providing food to the street dwellers become the conduit for providing psychiatric care by administering medicines, either with or without the person's knowledge. The medicines administered were haloperdidol, amisulpride, clozapine (antipsychotics), fluoxetine (an antidepressant), sodium valproate (a mood stabiliser) and Parkin (an anticholinergic medicine used to treat side effects of psychopharmaceuticals). The following anecdote throws light on the prioritisation of medicines by the psychiatrist at Shanthi:

> This programme is for those who beg on the pavements, for whom there is none to look after. So we decided that medical help can be given at the place of their stay. We thought of sensitising the people about this issue. Community is already giving them food and clothes. Medicines also need to be given. Building rapport with the community is paramount. We have been successful in this attempt. If patients resist medicines, we go for covert medication[11] with the help of caregivers.

The social worker also chiefly 'prescribes' medicines:

> We meet them [people living on the streets] every day, build rapport, after which they take [medicines] on their own. One of my patients didn't take medicines from me. I tried to persuade him, but in vain. One day I asked him what he wants. He replied *bhujiya* [a north Indian snack]. The next day, I brought it for him. Now he takes medicines daily from me.

Medicines are represented as good things by the social worker when people complain about side effects: 'When I tell Binoy with love, he will take medicine. Side effects do happen, but medicines will not harm. We provide medicines and counselling on the street and, later, vocational rehabilitation and resettlement' (male social worker). Social workers do admit that medicines can cause side effects, but they are obliged to administer the medicines on time as part of their assigned care work. A social worker was teary eyed when he said: 'When I am on leave, I remember my patients. I worry about whether they have taken medicines.' Due to the overwhelming task of medicine administration,[12] and its careful documentation, they equate the core of their work with *davai khilana* (feeding medicines) and ensuring compliance with this. In this way, caregivers move from 'feeding food' to 'feeding medicines', quite like the psychiatrists in Kolkata, who equated drugs with food, utilising the Bengali cultural connotations about belly and food (Ecks 2014).

After administering medicines, the priority of the NGO shifts to finding employment for the client. Life without labour is unacceptable, and vagrancy is a crime according to the colonial Vagrancy Act 1838[13] and Indian Penal Code Section 283 (danger or obstruction in public way or line of navigation). The persistence of coloniality in contemporary, post-independence India is indicated by the dominance of biomedicine over Indigenous healing practices, the seepage of English psychiatric nomenclature among laypersons (Mills 2014) and the realignment of Indian systems of medicine such as Ayurveda with the dominant allopathic systems (Lang 2017).[14] Scholars working on development aid organisations in the Global South have written critically about how development programmes in the Global South, often drawing on international funding or international support, become extensions of colonisation, leading to a continuing of colonisation in the contemporary (for example, Escobar 1995; Grech 2015). Escobar (1995, 13) presses on the need for 'local ethnographies of development and modernity'. Working on disability in the Global South, Grech (2015, 20) invites attention to 'development's own disabling practices, including the fact that it remains a source of much impairment, for example through displacement, industrial practices and environmental degradation'.

The obligation to work and earn is another form of social pressure that street dwellers face, just like any other modern neoliberal citizen. Psychiatry, like the state, is disturbed not only by deviant behaviour, but also by the unproductiveness of the lazy street dweller, who 'eats without doing any work'. The NGO strives to employ 'patients' with their shopkeeper-caregivers, for some sort of menial work, mostly cleaning vessels and drawing water from wells in restaurants. They are often overworked and underpaid, and they have to endure side effects, forced labour and subjugation silently without proper food and wages. Other aspects of their lives beyond medicine compliance and work are neglected. This shows an assemblage between disparate actors – the state, NGOs, mental health professionals, community social workers and shopkeepers (civil society) – who work together to silence the voices of 'homeless mentally ill' people.

Non-compliance triggers frictions in the relationship between providers and users. In an ethnography of a government-run community mental health programme in north India, Jain and Jadhav (2009, 71) explain that:

> patients who do not visit the clinic or are non-compliant with medication were viewed as 'irresponsible' (rural, uneducated) as opposed to the 'responsible' (urban, educated) professional. Conversely, clinicians view patients' non-compliance as antithetical to progress and advancement, construing patients as backward, uneducated, and irresponsible.

Whyte et al. (2002) talk about the ambiguity of psychopharmacy, where it suppresses disturbing symptoms but produces disastrous side effects of varying nature – pills make illnesses (Whitaker 2011). Breggin (2007) describes deactivation syndrome, referring to the reduction in the intensity of psychotic symptoms by medicines, along with the diminishing of other physical and emotional functions integral to mental activity. Applbaum (2015) argues that side effects and withdrawal syndromes have not received sufficient attention in clinical research.

While on a field visit, a social worker gave two *rotis* to an older man who was dozing off due to the side effect of medicines. He was found tired and sleeping, with swollen eyes and slurred speech. He was unable to drink water from a tumbler due to hand tremors. It seemed to be an effort for him even to open his eyes. We asked the social worker how the man got food:

Social Worker: He gets it from the shop.

Researcher: Does he need to pay for it?

[The social worker had no answer and was confused.]

Social worker to 'patient': Do you get food from the shop?

[The 'patient' nodded his head affirmatively.]

Social worker: He is taking medicines; that is why he sleeps.

Two weeks before, while on a doctor's visit, the man was so drained, sleepy and emaciated that the psychiatrist had prescribed multivitamins, oral rehydration solution and antibiotics. The side effects incapacitate him, preventing him from begging and fetching food, because he dozes off.

When concern was raised about side effects of medicines, the Assistant Director of the NGO replied that it is a necessary evil. The senior psychiatrist was in agreement:

> There are side effects for medicines, and risks can't be taken. We try to give medicines in low dosage. But that doesn't mean that we always prefer low dosage or give medicines only once a day. These matters are decided after taking feedback from the social worker and community caregivers.

As mentioned above, after administering medicines, the priority of the NGO shifts to employing the client with the shopkeeper for some sort of menial work. The whole dynamic of the shopkeeper–street dweller relationship shifted with the advent of the NGO, as shopkeepers were transformed from individuals who expressed their primordial affinity with fellow beings living on the streets, into official overseers of medication and employers for the 'homeless mentally ill'. A weak welfare state thus tasks the 'productive' members of society to take care of 'non-productive' members, mediating action through the NGO and various other actors in precarious and yet capillary chains of 'care' that assume a hierarchical structure. Talking about the dispersal of development activities among NGOs, donors, informal institutions, social entrepreneurs and the private sector, Mosse (2013, 236) comments: 'In the age of neoliberal reform, the terms weak state, fragile state, crisis state, and collapsed state are especially prominent in the development policy lexicon.'

Once, when the ambulance stopped at a shop where a patient was working, he continued doing work even after he saw us, fearing reprimand from the shopkeeper for interrupting work. He stopped work only when the shopkeeper called him. When the social worker gave him two *rotis*, he ate them at once, standing, holding them in one hand, bearing a large vessel for carrying water in the other hand. When we broached the issue of exploitation, the psychiatrist maintained that it is a reality: 'In the name of caregiving, there is also exploitation – they are made to work a lot without adequate pay. He gets food very late. The hotel owner gives him food at the end [after all the tasks].' In another instance, a social worker explained: 'Those who are employed get to have food only while they clean vessels, as they have to work continuously with minimal wages. When I tell the employers about this, they say that they are giving food and shelter.' However, the same psychiatrist complained that the caregiver was not forcing the patient to take medicines: 'Both the caregiver and patient are having conflict. Caregiver doesn't want to give medicines to him.' While on the streets, medicines are fed without a break by the caregiver-shopkeepers; once the person is employed under them, the caregiver-shopkeepers stop giving medicines, or taper the dosage, as the side effects badly affect the work of the street dweller.

A social worker commented on the lives of street dwellers: 'If they maintain hygiene, nobody will offer them money; they have to get up, work and earn money to get food. They want to earn maximum with minimum effort.' In this rendering, the social worker acts as an agent of psychiatric capitalism[15] by 'labeling as deviant those who defy or challenge the prevailing capitalist socioeconomic formation. The homeless defy and challenge by their mere existence, their mere presence' (Wilson 2018, 7). Writing on capitalist commodification of homeless people, where value is extracted from deviancy, Wilson (2018) expands her argument by saying that capitalism commodifies not only the proletariat, but also those who are unpredictably un/employed, such as people living on the streets. We do not deny the importance of good psychiatric care for those who need it, which can lead to a resumption of social roles and respect. Judicious use of medicines on a case-by-case basis by sensitive psychiatrists is beneficial. Our concern has more to do with essentialised assumptions that medical treatment is automatically equivalent to 'care', a point on which we elaborate later.

Chronic illness or chronic suffering? Medical, social and experiential understandings of homelessness

While social workers are aware of the everyday struggles and lived experiences of the street dwellers, with training received from the mental health professionals from the NGOs, they begin to develop a 'psychiatric eye' for 'symptoms' exhibited by street dwellers. The following excerpts illustrate the discordance between the perspectives of social workers and mental health professionals regarding homelessness and/or mental illness:

> They have become homeless due to the extreme pain that they have suffered in their lives. Muzammil was so poor that he didn't get enough food to eat during childhood, due to which he started stealing fish and crops in the field. He went to Delhi and worked

as a rickshaw puller, but he was not given salary. He was married, but he was not happy in that relationship. He didn't get satisfaction from anything in life. Due to all these problems, he got schizophrenia. Now he has property disputes with his brother. I have seen that trauma is linked to relationships. Mental illness does not develop out of thin air. Some are unable to tolerate these stresses, and they become mentally ill. (Male social worker)

The most senior psychiatrist's explanation of homelessness, however, took a more medical perspective:

Homelessness happens because they become mentally ill and leave home. I have not seen cases the other way, where homelessness leads to mental illness. Once a person in a low socioeconomic status becomes ill, their family is unable to take care of them and bear the cost of treatment. The patient also becomes uncooperative due to the disease process. They also stop medicines, leading to relapses. Proper treatment is not given, so problems become chronic. For those who don't even get one square meal a day, mental health is not a priority for them – surviving from day to day is more important. Genetic predisposition is also a reason.

Homelessness is as complex as any other social problem in India. Our participants had histories of immense trauma, mainly regarding family conflicts, property disputes, domestic violence, poverty, migration for work, sex trafficking and elder abuse. Many of them had homes in the vicinity but still preferred to live on the streets, demonstrating the fact that, for some people, a home with a roof is more traumatic than a home without a roof. Many were disturbed when asked about their families. Many responded with memories of torture and conflicts at home, which propelled them to leave. The following narratives by street dwellers reveal their negotiations between home and the streets:

I am not attached to family at my home. I am not close to anyone at home. I am being sent back home. I had to discontinue my education in 3rd class due to poverty. Life is hopeless. (Shankar, male, 55)

My father and mother passed away. Wife too died of cancer. I was working as a security guard after reaching here. I used to be tortured by hooligans because I did my job sincerely. Everything was stolen from me. (Debnath, male, 50)

These accounts attest that many people have assimilated the identity of being a street dweller. For Shiva, being in self-exile through homelessness is a response to his existential crisis.[16] For Bichitra, however, it is hard to get along without a home after it was trampled by elephants, an instance of recurring stories of human–animal conflicts in Assam.

The contrast in perspectives among the various actors raises the question of what is chronicity – chronic suffering or chronic illness? On the one hand, mental health discourse is bombarded with the 'chronicity' narrative and the need for lifelong 'care'. On the other hand, in the light of the increased commodification of health-care practices and declining welfare states, increasing social inequalities have complicated the easy distinction between chronic and acute conditions. Examining India's disturbing socioeconomic realities shows that it performs poorly on various development indicators[17] related to health, gender commitment, environmental performance, democracy and equality.

A study of homeless people in Australia found that the widely held belief that homeless people have mental health issues and that mental illness is a primary cause of homelessness is flawed (Johnson and Chamberlain 2011). Another study concluded that mental illness is only one of several vulnerabilities, along with childhood histories of family instability, violence, and economic and social disadvantage. Those who became homeless before becoming mentally ill have the highest levels of disadvantage and disruption (Sullivan et al. 2000). Cohen and Thompson (1992, 817) argue that 'the conceptual dichotomy between homeless persons with and without mental illness is largely illusory'. The increasing gap between rich and poor, and other sociopolitical shifts, contribute to homelessness across all groups, regardless of mental illness. As social workers from diverse backgrounds are trained by mental health experts, their focus shifts from the sociopolitical contexts of homelessness to signs, symptoms and diagnosis of mental illness. For social workers, their experiential knowledge becomes invalid, and the knowledge acquired from professionals becomes valid and actionable. As a result, they fail to acknowledge the strategies that people use to live on the streets, which almost always mimic 'mental illness'.

Caregiver–social worker alliance: 'Chronicity' as the ground for care

As critical stakeholders in the care of people living on the streets, shopkeepers are regularly sensitised to mental illness and the need for a regular supply of medicines to the street dwellers under their care. The role of the shopkeeper-caregiver becomes central, since most of the street dwellers do not take medicines provided by the social worker except when given by caregivers. The local caregiver community in Kolkata, who unconditionally fed and clothed the street dwellers before the coming of the NGO, typically have small shops that line the busy streets of Kolkata. The NGO workers were vocal about the shopkeeper community's pivotal role, which sustains their community mental health programme. The director said: 'It is each shopkeeper who helps us, and we believe that philanthropy can also be done by the poor like the rich.' For the shop-keepers, social workers are 'educated experts' on a noble mission. They listen to the social workers' advice carefully with reverence, as they see them as the executive arm of the psychiatrist who visits once a week. Questions are rarely asked, and clarifications are very rarely sought. The very visit of the doctor to the streets is seen as an extraordinary gesture of care, which should be deeply appreciated. Local people strive to help the team in this 'humanitarian' mission by following the instructions of the experts. The social workers explained their care work involving the care-givers: 'If there is resistance to take medicine, we find out from where s/he gets food. We approach those caregivers and ask them to mix medicine in food and give.'

Caregivers are instructed to administer medicines by hook or by crook. There is no discussion about side effects of medicines, or the need to identify side effects and report them. One of the caregivers thought that medicines were not good for the street dweller, and that he was entirely all right. The social worker spent about an hour convincing the 'erring' caregiver that mental illness is incurable and requires lifelong management with medicines. As the social worker failed to convince the caregiver, he asked the street dweller to swallow medicines without water. His mouth was inspected to ensure that the tablet was ingested. The social trauma which defined the homeless person for the layperson-social worker was divorced from the 'illness' from which he is suffering.

The chronicity narrative is pervasive among mental health profes-sionals. Beyond the right to free medicines and to employment (often exploitative bonded labour), their lives revolve around the priorities set for them by the NGO. The perspective that mental distress is something chronic requiring a standardised protocol for rehabilitation is directly lifted from training programmes imparted by the mental health profes-sionals. Attributing 'lifelong' temporality to individual deficiencies alone fails to acknowledge the situated, shifting and ephemeral nature of 'chronic' beings (von Peter 2013). Studying heterogeneity in the course of schizophrenia in Indonesia, Good et al. (2010) argue that chronicity is not inevitable for psychotic illness. The chronicity narrative of mental illness acts as political grounds for psychiatry to obliterate social structures and institutions, legal violence and human rights violations, and to replace it with a straightforward brain-based disease narrative of mental illness.

The caregivers and social workers collaborated in persuading and insisting that street dwellers take medicines regularly, reducing caregiving to medicine-giving. One major emphasis of treatment is work: employing the person in some form of occupation and reintegrating them with their families. Until the person is employed, shopkeepers aligned with social workers in imposing medicine compliance without concern about the complaints of side effects expressed by street dwellers. When street dwellers tried their level best to voice their troubles with medicines, the caregiver-shopkeeper joined the social worker in silencing them. However, once they were employed, side effects disrupted their work, which pushed shopkeepers to taper off the medicines, or to align with the street dweller in voicing concerns about the side effects. Hence, the tension between medicine compliance and the need to become 'active' and productive members of society ensues only after their employment with the shopkeepers.

This realignment of the street dweller–shopkeeper relationship into that of a caregiver–care receiver one disrupts their shared consciousness. Ironically, once the shopkeeper becomes defined by the NGO as a 'caregiver', we see the transformation of organic, spontaneous and individually tailored care into the adoption of routinised and standardised protocols of medical treatment. As highlighted in the Introduction to this volume, Mol's (2008) insightful analysis of 'tinkering', that is, constantly making adjustments and modifications based on individual requirements, is crucial to the concept of 'care'. While these carers previously used to spontaneously provide food, water and refuge to the homeless, after the entry of the NGO, their focus shifted from 'care' to 'treatment' of mental illness, primarily through psychiatric medicines. Medicines now become the *sine qua non* for the street dweller, and the local carers, in effect, become the official medicine overseers. Mental illness thus becomes a means of social control. When street dwellers are left medicated on the streets without adequate medical monitoring, side effects disable their capacity to fetch food and to carry on daily activities as before. After administering medicines, the shopkeepers play fast and loose with the provisioning of food, as 'patients' are now found asleep when they happen to offer food, and thus go hungry. Those who used to work or beg are now out of this routine due to the side effects. This increases the dependency of the street dwellers on everyone, including the NGO, which adds to their perceived 'chronicity', further compounding the need for 'care'. Yet this 'care' has now become 'medicalised care', because the NGO responds with psychiatric medicines interspersed with multivitamins and oral rehydration solution. Thus, the texture of care alters when particularities of deservingness are attached to the especially vulnerable category of people living on the streets. When care is articulated in a biomedical paradigm of mental illness, and relayed to the cared-for through community social workers and lay shopkeepers, it results in increased vulnerabilities for the cared-for. Care and chronicity need to be rethought critically as modern forms of biopolitical surveillance to sanitise the different and the deviant, sugarcoating the larger violations of the modernising state.

Conclusion

This chapter has critically examined the role of psychiatry in restraining people living on the streets both physically and chemically, often with questionable effects. As we have demonstrated, homelessness is not just a mental health problem, but one inescapably intertwined with poverty, domestic violence, trafficking, communal violence, international politics and allegiance to the free market and inequalities. In the Commitment to Reducing Inequality Index, India ranked 147th of 157 countries analysed, with the country's level of commitment to reducing inequality described as 'a very worrying situation given that it is home to 1.3 billion people, many of whom live in extreme poverty' (Oxfam International 2018, 10). 'Government spending on health, education and social protection is woefully low and often subsidises the private sector. Civil society has consistently campaigned for increased spending,' it reported, indicating a long way to go for India to achieve the United Nations Sustainable Development Goals on reducing inequality (Oxfam International 2018, 10). The high rate of diagnosis of mental illness in the homeless population is a cause for grave concern, especially in the context of India, where the psychiatric system is particularly medicalising in its approach to mental health and illness (Samudre et al. 2016). The cases examined in this chapter suggest that caution is necessary to ensure that the inclusion of homelessness in the National Mental Health Policy (Government of India 2014, 6) does not lead to psychiatric overreach.

As this chapter has shown, there is a dire need to resist the gravitational pull of psychiatry in defining and redefining the political economy of increasing inequalities, hunger and homelessness (Mander 2012). We suggest a shift away from psychiatric forms of knowledge-making about homelessness that would help us to ensure mental health care for those who are really in need of psychiatric services.

Notes

1. The terms 'homeless' and 'homeless mentally ill' emerge from the narratives of NGO personnel.
2. The social workers are hired from the city itself and trained by mental health professionals from the NGO in the mainstream biopsychiatric paradigm.
3. *Roti* (also known as *chapati*) is a round flatbread native to the Indian subcontinent made from wheat flour and water combined into a dough.
4. The identification of a person as homeless authorises the police to arrest them without a warrant, leaving them in a persistent state of exclusion and fear. As homelessness is perceived as a crime in India, prevention of beggary laws (Bombay Prevention of Begging Act 1959) allow the forcible removal of homeless people to 'sanitise' the streets. The homeless identity in India is often enmeshed with that of migrant populations within and outside the country, those living in slum areas, pavement dwellers and transient populations such as transgender persons who beg on the streets and the spiritual pontiffs who leave their homes in search of enlightenment. Such people are excluded from the census as they do not live in a census house, rendering them non-citizens and prone to state surveillance and police atrocities. In recent times, the state has been engaging in a welfare-centric approach towards homelessness – removing people living on the streets to mental health institutions and the shelter homes built for their rehabilitation – rather than a rights-based approach that promotes their agency in deciding about their course of life.
5. This risk thinking has also been a central feature of the Indian state in recent times, evidenced by the National Registry of Citizens – an exercise carried out in Assam to remove 1.9 million 'illegal Bangladeshis' (for whom detention centres have been set up) and the enactment of the Citizenship Amendment Act 2019, which enables Indian citizenship to be granted to non-Muslim migrants/refugees from Pakistan, Bangladesh and Afghanistan that has ruffled feathers en masse in India. The process of ascertaining citizenship through the state's definitions of identity through family lineage is exclusionary, as it runs the risk of including only those who fit into the heteronormative family structure as citizens. See Sharma (2019) for a detailed account.
6. Aadhar is a 12-digit individual identification number issued by the Government of India that serves as a proof of identity and address across the country. It is the largest biometric identification project in the world. The Supreme Court of India partially struck down provisions of the Aadhar Act in 2018. The dissenting judgement by Justice Chandrachud termed the whole Aadhar project unconstitutional. 'Technology deployed in the Aadhar scheme reduces different constitutional identities into a single identity of a 12-digit number and infringes the right of an individual to identify herself/himself through a chosen means' (Chandrachud 2018, 480).
7. Massive protests, shutdowns and public outcry are continuing as citizenship debates have taken centre stage in India after the enactment of the controversial Citizenship Amendment Act in 2019.
8. In a different context, there have been critiques of the National Population Register, National Registry of Citizens and the Citizenship Amendment Act 2019 brought out by the federal government, which dilute the broad definition of citizenship and employ religion as a criterion for citizenship, thus violating the basic structure of India's secular constitution (see Desai 2020; Karmakar 2019; Muktiar et al. 2018).
9. Most of the social workers in these NGOs are men who traverse the city streets on beats. There are only two women social workers who conduct street beats. The woman street dwellers in Kolkata are rescued and housed in the shelter home as a matter of safety. The shelter home for

women came into existence after a street dweller who was treated and reformed by the NGO (given medicines, hygiene care, new clothes and later employed at a wayside shop in the city) was gang raped and killed. In our fieldwork in Kolkata, we have seen only one woman who lives on the streets.

10. The mental health workers develop their knowledge about psychosocial disability through the hands-on training in the biopsychiatric paradigm from the mainstream mental health professionals in the NGO. They identify 'homeless mentally ill' people by observing their behaviour and employing psychiatric rating scales.

11. Medicines are mixed in with the food following the instructions of the social worker, and are given to the street dwellers by the shopkeepers who were already caring for them out of compassion. The shopkeepers are now redesignated as caregivers by the NGO for the care work.

12. The most common psychiatric medicines administered on the streets by the NGO are olanzapine, amisulpride, Parkin and risperidone. When patients are found very tired, we saw the psychiatrist prescribing B-complex, multivitamins and oral rehydration solution. We were not allowed access to the case records, so we have limited information regarding the range of medicines being prescribed.

13. Another colonial act, the Bengal Vagrancy Act 1943, defines vagrants as not only those people roaming in public places seeking alms, but also people 'wandering about or remaining in any public place in such condition or manner as makes it likely that such person exists by asking for alms'. Other than this, there are scores of similar pieces of legislation in India that draw on the colonial legacy and state paternalism to criminalise vagrancy – for example, the Bombay Prevention of Begging Act 1959, the Himachal Pradesh Prevention of Begging Act 1971 and the Karnataka Prevention of Begging Act 1975. (See Mukherjee (2008) and Raghavan and Tarique (2018) for a critical review of anti-begging laws in India.) In 2018, the Delhi High Court struck down several provisions of the Bombay Prevention of Begging Act that criminalise begging, observing that 'Criminalizing begging violates the most fundamental rights of some of the most vulnerable people in our society' (*In the High Court of Delhi at New Delhi* 2018, 15).

14. See also Lang and Jensen (2013) and Lang (2018) on how depression is appropriated and institutionalised by Ayurvedic psychiatry, and how Ayurveda practitioners creatively appropriate International Classification of Diseases categories and reinterpret Ayurvedic scriptures and practices in the light of biopsychiatric categories to reframe 'depression' according to local contexts in India.

15. Psychiatric capitalism exposes the myriad ways in which psychiatry and capitalism are related to each other. Scholars have shown the direct impact of capitalism on mental health, as well as how psychiatry is driven by the profitability motive, akin to capitalism focusing on individualism, work and consumption, thus enlarging markets for psychiatric services, which in turn serve neoliberal capitalist system. See U'Ren (1997) and Cohen (2016) for detailed analysis of the topic.

16. Shiva has been living on the footpaths for 22 years voluntarily. He rescues people who jump into the famous Hussainsagar Lake in Hyderabad to attempt suicide. To date, he has rescued 99 persons. He also helps Hyderabad police remove dead bodies from the lake. In an interview with a national daily newspaper, he explained that the death of his younger brother was the cause of his 'homelessness': 'My brother, who came to live with me, drowned in a lake near Monda Market, and nobody helped me to fetch the body out. I ran to more than one police station, but they asked me to come the next day. Finally, I had to fish the body out myself. I vowed then to shift totally to Tank Bund [a place in the city] and engage myself in this work. I am not a beggar or a thief. I stay here out of my own volition' (Vadlamudi 2018, n.p.).

17. India was ranked 103rd out of 119 qualifying countries in the peer-reviewed Global Hunger Index 2018. According to the report, India is among the 45 countries that have 'serious levels of hunger'. At least one in five Indian children under the age of 5 are wasted, reflecting acute under-nutrition. The only country with a higher prevalence of child wasting is the war-torn nation of South Sudan. The report notes that 'factors that could reduce child stunting in South Asia include increased consumption of non-staple foods, access to sanitation, women's education, access to safe water, gender equality, and national food availability' (von Grebmer et al. 2018, 12). India ranked 95th out of a total 129 countries in the first-ever Sustainable Development Goals Gender Index, which measures strides made in achieving gender commitments against internationally set targets. India's score of 56.2 means that it is among 43 countries in the 'very poor' category (Equal Measures 2030 2019).

References

Applbaum, Kalman. 2015. 'Solving global mental health as a delivery problem'. In *Re-Visioning Psychiatry: Cultural phenomenology, critical neuroscience, and global mental health*, edited by Laurence J. Kirmayer, Robert Lemelson and Constance A. Cummings, 544–74. Cambridge: Cambridge University Press.

Bradley, Bridget and Lilian Kennedy. 2017. 'Why should we care? A discussion', *Somatosphere*, 10 January. Accessed 1 June 2021. http://somatosphere.net/forumpost/why-should-we-care-a-discussion/.

Breggin, Peter R. 2007. *Brain-Disabling Treatments in Psychiatry: Drugs, electroshock, and the psychopharmaceutical complex*. New York: Springer.

Chandrachud, Dhananjaya Yeshwant. 2018. *Justice K.S. Puttaswamy (Retd) and another versus Union of India and others*. Supreme Court of India Case. Accessed 27 December 2019. https://uidai.gov.in/images/news/Judgement_26-Sep-2018.pdf.

Christensen, Richard C. 2009. 'Psychiatric street outreach to homeless people: Fostering relationship, reconnection, and recovery', *Journal of Health Care for the Poor and Underserved* 20 (4): 1036–40. https://doi.org/10.1353/hpu.0.0216.

Cohen, Bruce M.Z. 2016. *Psychiatric Hegemony: A Marxist theory of mental illness*. London: Palgrave Macmillan.

Cohen, Carl I. and Kenneth S. Thompson. 1992. 'Homeless mentally ill or mentally ill homeless?', *American Journal of Psychiatry* 149 (6): 816–23. http://hdl.handle.net/10822/856342.

Davar, Bhargavi. V. 2012. 'Gender and community mental health: Sharing experiences from our service programmme'. In *Community Mental Health in India*, edited by B.S. Chavan, Nitin Gupta, Priti Arun, Ajeet Sidana and Sushrut Jadhav, 136–47. New Delhi: Jaypee.

Dej, Erin. 2016. 'Psychocentrism and homelessness: The pathologization/responsibilization paradox', *Studies in Social Justice* 10 (1): 117–35. https://doi.org/10.26522/ssj.v10i1.1349.

Desai, Mihir. 2020. 'CAA-NRC-NPR and its discontents', *Economic and Political Weekly* 55 (7): 25–30. Accessed 1 June 2021. https://www.epw.in/journal/2020/7/perspectives/caa%E2%80%93nrc%E2%80%93npr-and-its-discontents.html.

Dhanda, Amita. 2000. *Legal Order and Mental Disorder*. New Delhi: Sage.

Ecks, Stefan. 2014. *Eating Drugs: Psychopharmaceutical pluralism in India*. New York: NYU Press.

Equal Measures 2030. 2019. *Harnessing the Power of Data for Gender Equality: Introducing the 2019 EM2030 SDG Gender Index*. Accessed 6 July 2021. https://www.equalmeasures2030.org/products/global-report-2019/.

Escobar, Arturo. 1995. *Encountering Development: The making and unmaking of the Third World*. Princeton, NJ: Princeton University Press.

Etter, Connie. 2012. '"Women with no one": Community and Christianity in a secular south Indian homeless shelter'. PhD thesis, Syracuse University. Accessed 29 September 2019. https://surface.syr.edu/ant_etd/96.

Goffman, Erving. 1961. *Asylums: Essays on the social situation of mental patients and other inmates*. Garden City, NY: Anchor Books.

Good, Byron J., Carla Raymondalexis Marchira, Nida Ul Hasanat, Muhana Sofiati Utami and S. Subandi. 2010. 'Is "chronicity" inevitable for psychotic illness? Studying heterogeneity in the course of schizophrenia in Yogyakarta'. In *Chronic Conditions, Fluid States: Chronicity and the anthropology of illness*, edited by Lenore Manderson and Carolyn Smith-Morris, 54–74. New Brunswick, NJ: Rutgers University Press.

Government of India. 2014. National Mental Health Policy. Accessed 29 September 2019. https://www.nhp.gov.in/sites/default/files/pdf/national%20mental%20health%20policy%20of%20india%202014.pdf.

Grech, Shaun. 2015. *Disability and Poverty in the Global South: Renegotiating development in Guatemala*. Basingstoke: Palgrave Macmillan.

In the High Court of Delhi at New Delhi. 2018. Accessed 1 June 2021. https://www.hlrn.org.in/documents/HC_Delhi_Decriminalisation_of_Begging.pdf.

Jacob, K.S. 2016. 'Movement for global mental health: The crusade and its critique', *National Medical Journal of India* 29 (5): 290–2. http://www.nmji.in/text.asp?2016/29/5/290/197816.

Jain, Sumeet and Sushrut Jadhav. 2009. 'Pills that swallow policy: Clinical ethnography of a community mental health programme in northern India', *Transcultural Psychiatry* 46 (1): 60–85. https://doi.org/10.1177/1363461509102287.

Johnson, Guy and Chris Chamberlain. 2011. 'Are the homeless mentally ill?', *Australian Journal of Social Issues* 46 (1): 29–48. https://doi.org/10.1002/j.1839-4655.2011.tb00204.x.

Karmakar, Rahul. 2019. 'National register of citizens: Assam man suffers double blow', *The Hindu*, 7 July. Accessed 29 May 2021. https://www.thehindu.com/news/national/other-states/national-register-of-citizens-assam-man-suffers-double-blow/article28313511.ece.

Kittay, Eva Feder. 1999. *Love's Labor: Essays on women, equality and dependency*. Routledge.

Lang, Claudia. 2017. 'Translation and purification: Ayurvedic psychiatry, allopathic psychiatry, spirits and occult violence in Kerala, south India', *Anthropology & Medicine* 25 (2): 141–61. https://doi.org/10.1080/13648470.2017.1285001.

Lang, Claudia. 2018. *Depression in Kerala: Ayurveda and mental health care in 21st century India*. London: Routledge.

Lang, Claudia and Eva Jansen. 2013. 'Appropriating depression: Biomedicalizing Ayurvedic psychiatry in Kerala, India', *Medical Anthropology* 32 (1): 25–45. https://doi.org/10.1080/01459740.2012.674584.

Mander, Harsh. 2012. *Ash in the Belly: India's unfinished battle against hunger*. New Delhi: Penguin.

Manderson, Lenore and Carolyn Smith-Morris. 2010. 'Introduction: Chronicity and the experience of illness'. In *Chronic Conditions, Fluid States: Chronicity and the anthropology of illness*, edited by Lenore Manderson and Carolyn Smith-Morris, 54–74. New Brunswick, NJ: Rutgers University Press.

Manderson, Lenore and Narelle Warren. 2016. '"Just one thing after another": Recursive cascades and chronic conditions', *Medical Anthropology Quarterly* 30 (4): 479–97. https://doi.org/10.1111/maq.12277.

Mattingly, Cheryl. 1998. *Healing Dramas and Clinical Plots: The narrative structure of experience*. Cambridge: Cambridge University Press.

Mills, China. 2014. *Decolonizing Global Mental Health: The psychiatrization of the majority world*. London: Routledge.

Ministry of Law and Justice. 2017. 'Mental Health Care Act 2017'. Accessed 29 September 2019. https://www.prsindia.org/uploads/media/Mental%20Health/Mental%20Healthcare%20Act,%202017.pdf.

Mol, Annemarie. 2008. *The Logic of Care: Health and the problem of patient choice*. London: Routledge.

Mosse, David. 2013. 'The anthropology of international development', *Annual Review of Anthropology* 42: 227–46. https://doi.org/10.1146/annurev-anthro-092412-155553.

Mukherjee, Dyutimoy. 2008. 'Laws for beggars, justice for whom: A critical review of the Bombay Prevention of Begging Act 1959', *International Journal of Human Rights* 12 (2): 279–88. https://doi.org/10.1080/13642980801899709.

Muktiar, Pinku, Prafulla Nath and Mahesh Deka. 2018. 'The communal politics of eviction drives in Assam', *Economic and Political Weekly* 53 (8). Accessed 1 June 2021. https://www.epw.in/engage/article/communal-politics-eviction-drives-assam.

Oxfam International. 2018. *The Commitment to Reducing Inequality Index 2018*. Accessed 1 June 2021. https://oxfamilibrary.openrepository.com/bitstream/handle/10546/620553/rr-commitment-reducing-inequality-index-2018-091018-en.pdf.

Raghavan, Vijay and Mohammed Tarique. 2018. 'Penalising poverty: The case of the Bombay Prevention of Begging Act, 1959', *Economic and Political Weekly* 53 (22). Accessed 1 June 2021. https://www.epw.in/journal/2018/22/perspectives/penalising-poverty.html.

Ravenhill, Megan. 2003. 'The culture of the homeless: An ethnographic study'. PhD thesis, London School of Economics. Accessed 1 June 2021. http://etheses.lse.ac.uk/2665/1/U615614.pdf.

Rose, Nikolas. 1998. 'Governing risky individuals: The role of psychiatry in new regimes of control', *Psychiatry, Psychology and Law* 5 (2): 177–95. https://doi.org/10.1080/13218719809524933.

Rose, Nikolas. 2011. *What is Mental Health Today – Psychiatry, Neuroscience & Society – Nikolas Rose* [video]. Accessed 1 June 2021. https://www.youtube.com/watch?v=P8mkcXdTZ_g.

Samudre, Sandesh, Rahul Shidhaye, Shalini Ahuja, Sharmishtha Nanda, Azaz Khan, Sara Evans-Lacko and Charlotte Hanlon. 2016. 'Service user involvement for mental health system strengthening in India: A qualitative study', *BMC Psychiatry* 16 (1): 269. https://doi.org/10.1186/s12888-016-0981-8.

Sharma, Ditilekha. 2019. 'Determination of citizenship through lineage in the Assam NRC is inherently exclusionary', *Economic and Political Weekly Engage* 54 (14). Accessed 1 June 2021. https://www.epw.in/node/154137/pdf.

Sriraman, Tarangini. 2018. *In Pursuit of Proof: A history of identification documents in India*. Delhi: Oxford University Press.

Sullivan, Greer, Audrey Burnam and Paul Koegel. 2000. 'Pathways to homelessness among the mentally ill', *Social Psychiatry and Psychiatric Epidemiology* 35 (10): 444–50. Accessed 1 June 2021. https://www.rand.org/pubs/external_publications/EP20001006.html.

Summerfield, Derek. 2012. 'Afterword: Against "global mental health"', *Transcultural Psychiatry* 49 (3–4): 519–30. https://doi.org/10.1177/1363461512454701.

U'Ren, Richard. 1997. 'Psychiatry and capitalism', *Journal of Mind and Behavior* 18 (1): 1–12. https://www.jstor.org/stable/43853806.

Vadlamudi, Swathi. 2018. 'Good Samaritan from the margins felicitated', *The Hindu*, 30 July. Accessed 1 June 2021. https://www.thehindu.com/news/cities/Hyderabad/good-samaritan-from-the-margins-felicitated/article24556328.ece.

Visse, Merel. 2017. 'Nested tensions in care', *AMA Journal of Ethics* 19 (4): 399–405. https://doi.org/10.1001/journalofethics.2017.19.4.imhl1-1704.

von Grebmer, Klaus, Jil Bernstein, Laura Hammond, Fraser Patterson, Andrea Sonntag, Lisa M. Klaus, Jan Fahlbusch, Olive Towey, Connell Foley, Seth Gitter, Kierstin Ekstrom and Heidi Fritschel. 2018. *2018 Global Hunger Index: Forced migration and hunger*. Bonn and Dublin: Welthungerhilfe and Concern Worldwide. Accessed 6 July 2021. https://www.globalhungerindex.org/pdf/en/2018.pdf.

von Peter, Sebastian. 2013. 'Chronic identities in mental illness', *Anthropology & Medicine* 20 (1): 48–58. https://doi.org/0.1080/13648470.2013.772493.

Whitaker, Robert. 2011. *Anatomy of an Epidemic: Magic bullets, psychiatric drugs, and the astonishing rise of mental illness in America*. New York: Random House.

Whitley, Rob. 2015. 'Global mental health: Concepts, conflicts and controversies', *Epidemiology and Psychiatric Sciences* 24 (4): 285–91. https://doi.org/10.1017/S2045796015000451.

Whyte, Susan Reynolds. 2012. 'Chronicity and control: Framing "noncommunicable diseases" in Africa', *Anthropology & Medicine* 19 (1): 63–74. https://doi.org/10.1080/13648470.2012.660465.

Whyte, Susan Reynolds, Sjaak van der Geest and Anita Hardon. 2002. *Social Lives of Medicines*. New York: Cambridge University Press.

Wilson, Tamar Diana. 2018. 'A note on capitalist commodification of the homeless', *Review of Radical Political Economics* 51 (2): 298–309. https://doi.org/10.1177/0486613417741308.

8

'My body is my laboratory': Care experiments among persons who use drugs in Downtown Montreal

Rossio Motta-Ochoa and Nelson Arruda[1]

To Carl and François, who cared for us.

Carl,[2] a man in his early fifties and one of our close research participants, was hospitalized for almost five months due to life-threatening complications associated with a chronic infection. As he explained to us, he caught a rare infection by injecting cocaine that, at a certain point, manifested as an endocarditis (infection of the inner lining of the heart's chambers and valves). He did not want to go to the hospital, and his friends brought him to the emergency room when the infection had already advanced. During one of our visits at the time of his hospitalization, Carl noticed that Rossio, one of the members of our research team, was particularly tired: 'I swear, you are working too much and not sleeping enough. Look at you!' Rossio laughed, and told him that she has trouble falling asleep. 'If I don't take my Serax, I also can't fall asleep ... why don't you take a Xanax, a Rivo [Rivoltril] or another benzo [benzodiazepine[3]]?', Carl suggested. Rossio declined politely, saying that she could not take a benzodiazepine because she did not have a prescription. A couple of days later, when Rossio visited Carl again, he noticed that she looked even more tired: 'Look at the bags under your eyes! You really need a good night of sleep.' At the end of the visit, Carl offered to give Rossio his dose of Serax. Rossio was surprised because Carl had told the research team that the only 'drug' he does not share with anybody is his Serax. He explained to her with a half-smile in his face: 'I'm offering you my Serax because at this point you are my friend.' He made a pause, and then added timidly: 'And I care for you.' (Fieldnote excerpt)

In this chapter, we will examine how psychiatric drugs such as Serax (oxazepam) are used among street-drug consumers in Downtown Montreal, Canada. We have observed that our research participants use psychiatric medication to perform care for themselves and others in a complex interplay of intimate moral reckonings and socioeconomic constraints. Although the use of psychiatric medication in combination with street drugs can be seen as a set of self-destructive and risky behaviours at first, a deep understanding of these practices could unsettle common-sense assumptions of so-called addicts as purely self-harming and uncaring subjects. We suggest that if we shift our understanding of care away from its exclusive association with morally life-sustaining actions, and include its disruptive ambivalences (Stevenson 2014), there is room to see these so-called destructive and risky practices as care. Furthermore, how our participants use psychiatric drugs could challenge a few limitations of common notions of care, expanding its conceptual range by showing how care can be configured by practices in which what is usually 'considered good and bad may be intertwined' (Mol et al. 2010, 12). In line with the introduction of this book, we understand care as complex human activity where moral, affective and sociopolitical forces intersect, coalesce and collide, constituting an ambivalent ground.

We will also explore how persons who use drugs in Downtown Montreal enact these practices to manage the persistence of their addiction over time. Biomedicine defines addiction as a chronic brain disease characterised by compulsive drug seeking and use, despite its harmful consequences (National Institute on Drug Abuse 2007). Based on this approach, public policies and interventions aim to reduce drug abuse and its associated harms over the lifespan of the addicted person. However, politics of deservingness crucially influence how these policies are implemented, and to which extent they provide the comprehensive care that persons who use drugs need. Here, we will examine how despite Canada's robust welfare system, its public policies limit access to state-funded support for persons who use drugs, and how, under these conditions, our participants use psychiatric medication to provide care for themselves and others. In addition, we will reflect on harm-reduction strategies and interventions that, despite being far-reaching and effective in the control of blood-borne diseases, locate addiction and related health issues in the individual, rather than in socioeconomic inequalities, which have been widely acknowledged as the greatest determinants of ill health (Mackenbach 2012). Finally, we will understand the chronicity of our research participants' problematic drug use through a syndemic lens (Singer 1994, 1996), positing that addiction is not a single biological disease, but a biosocial phenomenon that interacts with other health conditions and is sustained by structural forces and social inequalities (Singer and Clair 2003).

Fieldwork and research strategy

Our research was conducted by an interdisciplinary team composed of two anthropologists (the authors of this chapter, Rossio Motta-Ochoa and Nelson Arruda), a public health physician, a psychologist and a psychiatrist. Members of the research team with a medical background had a critical public health perspective, were aware of the benefits of the cross-disciplinary dialogue between public health and ethnography (Bourgois and Bruneau 2000), and had been previously involved in multi/interdisciplinary projects that included ethnography (Roy et al. 2011; Roy and Arruda 2015).

We did 10 months of fieldwork (from May 2015 to January 2016) in several sites frequented by persons who use drugs in Downtown Montreal (living places, injection and crack-smoking sites, locations where drugs and psychiatric medications were sold, pharmacies and community-based organisations). We conducted participant observation to describe the use of psychiatric medication among 50 individuals, and closely followed 10 of them across their everyday routines. Additionally, we conducted semi-structured interviews with 25 participants to further explore their perceptions of psychiatric medication and related practices. Nelson Arruda knew most of the research participants from previous studies, and he had already established relationships of trust and friendship with them, which facilitated the development of our research.

Research participants' background, public policies and deservingness

A significant number of the study participants were men between 20 and 60 years old. They were white Canadian citizens, born in the province of Quebec, and spoke French as their first language. All used more than one drug, and their preferred mode of drug administration was injection. They were regular cocaine consumers (crack, cocaine or both), but they largely used heroin and prescription opioids. To a lesser degree, they also used cannabis, amphetamines, methamphetamines, ecstasy, ketamine, GHB, hallucinogens and alcohol. Additionally, several participants were in opioid substitution therapy (methadone or suboxone) for heroin and prescription opioids, although this treatment did not preclude them from using these and other drugs. Although some of our participants had previously joined rehabilitation programmes, at the time of our research none of them wanted to stop their drug use, and they did not envision their lives without drugs. François, a man in his early forties and one of our close research participants, eloquently described this desire, alluding to the chronicity of his drug use over his life time: 'I began using drugs when I was a teenager, and I loved their effects ... I have been in detox, in rehab programmes a few times, mostly because of external pressure. I was never so convinced, because I love drugs, they are part of my life and I can't imagine my life without drugs.' From a public health perspective, our participants would be labelled as refractory drug injectors and polydrug users, who simultaneously and strategically manage multiple addictions.

Like most persons who use drugs in Downtown Montreal, our participants were homeless and/or lived in precarious and temporary housing, such as illegal squats, cheap hotel rooms[4] and friends' places (Roy et al. 2011; Motta-Ochoa et al. 2017). This co-occurrence of addiction and homelessness observed in our participants is a frequently reported phenomenon: numerous studies show that substance use is prevalent among persons who are homeless (Palepu et al. 2010; van Laere et al. 2009), and homelessness is associated with drug use, particularly with drug injection (Bourgois 1998). According to our participants, the harsh conditions of living on the streets (cold weather, difficulties obtaining food, exposure to police and drug dealer harassment, as well as robbery and other forms of violence) and associated stress increased their drug use.

Of note during our fieldwork, homeless persons who use drugs were progressively displaced from their living quarters due to an ongoing gentrification process. Until recently, the municipal programmes designed to revitalise Downtown Montreal were deliberately socially mixed, where middle-/upper-income gentrifiers owned properties next to social housing and homeless encampments (Rose 2004). However, a few years prior to our research, the municipality began promoting the development of new condominium buildings and the transformation of public places in tourist destinations, favouring more aggressive gentrification dynamics. 'Livability' for a few who deserved to occupy Downtown Montreal replaced the prior inclusive approach of inner city revitalisation (Wyly and Hammel 2004). In the last decade, measures to create such livability, including the removal of marginalised groups from public areas, or so-called social cleansing (Lees and White 2020), were implemented. When we conducted fieldwork, most participants gathered in small encampments located in Saint-Paul Square, which was one of the last public places occupied by homeless persons who use drugs in Downtown Montreal.[5] As suggested by Kottai and Rangathan in this volume, homeless people were seen as deviant, and consequently rendered invisible in public areas, and their care needed to be managed in concealment.

All our participants lived under the poverty line.[6] They were unemployed, and their main income source was social welfare. However, they were often excluded from welfare support for short and/or long periods of time due to its internal rules, such as the need of an address to apply for welfare and the suspension of welfare payments to anyone who leaves the province of Quebec for more than seven days (Government of Quebec 2020). In addition to welfare, all our participants had as complementary sources of income street-based economic activities, including panhandling, 'squeegeeing' (wiping the windshields of cars stopped in traffic in exchange for money), sex work and petty drug trade.

Due to drug-related petty crime, our participants were periodically incarcerated in provincial and federal prisons. Although incarceration is a frequently reported phenomenon among persons who use drugs (Beyrer et al. 2003), it was striking for us to find out that almost all our participants had experienced detention, and some had spent the most part of their adult lives in prison. According to them, their criminal records precluded them from being employed within the formal economy.

Our participants had health issues commonly associated with injection drug use, including viral and bacterial blood-borne infections (for example, hepatitis C, HIV, chronic infections) and injection-related injuries (Islam et al. 2012). Some of them also had chronic pain that they linked to their harsh living conditions and exposure to violence. As residents of the province of Quebec, they were covered by the public health insurance plan to treat their health problems, and they sporadically visited health services, mostly primary care. However, the stigma associated with illicit drug users strongly influenced how health providers related with our participants. Most were reluctant to seek institutional care, particularly for drug-related issues, because they feared being mistreated and discriminated against.

Contrary to their refusal to attend institutional health services, our participants partook in various harm reduction programmes provided by the government of Quebec through community-based organisations. The staff of these organisations had a non-judgemental attitude toward persons who use drugs, which contributed to create an environment in which our participants felt comfortable and welcomed. They participated in needle and syringe programmes, crack equipment distribution programmes and opioid substitution treatment, among others. Our participants considered that some of these programmes had reduced certain risks associated with drug use, including HIV and hepatitis C transmission, which is consistent with the extensive evidence about harm reduction interventions (Wilson et al. 2015). Despite the wide availability of harm reduction programmes and their beneficial effects, current harm reduction in Canada mostly focuses on medical outcomes, without addressing the structural conditions at the root of substance use and health inequalities. This version of harm reduction privileges the biomedical brain disease model of addiction, central to public health policy, as well as the bio-corporal risks of injection (for example, blood-borne disease transmission), locating the problematic substance use in the individual and dismissing larger political issues that crucially influence people's health and wellbeing (Carrier and Quirion 2003; Roe 2005).

Most of our participants reported having mental health problems, and over half of them were diagnosed with one or more psychiatric disorders at certain point(s) of their lives, with anxiety disorder and depression being the most frequent. The co-occurrence of mental health problems and addictions has been extensively reported in the literature, and it is particularly prevalent among homeless persons (Drake et al. 1991; Palepu et al. 2013). As pointed out in this volume by Kottai and Ranganathan, high rates of diagnosis of mental illness among homeless populations are constitutive of a medicalising approach that aims to individualise a social problem that is inescapably intertwined with poverty, violence, international politics and free market inequalities. Our participants were also aware of the close association between mental health problems and addictions, and they pointed out that this association was widespread among health providers, shaping the diagnosis and prescription practice of doctors in Montreal. In the words of François, who had been diagnosed with four different psychiatric disorders in recent years: 'If you are a drug addict, doctors almost immediately rate you as mentally ill, they will diagnose you with at least one psychiatric disease and will prescribe you pills.' The dominant biomedical model of addiction that conceptualises it as a brain disease has progressively equated addiction with mental illness, psychiatrising the diagnosis of addiction and its treatment (Becoña 2016). Those participants who had the 'dual diagnosis' (mental disorder(s) and addiction) received psychiatric treatment that was mostly pharmacological, of which the costs were fully covered by the public drug insurance of the Province of Quebec for people in social welfare (Régie de l'assurance maladie du Québec n.d.). None of our participants received psychological services, despite the fact that several of them wanted psychotherapy. Publicly funded psychological services are very limited and difficult to access (Chodos 2017). They are mostly restricted to a few regular users of mental health services and/ or those with psychological conditions that cannot be treated pharmacologically (for example, borderline personality disorder). As the biomedical model of addiction has reduced it to a brain disease, divorced from its psychological dimension (among other dimensions), persons who use drugs were not suitable candidates for receiving psychotherapy.

In keeping with the approach of Singer (1994, 1996), we understand our participants' drug use not as an isolated health issue, but as constitutive of a syndemic, or a set of closely intertwined and mutually enhancing health problems that are developed and sustained in this group of individuals because of structural forces (for additional descriptions of syndemic clusters that include addictions, see Bresciani's chapter in this volume). For example, Carl's chronic infection that manifested as endocarditis and his drug use were not two distinct conditions that happened to occur in the same body. As we will see later in the chapter, both health issues interacted with each other and with other illnesses in complex ways, as well as with the socioeconomic conditions in which they took place. Moreover, these interactions changed over time, shaping the ways in which Carl experienced both conditions from day to day, and cared for himself.

We have also described how the public services to which our participants were entitled as Canadian citizens and residents of the Province of Quebec (social welfare, housing, health services, psychiatric services and harm reduction programmes) operated, and failed to provide them with the care they needed. Noticeably, social and health policies that regulated access to care services were influenced by ideas of deservingness that distinguish between those that are worthy and unworthy of receiving support (Bambra and Smith 2010; Petersen et al. 2011). Except for harm reduction programmes, in most publicly funded services, so-called drug addicts were stigmatised and perceived as undeserving of state support. These perceptions reflected on the over-regulation of the welfare service that periodically excluded our participants from financial help, the systematic displacement from their living quarters, and the discriminatory treatment they received in health services. Thus, despite their citizenship status, our participants somehow fell through the policy safety net of the state, and they had to create their own ways to provide care for themselves.

Street-level psychiatric drug circulation

As previously mentioned, most of our participants were diagnosed with one or more psychiatric disorders and had a prescription for psychiatric drugs, which were covered by the public drug insurance of the Province of Quebec. However, at the beginning of our fieldwork, we did not exactly know how widespread the use of psychiatric drugs was. The prescription drugs most widely used and sold at the street market were opioid-based painkillers such as Dilaudid (hydromorphone hydrochloride tablets) and Hydromorph Contin (hydromorphone hydrochloride time-release capsules), which persons who use drugs dissolved and administered through injection, obtaining effects similar to heroin at a lower cost (Roy et al. 2011).[7]

We started by asking our participants if they took psychiatric drugs. Their first reaction was to say that they were not using this type of drugs because they were for 'the crazies'. There was a strong stigma attached to psychiatric medication due to its direct association with mental illness, but during subsequent conversations they often remembered having taken a Rivotril (clonazepam) or the second-generation antipsychotic Seroquel (quetiapine)[8] in the week due to problems sleeping after injecting or smoking cocaine. Thus, we came to learn that the use of psychiatric medications was pervasive, and that all our participants were taking them regularly. In a continuum of psychoactive substances, where the divide between illicit and prescription drugs was sometimes blurred, psychiatric drugs seemed to be at the bottom of the hierarchy. Yet psychiatric medication was also considered to be safe and trustable. In contrast with street drugs, whose origin and composition is uncertain, psychiatric medication is produced by renowned pharmaceutical companies. As stated by Carl: 'We can be sure of what the medication contains, we don't have bad surprises, we get the substance and quantity of the substance that are written in the box.'

We also followed the commercial circuit of psychiatric drugs, which was not always obvious. The sale of these substances occurred in spots already known by users and in relaxed environments, which were not controlled by criminal groups through violent procedures, but by small dealers or individual sellers who exchanged a portion of their own prescriptions. Nonetheless, the place of psychiatric drugs within the street drug market was marginal: neither the demand nor their prices were high. A 2 mg Rivotril, the most popular psychiatric drug, costs around CA$2. Additionally, other prescription drugs such as Seroquel, and even the replacement treatment methadone, did not have an established monetary cost.

As fieldwork developed, we learned that the low cost and demand of psychiatric medication was related to the significant number of drug users who had prescriptions for psychiatric drugs, free of cost. Moreover, the availability of psychiatric medication generated circuits of exchange that exceeded the commercial ones. Persons who use drugs bartered psychiatric medication, according to Carl, 'for cigarettes, food or small favours'. And, as we will see in the following sections, they also gave psychiatric medication for free to their friends, turning these drugs into substances through which they performed care.

Para-pharmacologists

Kyle, another of our participants, had a large knowledge of psychiatric medication, its interactions with street drugs and their combined effects on brain chemistry. He dedicated a fair amount of his time to reading about these topics and experimenting with unthinkable drug combinations. His friends told us that he had studied science at university, but that his habitual drug use did not allow him to complete his degree. Due to his vast expertise in drug-related matters, they called him 'para-pharmacologist'.

Kyle knew how to mix psychiatric drugs with street drugs in ways that potentiate the effects of the latter while reducing their side effects. For example, he explained to us that he sometimes liked to use heroin and benzodiazepines together. While dissolving heroin for injection, Kyle added a little bit of benzodiazepine to simultaneously increase the pleasurable effects of heroin and reduce some of its side effects, such as drowsiness. Although the combination of heroin and benzodiazepine largely increases the risk of overdose, through experimentation, Kyle found how much of each substance he had to put in the mix so as not to overdose. He also used to add 'a pinch' of benzodiazepine when preparing a combination of heroin and cocaine, which is known as a speedball. The interaction between the stimulant effects of cocaine and the depressant effects of heroin can trigger a fatal respiratory depression, so this mix is considered particularly dangerous. According to Kyle, however, the pinch of benzodiazepine he added made it possible to decrease the amount of heroin in the mix, reducing the potential negative interactions of heroin and cocaine.

Kyle's knowledge on how to mix different drugs to get the best possible effects was the result of endless processes of experimentation. 'My body is my laboratory,' he told us in a conversation about his pharmacological experiments. When he obtained the expected results, he made a mental note of the different amounts of drugs that he had used. Afterwards, he experimented again in his body/laboratory to reproduce the results. He liked to share his knowledge with his peers, but given that each of their bodies was a different laboratory, every one of them had to run their own separate experiments. 'Every drug addict has to become a little bit of a pharmacologist,' said Kyle, and then he added that this was because drugs, including psychiatric medication, were 'dangerous substances'. Experimentation was the only way in which persons who use drugs tamed drugs; through experimentation, they could enhance the effects of drugs, minimise their risks and thus take care of themselves.

In Kyle's description, drugs have the capacity to be beneficial and detrimental for the same person at the same time. Drugs are both medicine and poison. This refers us to the polyvalent figure of the *pharmakon*, which in philosophy and critical theory has been associated with scapegoat, remedy and venom (Biehl 2011; Derrida 1981). Anthropologist João Biehl (2011) uses the notion of 'human pharmakon' to speak of Catarina, a woman with an unknown degenerative disease who was misdiagnosed and overmedicalised within the Brazilian public mental health system, and finally dumped in Vita, a zone of social abandonment where the unwanted of society were left to die. Catarina described herself in Vita as becoming one with the psychiatric medication she took, Akineton, changing her name to Catkine. According to Biehl (2011, 224), after the pharmacological interventions did not improve Catarina's condition, she was cast out in Vita by her family; she became a 'failed medication that, paradoxically, allowed the life, sentiment and values of others to continue in other terms'.

It is tempting to see Kyle and our other participants as human pharmakons. There are several resemblances. Like Catarina, they are social outcasts, with addictions and other medical conditions that have been mostly addressed by somehow failed pharmacological interventions. However, they are not only human pharmakons, but also para-pharmacologists. More than pure objects of pharmacological experimentation, they had the ability to experiment themselves with drugs in their own bodies/

laboratories. And in these ongoing experiments, they attempt to control the poisonous capacities of drugs. In this context, using psychiatric medication enacts their attempts at taking care of themselves.

Caring for oneself: Practices of psychiatric drug use

Our participants were seen as undeserving of state support and excluded from several public services, which strongly affected the ways in which they cared for themselves. Other chapters in this volume explore how non-state actors provide care to marginalised groups, filling the gaps left by deficient public health systems (see Bresciani, and Kottai and Ranganathan). Conversely, our participants assumed several of the duties associated with their own self-care. Moreover, the chronicity of their addictions influenced their care practices: they did not envision a life without drugs, rather they wanted a good life using drugs. Although the overall goal of harm reduction is providing care while minimising the negative harms associated with substance use (Pauly et al. 2007), its narrow focus on medical outcomes failed to address crucial dimensions of our participants' lives that also required care. Through our fieldwork, we observed several practices of psychiatric drug use that were related to forms of self-care, and four of these practices were part of their day-to-day lives, as discussed below.

Downing from a high

Once François told us jokingly that in the last years, he had received a 'collection' of psychiatric diagnoses, including depression, bipolar disorder, borderline personality disorder and antisocial personality disorder. He was hospitalised for a drug-related injury, and during that time, a psychiatrist evaluated him and diagnosed him with depression and borderline personality disorder. Later, he was incarcerated for drug possession: 'I got into a few fights, I was sent to the psychiatrist and he told me I had antisocial personality disorder. Then, I was depressed because I was in jail! I saw the psychiatrist again and I came back with a diagnosis of bipolar disorder.' Because of these diagnoses, he had prescriptions for several psychiatric drugs. Although these psychiatric drugs were prescribed to treat his multiple diagnoses, he used them to 'come down from cocaine highs'. He used to take Rivotril and Seroquel to be able to sleep when he used 'too much cocaine' and was particularly agitated and overexcited. François opened his hands beside his eyes to graphically describe this state: 'I get these gigantic eyes, I cannot close them, but with some Rivos or one Seroquel I can fall asleep.' He explained to us that getting a good night's sleep when a person lives on the streets was by default a 'big challenge', which often becomes impossible under the effects of cocaine. Without ensuring some hours of sleep, François was not able to function the following day, when 'you really need to wake up with some energy to go around and do something to get money for your next hit'.

François and several of our participants also used benzodiazepines and Seroquel to counter the side effects of a cocaine high or the after-effects endured while 'coming down', a period commonly known as 'the down'. While François described cocaine as his 'drug of choice' because it gave him more 'excitement', 'pleasure' and 'self-confidence' than any other drug, he also pointed out that the after-effects can be very distressing: 'I become very anxious and paranoid.' To limit his down, François takes benzodiazepines: 'I take two, three Rivos [Rivotril 2 mg] to cut the mess ... the Rivos help me to calm down a bit, to relax, and sometimes I just fall asleep and ... the day after, I am fine.'

Managing withdrawal

Our participants told us that when they were not able to buy heroin or prescription opioids, they took benzodiazepines to supress or reduce their withdrawal symptoms. Kristelle, a young woman in her early twenties and a good friend of François, vividly described the disabling effects of being 'dope sick', or heroin withdrawal: 'It's just unbearable! I feel so drowsy, I cannot breathe well, I vomit my guts ... I feel so cold ... I shake like a leaf.' She always kept a couple of benzodiazepine pills to stave off the withdrawal: 'Some days I don't have money for my next shot, and if I don't wake up in shape, which is generally the case [laughs], I can't go squeegee to make a couple of bucks, so I take some benzos.'

Kristelle was one of the few participants who did not have a prescription for benzodiazepines. She usually got benzodiazepine pills for free from François and other experienced drug users, who also advised her to keep these pills to manage her withdrawal symptoms: 'They give [benzos] to me, and say: "Save it until you are sick."' Like any good student would, Kristelle showed us a small pocket in her backpack where she kept her benzodiazepine pills along with other medications 'for fever, stomach ache and PMS [premenstrual syndrome]'. She explained to us that benzodiazepines worked as an insurance or last resource against withdrawal: 'I would prefer to get my dope [heroin], but if I don't have it, Rivos will help me out.'

Detoxing from drug use

Our participants also use benzodiazepines to do what they call 'Rivotrips'. Carl told us that sometimes he wants to take a break from heavy drugs: 'When I felt sick of cocaine, you know injecting coke is hard on the body, so I need to stop from time to time. I go to my little corner, I prepare everything to be comfortable and I take several Rivos [Rivotril 2 mg] – four, seven, eight, no more than that.' He did not take all the Rivotril pills in a shot: 'It's not about getting high, it's to clean yourself, so you take your time. You take one Rivo first, you wait. One hour later, one or two more Rivos, and you continue like this.' Carl described the Rivotrip as a process of 'making a fire', in which he regularly and patiently had to 'add wood to keep it burning'. Benzodiazepines, taken this way, bring him another type of 'buzz' that he described as relaxing and safe. This way, Carl 'detoxed' from cocaine without craving it too much.

Carl has had a prescription for Serax for 20 years, and recently he also got a prescription for Rivotril. He had sleep problems because of chronic back pain: 'I was hit in my back a long time ago during a riot in the Lyon Prison. I was distracted, so a guy caught me by surprise and hit me ... with a piece of wood. I've never fully recovered, and as I get older, I feel more pain.' Ageing, and the harsh living conditions of the streets, had increased Carl's back pain. His refusal to seek institutional health care due to previous experiences of exclusion left his back pain undertreated (he only received sleep aid pills, and not chronic pain treatment). In addition, his back pain interacted with other chronic health issues, such as his infection that manifested as endocarditis and his drug use, which strongly influenced his day-to-day care choices. For example, sleeping well was crucial for Carl, and he used Serax as a sleep aid: 'If I don't take my Serax, I'm not able to sleep. I don't use it for anything else, I don't share it, I kept it for myself.' However, he did not use his Rivotril pills for sleeping as prescribed by the doctor, because he also had to take care of other needs related to his drug consumption and used them to do Rivotrips: 'Sometimes, I kept my Rivos for a few days, three, four, five days, and then I have enough to go to my little corner, relax and clean myself.' We asked Carl if he could use Serax for detoxing. He said that it was 'technically possible', but that: 'My Serax does not feel, anymore. It just relaxes my back a little bit and helps me to sleep because I've had it for 20 years ... my body is used to it. When you eat peanut butter on toast the first time, it is good. If you eat it for 20 years, it tastes like yesterday.' Although Serax and Rivotril are both benzodiazepine-based drugs, they can produce different effects and fulfil separate care purposes: 'They are from the same family but … it is like two sisters. They have their own character each of them: they are cute, but they have their own qualities.' Carl built a different relationship with each of these two benzodiazepines, based on his body's habituation to each substance and his care choices: 'I'm going to feel the Rivotril more than the Serax, so I use Rivotril to clean myself.'

Medicating mental health problems

Most of our participants used benzodiazepines and Seroquel to treat mental health issues. Almost all of them told us that they had sleeping problems, were stressed, felt depressed or could not control their aggression. One of these participants was Étienne, a young man in his late twenties, who was the running partner of François. When we started our research, we told Étienne that we were looking for people who used psychiatric medication. He looked at us overly suspiciously, and asked in an inquisitive tone: 'Who told you that I'm taking psychiatric meds? It was François, right?' We calmed Étienne down and told him that we were just searching for participants for a study. He apologised for being so 'paranoid', went to a nearby trashcan, started digging inside and came back with a bottle of Ibuprofen. He opened the bottle and took out three benzodiazepine pills, a couple of Seroquel pills, one Effexor (antidepressant), a rock of crack and a small Ziploc bag containing cocaine powder. With a nervous laugh, he said that he liked to keep his drugs in a safe place. In the insecure conditions of the streets, Étienne feared being robbed, and he temporarily hid his belongings in unexpected places, such as the bottom of a trashcan. While showing us his drugs, his hands were shaking. He suddenly put all his psychiatric pills in one of his trembling palms, brought them closer to us and asked: 'What do you wanna know about my meds?'

Étienne defined himself as an anguished man: 'I worry all the time, I'm always fearful … it's like living with a heavy weight inside of me.' He connected these feelings with childhood experiences of abandonment: 'My parents never cared for me, I am the product of a one-night stand! [laughs] My mother dumped me at my grandmother's place for a while, then I bounced from one foster home to another, then back to my grandma … I'm not mad at my parents anymore, I'm in contact with them … but it hurts, it still hurts.' Since childhood, Étienne has had frequent and short 'panic attacks', which although uncomfortable were not disabling. But five years ago, he had a major breakdown, after his girlfriend left him: 'I had this big panic attack, I couldn't breathe and I fainted.

I ended up in the hospital.' His doctor diagnosed Étienne with anxiety disorder, and prescribed him benzodiazepines and Effexor (also used for anxiety and panic attacks), as well as Seroquel to improve his sleep.

When we were doing fieldwork, Étienne only used cocaine. He injected powder cocaine and smoked crack. A couple of years ago, he had entered a methadone programme to stop his heroin and prescription opioid consumption. Étienne noticed that, since he had been in methadone treatment, his cocaine use had increased: 'Methadone ended my heroin cravings, but my hunger for cocaine is bigger now. I shoot up 50 per cent more than before.' Because of his higher cocaine intake, 'The anxiety is always present and I can become extremely aggressive, dangerous ... and I easily get into troubles.' He also felt more stressed: 'I don't take heroin now, and the bad side is that I'm more nervous because heroin really relaxed me.' Additionally, his sleeping problems increased: 'The good side [of not taking heroin] is that I save a bunch of money ... but then I take more coke, that is cheaper, but still, then I'm wondering at night how to get the money, and I can't sleep.'

Étienne told us that benzodiazepine helped him control his anxiety and aggression, and that Seroquel: 'Knocks me like a hammer. I take 300 mg and it's like a massive blow to my forehead, I sleep deeply.' He used psychiatric medication to treat the mental health issues for which these drugs are prescribed: 'I don't mess up with my meds. Before I mixed benzos with heroin, but now there is no need, I follow my doctor's prescription.' However, Étienne could not follow the instructions for use because of the increase in his cocaine intake: 'Sometimes, my anxiety is too big. After shooting up, my anxiety is huge and to really calm down I should take more benzos ... Same thing with Seroquel, I have to take more to fall asleep'. He needed to take more psychiatric drugs, but 'not too many because I'm not going to wake up the day after or I'm going to be too sleepy'. Étienne kept experimenting to find a balance between the quantity of cocaine he took and the right amount of psychiatric medication.

The four practices described above illustrate how our participants experiment with psychiatric drugs to counteract the side effects of street drugs. As undeserving subjects differentially excluded from state support, their use of psychiatric medication to control the after-effects of cocaine, to reduce or suppress the heroin and prescription opioid withdrawal symptoms, to detox from their use of heavy drugs and to medicate their mental health issues, reflect their somewhat messy attempts to care for themselves without having to renounce their poly-drug consumption. Nonetheless, the combination of benzodiazepines and street drugs entails risks of overdose and accidental death, and from a purely public health perspective, rather than care, these practices are described as harmful and even lethal. The elevated health risks of these practices also exceed the scope of harm reduction that, although comprehensive of a variety of interventions, aims to minimise the health impacts of drug use without threatening the lives of persons who use drugs (Lenton and Single 1998). However, if we stop associating care only with morally life-sustaining actions, and include its ambivalences, such practices can be understood as care. There are also other ways in which our participants use psychiatric drugs that could be more directly associated with forms of compassionate, altruistic and life-affirming care.

Caring for others: The moral value of psychiatric medication

> We met Kristelle at night in a community-based organisation, when she was picking up sterile injection material. She had virtually disappeared from our field site after a big argument with François around drug sharing. We already knew François's version of the story. According to him, Kristelle was a 'messy girl' who did not know how to manage her drug use. She 'burned all her money' on cocaine. She never saved for heroin or prescription opioids and, consequently, she often had withdrawal symptoms. When Kristelle found herself in these situations, François helped her out, giving her heroin or prescription opioids. But when Kristelle was 'back in shape' and had cocaine, she did not want to share it with François. That night, we learnt Kristelle's version of their argument. According to Kristelle, François was 'getting old', and forgetting 'how to enjoy life'. He was 'obsessed' with saving money for heroin or prescription opioids, and tried to control how Kristelle administered her money: 'I left my parents' house because I was fed up of someone telling me what to do, and François is even worse than my parents!' Thus, Kristelle rebelled against François' control by withholding her cocaine from him: 'I wanted to show him that buying cocaine makes sense; he also likes cocaine! … We can't just think about having money for heroin or Dilaus [Dilaudid].' (Fieldnote excerpt)

That night, Kristelle told us that a few days before, she had reconciled her differences with François. She started her account by acknowledging that, although controlling, François was often 'right, because he has lived on the street for much, much longer than I'. To avoid withdrawal symptoms, François had advised Kristelle not only to save money for heroin or prescription opioids, but also to keep benzodiazepine pills. As she had shown us, Kristelle used to carry benzodiazepines in her backpack, but one morning, after losing her backpack and having forgotten to get new pills, she woke up: 'Totally dope sick, with no strength in my body to score heroin or Dilaus.' Despite being angry at Kristelle, François helped her out: 'François brought me ... Rivos, and I came back to life.' Excitedly, Kristelle told us that François was a 'good guy', incapable of 'holding grudges', and that they were friends again. According to Kristelle, by giving her Rivotril when she was sick, François had shown that he still cared for her.

In Kristelle's description, psychiatric medication did not have an economic value of exchange, but a moral one. It 'becomes the substance through which care is performed' (Garcia 2010, 128), and through which social ties are reinforced or rebuilt. By giving a 'gift of care' in crucial moments, persons who use drugs become part of a moral economy of gift exchange that facilitates their survival in the precarious conditions of the streets (Bourgois 1998; Roy et al. 2011). Their participation in this moral economy ensures the continuity of their existence not only in the present time, but also in the future. For example, Carl also told us that when a street friend was dope sick, he helped him out, giving him any psychiatric medication (except for his Serax): 'This is something I give to a buddy in need, because I know that later when I'll be dope sick, the favour will be returned.' The chronicity of addictions shaped the way in which they envisioned their future: although this future was uncertain, they could not imagine an upcoming life without drugs.

Knowledge of how to experiment with psychiatric medication and other drugs was also part of this moral economy. When Kyle gave his street friends information about the drugs and quantities they had to combine, or recommended that they test this information by running experiments with their own bodies, he contributed to reducing the harmful effects of drugs, and therefore cared for them. Additionally, this knowledge also circulated under the form of advice when experienced drug users such as François told younger ones such as Kristelle to keep benzodiazepines as insurance against heroin or prescription opioid withdrawal. Again, the chronicity of addictions among persons who use drugs shaped the transmission of the knowledge needed to survive on the streets, and what it meant to care for others in this context.

Deservingness, chronicity and care: Final reflections

Carl and François, our key informants and beloved friends, died in the last couple of years due to chronic health issues that co-occurred with their use of drugs. Carl's infection generalised, compromising vital organs, and François developed a throat cancer that he linked with crack smoking, which aggressively spread throughout his body. Carl's infection and François's cancer were part of syndemic clusters of mutually enhancing health problems sustained by the detrimental socioeconomic conditions in which they lived, and by limited access to health and social services. Similarly, from the 25 persons who we interviewed for this research, 13 have already passed away, and we estimate that we have lost more than half of the 50 individuals we followed during our fieldwork. This painful reality pushes our reflection in two different directions. First, it is possible that the care experiments of our participants failed in the long run. Most of them wanted to live and to keep using drugs. The care that our participants performed for themselves and others using psychiatric medication allowed them to live their lives using drugs and, consequently, to ensure the chronicity of their addictions. But addictions are chronic, not endless. The chronicity of addictions has a final point. They can only last the lifetime of the addicted person. Psychiatric medications enabled our participants to inscribe addictions within the length of their lifetime, but did not allow them to extend their lives for much longer.

Our second train of thought brings us to question how politics of deservingness influence public policies that target homeless polydrug users in Canada, a country with a still robust welfare state, and one of the leading countries in harm reduction interventions. If our participants are dying at such a pace, these policies might be disserving one of the most vulnerable populations of the country. Due to their drug addict status, our participants were perceived as not deserving state support and, therefore, were excluded from several public services. Conversely, harm reduction programmes reached our participants and had positive outcomes on blood-borne disease transmission. Nonetheless, these programmes neglected not only the larger structural forces that influence our participants' drug use, but also critical medical areas closely linked to the harm reduction approach. For example, several of our participants discussed with us their need to treat the psychological issues that they saw as the root of their addictions, and their desire to receive psychotherapy in the community-based organisations that provided harm reduction programmes. They could not access the limited state-funded psychological services, and the only mental health resource they received was free psychiatric medication. As described in other anthropological studies, this availability of psychiatric medication is part of an ongoing global process of 'pharmaceuticalization of public health' (Biehl 2007), which aims to circumscribe chronic conditions to the individual sphere and to overshadow the social inequalities that shape these very conditions. However, we would like to conclude this chapter not only by criticising the scope of public policies, but also by asking for comprehensive interventions that include the needs and desires of chronic drug users and target the socioeconomic conditions that perpetuate health inequalities.

Acknowledgements

We thank the members of our research team, Élise Roy, Karine Bertrand and Didier Jutras-Aswad, for their support and guidance during our research. We presented a preliminary version of this chapter at the 2015 American Anthropological Association Annual Meeting on a panel organised by Danya Glabau. Thanks to her and to Andrea Lopez for a thought-provoking discussion of our paper. Thanks to Alissa Low and Alonso Gamarra for editing the English. Thanks to the community-based organisations (Cactus Montréal, Spectre de Rue and CRAN) and to our research participants, without whom this study would not have been possible. Ethical approval for this study was granted by the Comité d'éthique de la recherche en santé chez l'humain of the Centre hospitalier de l'Université de Sherbrooke. Support for this study was provided by the COSMO project (No. CBG101825).

Notes

1. The authors contributed equally to this work.
2. To ensure anonymity, we have changed the names of all participants, institutions and sites.
3. Benzodiazepine is a class of psychiatric substance that has sedative, hypnotic, anxiolytic, anticonvulsant and muscle relaxant effects. It is used to treat anxiety, insomnia, agitation and alcohol withdrawal symptoms. Examples of types of benzodiazepines distributed in Canada are clonazepam (Rivoltril), alprazolam (Xanax) and oxazepam (Serax).
4. A single room in a cheap hotel in Downtown Montreal costs around CA$30 per night. Persons who use drugs paid daily and did not permanently live in hotel rooms. They used hotel rooms strategically, for a few days, to 'take a break' from sleeping on the streets and to wash themselves.
5. At the time of this publication, persons who use drugs in Downtown Montreal have also been displaced from Saint-Paul Square.
6. Canada's official poverty line is the Market Basket Measure (MBM). According to the MBM, a family, or a person who is not in a family, lives in poverty if they cannot afford the cost of a basket of goods in their community. When we conducted this research, the annual income of all our participants was under CA$17,714, the MBM threshold for a person living in Montreal (Statistics Canada 2017).
7. The lowest dose of prescription opioids costs CA$5, and the lowest dose of heroin (half a 'point' or 0.05 grams) costs CA$30.

8. Quetiapine, commercialised in Canada under the name Seroquel, is a second-generation anti-psychotic prescribed for the treatment of schizophrenia, bipolar disorder and major depressive disorder, and off-label as sleep aid. It is considered that quetiapine has no abuse potential, and thus this medication is widely prescribed among persons who use drugs. However, increasing research shows that quetiapine has been abused among different populations (Hussain et al. 2005; Keltner and Vance 2008).

References

Bambra, Clare and Katherine E. Smith. 2010. 'No longer deserving? Sickness benefit reform and the politics of (ill) health', *Critical Public Health* 20 (1): 71–83. https://doi.org/10.1080/09581590902763265.

Becoña, Elisardo. 2016. 'Addiction is not a brain disease', *Papeles del Psicólogo* 37 (2): 118–25. Accessed 29 May 2021. http://www.papelesdelpsicologo.es/English/2696.pdf.

Beyrer, Chris, Jaroon Jittiwutikarn, Waranya Teokul, Myat Htoo Razak, Vinai Suriyanon, Namtip Srirak, Tasanai Vongchuk, Sodsai Tovanabutra, Teerada Sripaipan and David D. Celentano. 2003. 'Drug use, increasing incarceration rates and prison-associated HIV risks in Thailand', *AIDS and Behavior* 7 (2): 153–61. https://doi.org/10.1023/A:1023946324822.

Biehl, João. 2007. *Will to Live: AIDS therapies and the politics of survival*. Princeton, NJ: Princeton University Press.

Biehl, João. 2011. 'Human pharmakon: The anthropology of technological lives'. In *In Search of Self: Interdisciplinary perspectives on personhood*, edited by J. Wentzel Huyssteen and Erik P. Wiebe, 213–31. Grand Rapids, MI: William B. Eerdmans.

Bourgois, Philippe. 1998. 'The moral economies of homeless heroin addicts: Confronting ethnography, HIV risk and everyday violence in San Francisco shooting encampments', *Substance Use & Misuse* 33 (11): 2323–51. https://doi.org/10.3109/10826089809056260.

Bourgois, Philippe and Julie Bruneau. 2000. 'Needle exchange, HIV infection and the politics of science: Confronting Canada's cocaine injection epidemic with participant observation', *Medical Anthropology* 18 (4): 325–50. https://doi.org/10.1080/01459740.2000.9966161.

Carrier, Nicolas and Bastien Quirion. 2003. 'Les logiques de contrôle de l'usage des drogues illicites: La réduction des méfaits et l'efficience du langage de la périllisation', *Drogues, santé et société* 27 (1): 59–76. https://doi.org/10.7202/007181ar.

Chodos, Howard. 2017. *Options for Improving Access to Counselling, Psychotherapy and Psychological Services for Mental Health Problems and Illnesses*. Ottawa: Mental Health Commission of Canada.

Derrida, Jacques. 1981. *Dissemination*. Chicago: University of Chicago Press.

Drake, Robert. E., Fred C. Osher and Michael A. Wallach. 1991. 'Homelessness and dual diagnosis', *American Psychologist* 46 (11): 1149–58. https://doi.org/10.1037/0003-066X.46.11.1149.

Garcia, Angela. 2010. *The Pastoral Clinic: Addiction and dispossession along the Rio Grande*. Berkeley: University of California Press.

Government of Quebec. 2020. Individual and Family Assistance Act, Publications Québec. Accessed 21 June 2020. http://legisquebec.gouv.qc.ca/en/ShowDoc/cr/A-13.1.1,%20r.%201.

Hussain, M.Z., Waqar Waheed and Seema Hussain. 2005. 'Intravenous quetiapine abuse', *American Journal of Psychiatry*, 162: 1755–6. https://doi.org/10.1176/appi.ajp.162.9.1755-a.

Islam, M. Mofizul, Libby Topp, Carolyn A. Day, Angela Dawson and Katherine M. Conigrave. 2012. 'The accessibility, acceptability, health impact and cost implications of primary healthcare outlets that target injecting drug users: A narrative synthesis of literature', *International Journal on Drug Policy* 23 (2): 94–102. https://doi.org/10.1016/j.drugpo.2011.08.005.

Keltner, Normand L. and David E. Vance. 2008. 'Incarcerated care and quetiapine abuse', *Perspectives in Psychiatric Care* 44: 202–6. https://doi.org/10.1111/j.1744-6163.2008.00175.x.

Lees, Loretta and Hannah White. 2020. 'The social cleansing of London council estates: Everyday experiences of "accumulative dispossession"', *Housing Studies* 35 (10): 1701–22. https://doi.org/10.1080/02673037.2019.1680814.

Lenton, Simon and Eric Single. 1998. 'The definition of harm reduction', *Drug and Alcohol Review* 17 (2): 213–19. https://doi.org/10.1080/09595239800187011.

Mackenbach, Johan P. 2012. 'The persistence of health inequalities in modern welfare states: The explanation of a paradox', *Social Science & Medicine* 75 (4): 761–9. doi:10.1016/j.socscimed.2012.02.031.

Mol, Annemarie, Ingunn Moser and Jeannette Pols. 2010. 'Care: Putting practice into theory'. In *Care in Practice: On tinkering in clinics, homes and farms*, edited by Annemarie Mol, Ingunn Moser and Jeannette Pols, 7–25. Bielefeld: Transcript.

Motta-Ochoa, Rossio, Karine Bertrand, Nelson Arruda, Didier Jutras-Aswad and Élise Roy. 2017. '"I love having benzos after my coke shot": The use of psychotropic medication among cocaine users in downtown Montreal', *International Journal on Drug Policy* 49: 15–23. https://doi.org/10.1016/j.drugpo.2017.07.012.

National Institute on Drug Abuse. 2007. *Drugs, Brains, and Behavior: The science of addiction.* Bethesda, MD: National Institute on Drug Abuse.

Palepu, Anita, Brandon D. Marshall, Calvin Lai, Evan Wood and Thomas Kerr. 2010. 'Addiction treatment and stable housing among a cohort of injection drug users', *PloS One* 5 (7): 1–6. https://doi.org/10.1371/journal.pone.0011697.

Palepu, Anita, Michelle Patterson, Verena Strehlau, Akm Moniruzzamen, Jason Tan de Bibiana, James Frankish, Michael Krausz and Julian Somers. 2013. 'Daily substance use and mental health symptoms among a cohort of homeless adults in Vancouver, British Columbia', *Journal of Urban Health* 90 (4): 740–6. https://doi.org/10.1007/s11524-012-9775-6.

Pauly, Bernadette, Irene Goldstone, Jane McCall, Fiona Gold and Sarah Payne. 2007. 'The ethical, legal and social context of harm reduction', *Canadian Nurse*, 103: 19–23. Accessed 29 May 2021. http://europepmc.org/article/MED/17990401.

Petersen, Michael B., Rune Slothuus, Rune Stubager and Lise Togeby. 2011. 'Deservingness versus values in public opinion on welfare: The automaticity of the deservingness heuristic', *European Journal of Political Research* 50: 24–52. https://doi.org/10.1111/j.1475-6765.2010.01923.x.

Régie de l'assurance maladie du Québec. n.d. *Aid Programs: Free access to prescription drugs.* Accessed 5 July 2021. https://www.ramq.gouv.qc.ca/en/citizens/aid-programs/free-access-prescription-drugs.

Roe, Gordon. 2005. 'Harm reduction as paradigm: Is better than bad good enough? The origins of harm reduction', *Critical Public Health* 15 (3): 243–50. https://doi.org/10.1080/09581590500372188.

Rose, Damaris. 2004. 'Discourses and experiences of social mix in gentrifying neighbourhoods: A Montreal case study', *Canadian Journal of Urban Research* 13 (2): 278–316.

Roy, Élise and Nelson Arruda. 2015. 'Exploration of a crack use setting and its impact on drug users' risky drug use and sexual behaviors: The case of *piaules* in a Montréal neighborhood', *Substance Use & Misuse* 50 (5): 630–41. https://doi.org/10.3109/10826084.2014.997825.

Roy, Élise, Nelson Arruda and Philippe Bougois. 2011. 'The growing popularity of prescription opioid injection in downtown Montréal: New challenges for harm reduction', *Substance Use & Misuse* 46: 1142–50. https://doi.org/10.3109/10826084.2011.552932.

Singer, Merrill. 1994. 'Aids and the health crisis of the US urban poor: The perspective of critical medical anthropology', *Social Science & Medicine* 39 (7): 931–48. https://doi.org/10.1016/0277-9536(94)90205-4.

Singer, Merrill. 1996. 'A dose of drugs, a touch of violence, a case of AIDS: Conceptualizing the SAVA syndemic', *Free Inquiry in Creative Sociology* 24 (2): 99–110. Accessed 29 May 2021. https://ojs.library.okstate.edu/osu/index.php/FICS/article/view/1346.

Singer, Merrill and Scott Clair. 2003. 'Syndemics and public health: Reconceptualizing disease in bio-social context', *Medical Anthropology Quarterly* 17 (4): 423–41. https://doi.org/10.1525/maq.2003.17.4.423.

Statistics Canada. 2017. 'Table 4.5 Market Basket Measure (MBM) thresholds for economic families and persons not in economic families, 2015'. Accessed 27 February 2020. https://www12.statcan.gc.ca/census-recensement/2016/ref/dict/tab/t4_5-eng.cfm.

Stevenson, Lisa. 2014. *Life Beside Itself: Imagining care in the Canadian Arctic.* Oakland: University of California Press.

van Laere, Igor R., Matty. A. de Wit and Niek S. Klazinga. 2009. 'Pathways into homelessness: Recently homeless adults problems and service use before and after becoming homeless in Amsterdam', *BMC Public Health* 9 (3): 1–9. https://doi.org/10.1186/1471-2458-9-3.

Wilson, David P., Braedon Donald, Andrew J. Shattock, David Wilson, Nicole Fraser-Hurt. 2015. 'The cost-effectiveness of harm reduction', *International Journal on Drug Policy* 26 (1): 5–11. https://doi.org/10.1016/j.drugpo.2014.11.007.

Wyly, Elvin K. and Daniel J. Hammel. 2004. 'Gentrification, segregation and discrimination in the American urban system', *Environment and Planning A* 36: 1215–41. https://doi.org/10.1068/a3610.

9

'These doctors don't believe in PANS': Confronting uncertainty and a collapsing model of medical care

Maria LaRusso and César Abadía-Barrero[1]

Introduction

Diagnoses are products of history: they are both a classificatory tool and a process that shapes how societies think about diseases and act upon those who receive a given diagnosis. Rather than simple and uncontroversial, diagnoses are highly complex processes 'involving hierarchies, interests, paradigms, and power' (Juttel 2018, 9). Social scientists have demonstrated that disease entities, rather than existing in nature, are 'made' through the work of diagnosis classification and clinical practice (Mol 2002; Nissen and Risør 2018; Smith-Morris 2016). The irregular human experience that characterises living with illness, suffering or afflictions, is made to fit in to a particular nosology, a landscape of uniformity that hides the many ambiguities, guess work, uncertainty and 'tolerable' margin of error involved in setting boundaries for a set of signs and symptoms (Risør and Nissen 2018; Smith-Morris 2016).

When something is 'off' or 'wrong' with people's bodies and does not fit with neatly defined diagnoses, the unspecific umbrella terms 'disorder' or 'syndrome' are used to capture the lack of distinctiveness and variability across people (for example, HIV/AIDS, metabolic syndrome, restless leg syndrome and, in our case, paediatric acute-onset neuropsychiatric syndrome, or PANS). When new diagnoses emerge, or when biomedical standards of care fail to recognise patients' needs and demands (for example, Lyme disease, chronic fatigue syndrome), the whole medical system comes under scrutiny as scientists, clinicians, patients and relatives start confronting the unknown and disputing the meaning of specific signs and symptoms, what to call them, the disease causation and the best therapeutic options (Dumes 2020; Smith-Morris 2016). Even when the medical community agrees on specific diagnoses and treatment guidelines, the debates that surround specific conditions, including causes, progress and course of treatment, continue. Hence, diagnoses are ambiguous, and fluid in meaning and practice, with clinicians, patients and communities of care using a given diagnosis to mean different things (Nissen and Risør 2018; Smith-Morris 2016). The efforts of biomedicine to present diagnoses as 'value free' (Risør and Nissen 2018) and undisputable can be understood as reflecting how biomedicine deals with uncertainty, and how it has a hard time recognising its limits and, as the families we will present in this chapter argue, remaining open and being curious.

This chapter presents ethnographic research in the United States with families with children affected by PANS, a relatively new condition that is defying the disciplinary borders between infectious diseases, environmental causes of immune dysregulation, neurological problems and developmental psychopathology in paediatric care. PANS opens a window to examine critically why the hegemony of a biomedical model of care structured around sub-specialties is collapsing. In facing the uncertainty of the new condition, families' approach to care emphasises the need for comprehensiveness and immediacy; however, biomedicine seems to be ill equipped to meet those needs. Rather than offering support and facilitating a path to recovery, clinicians often challenge the knowledge of families, negate PANS as a viable diagnosis, and delay adequate care, which results in increased harm to both the child and the family. Furthermore, the chapter shows how families incur significant debt by trying several therapeutic options that are not covered by insurance. This signals how the inadequacy of the social welfare and broader safety nets in the United States further magnify children's and parents' suffering.

A brief description of PANS

In the early 1990s, researchers under the leadership of Susan Swedo of the Child Psychiatry Branch of the US National Institute of Mental Health reported on the first set of children who shared several psychological symptoms associated with GABHS (group A beta-hemolytic streptococci) (Swedo et al. 1993; Swedo 1994). She proposed to call this novel disease PANDAS: paediatric autoimmune neuropsychiatric disorder associated with streptococcus infections (Swedo et al. 1998). Importantly, all the children shared a very sudden, dramatic symptom onset, increased emotional lability, motoric hyperactivity, irritability, distractibility, age-regressive behaviour and, particularly, obsessive compulsive disorder (OCD). Over time, it became clear that other viral and bacterial infections, environmental factors, metabolic disorders and other conditions could also trigger similar symptoms, prompting Swedo's group to propose the new label PANS (NIH National Institute of Mental Health n.d.; Swedo 2012).

The most prevalent neuropsychiatric symptoms reported are OCD and/or a tic disorder, anxiety, emotional lability and/or depression, behavioural (developmental) regression, deterioration in school performance, attention deficit/hyperactivity disorder, sensory or motor abnormalities, and somatic signs and symptoms, including sleep disturbances, enuresis or urinary frequency (Calaprice et al. 2017; Swedo et al. 2015). The first episode typically lasts between 2 and 12 weeks, and is severe and incapacitating in about 50 per cent of cases. Recurrences, called PANS flares, vary in severity and are rather common (84 per cent of the cases) (Calaprice et al. 2017). Earlier diagnosis and treatment geared towards the specific trigger improves the chances for a full and complete recovery (Calaprice et al. 2017, 2018).

The fact that the condition has been recently established within the medical community, with the WHO including it very recently (October 2018) in its ICD-10 diagnosis code under 'disorders involving the immune mechanism', raises concerns about the preparedness of paediatricians, other health-care providers, and health-care systems as a whole to identify and adequately treat the children. Indeed, a study with 698 children with PANS indicated that clinicians struggled to 'identify and appropriately treat affected patients', which might explain why from age of onset to diagnosis, these authors found a significant time lag of between 1.1 and 3.8 years (Calaprice et al. 2017).

Our research focuses on the experiences of families with children affected by PANS, including how families make sense of the disease and what journeys they have embarked on to help their children recover while navigating the complexities of health-care systems. We examine what happens to families' search for answers when health-care professionals and health-care systems are being challenged by both market forces in health care and by the uncertainties brought about by a new condition. The acute presentation but chronic course of PANS, along with infectious or environmental triggers, neuropsychiatric symptoms and autoimmunity, add to anthropological debates about diagnostic fluidity, ambiguities, uncertainties and controversies that challenge the traditional biomedical separations between acute and chronic, and infectious and non-communicable, diseases (Manderson and Smith-Morris 2010; Nissen and Risør 2018; Smith-Morris 2016). Just as with diagnoses, as explained above, this edited volume highlights chronicity and care as socially constructed spaces that allow researchers to critically examine the culture of biomedicine and its increasing reliance on market forces (Manderson and Smith-Morris 2010; Mol 2008). In the case of PANS, then, chronicity merges with diagnostic uncertainty and complex care needs in powerful ways. In this chapter, we examine how health-care providers and families negotiate what is known and unknown about the diagnosis and clinical course of PANS within a context in which market forces determine how much families need to pay out of pocket to provide care for their children, if they even have sufficient social capital, economic resources or indebtedness capacity.

Ethnographic research

We started to investigate the rising 'epidemic' of childhood chronic conditions in 2017. From initial clinical reports and anthropological analysis (Bock et al. 2008; Perro and Adams 2017), it became evident that clinicians and researchers were acknowledging that environmental factors were affecting children's bodies immensely. Paediatricians saw dramatic shifts in their clinical practice, from acute and easy-to-treat conditions, to epidemics of complex conditions with long-lasting effects and difficult care needs. We started to follow some discussions in online forums where primarily families, but also some health-care professionals, debated the new conditions, offered support and shared information about local health-care networks. Parents would recommend clinicians (sometimes local, often not) who they considered knowledgeable and experienced with the diagnosis and treatment of PANS. It was also very common for families to share stories about health-care professionals who not only disregarded their concerns, but also became hostile if families challenged their knowledge or tried to propose that their children might have PANS. Online forums, it seemed to us, constituted web-based communities of care in which families confronted uncertainties through the sharing of knowledge and resources, and found much-needed recognition and emotional support.

In 2017 and 2018, we attended conferences in the United States and England in which researchers and clinicians presented advances in treatment and research, and explained different theories of the physiopathology of PANS. The conferences were attended by some practitioners, but they were significantly outnumbered by families with children with PANS. In both the online forums and the conferences, it became clear that families were suffering as they confronted the many unknowns that still characterise this condition, and the largely unresponsive health-care systems, both in the United States and Europe.

With the help of a graduate student, we conducted a more systematic analysis of the threads of a US-based online forum of families with children with PANS (Dolce et al. under review). This analysis, plus the other information we had collected, allowed us to develop a protocol for ethnographic interviews in which we focused our attention on families' experiences with PANS, their 'journeys' to access care, and their sources of support. We used 'family illness journeys' as a main data-gathering technique, an adaptation of 'illness narratives' (Kleinman 1988) and 'bureaucratic itineraries' (Abadía-Barrero and Oviedo 2009). In this chapter, we focus on these ethnographic interviews: mean length = 2 hours, 49 minutes each, 22 children diagnosed with PANS/PANDAS (9 girls, 13 boys), 85 per cent white, 10 per cent Latinx, 5 per cent black. All families were living in the United States, although two families had moved to the United States in recent years to get care from practitioners specialising in PANS/PANDAS. The results we present are from our analysis of both preliminary data collected and all 20 interviews, and we describe two families in detail as a way to represent what it is like to have a child affected by PANS, and the challenges to finding adequate sources of care and support. We use PANS, PANDAS and PANS/PANDAS interchangeably, since participating families may have received either diagnosis.

Making sense of the unknown

In the interviews, parents would quickly and vividly recall the moment when a dramatic and extremely intense cascade of odd behaviours and movements, severe anxiety and personality changes took over their children, and marked the before and after of a life of worries, anxiety and uncertainty. Leah remembered that her 11-year-old son Ethan had just started eighth grade and was working with the school district behaviourist to manage his anxiety and difficult transition to middle school. He also seemed sick, and over the course of a few days, red bumps had spread to his head and neck. At urgent care, the doctors prescribed an antihistamine. When the rash spread to his leg and they returned two days later, they prescribed a corticosteroid. At soccer, Ethan reported that he 'kind of blacked out'. He said 'he had moved and he had no idea what happened', which, Leah recalled, 'freaked the hell out of' her. Leah's worries increased, and by Saturday she had seen three or four of these episodes. The next morning, Ethan's breathing sounded awful, and they rushed him to urgent care, where the doctors said Ethan had two bacterial infections and prescribed antibiotics and full bed rest. It was discovered much later, however, that Ethan had hidden the antibiotics and had not taken them – another out of character behaviour that suggested PANS-related OCD. Ethan's parents continued to see episodes and, after consulting with an acquaintance who is a paediatric neurologist, Ethan was sent for an electroencephalogram (EEG). The neurologist concluded that Ethan had a complex movement tic, and that an unusual response to the prednisone might explain everything that had happened. The next morning, Leah called the school district behaviourist to let him know what was happening, and he asked if Ethan had been tested for PANDAS, which Leah had never heard of. He explained that he had seen kids who got sick and then developed mood swings and/or tics, and found that it was connected to a recent sickness.

Leah hung up, opened a browser in the computer and typed 'tics + odd behaviour + children', and retrieved pages and pages of information about PANS/PANDAS. She immediately called the paediatrician, sent him more videos of Ethan, and asked for him to be tested for PANDAS.[2] Based on the response she received on the phone, she doubted the paediatrician knew what PANDAS was. In a video she shared with us, we saw Ethan moving from one side of the exam room to the other, going up and down from the exam table, making noises and chewing his hands. Ethan's whole body was out of control, and his terrified little sister insisted to Leah, almost yelling, that Ethan was choking. According to Leah, the paediatrician had no idea what he was looking at, and just said, 'he will be OK'. That night, Ethan almost choked himself brushing his teeth. Leah managed to page the neurologist on call, who said that it sounded like Ethan had OCD. Leah asked, '"Do you mean PANDAS?, and he's like, 'Oh, we don't believe that exists.'"

Both in the online forum and in our interviews, parents described many similar interactions with health-care professionals who 'do not believe' in PANS/PANDAS as a diagnosis. OCD, anxiety and complex tic disorders, among others, are offered as possible diagnoses, and referrals to neurology, psychiatry, cognitive behavioural therapy programmes and so on are recommended as part of the therapeutic plan. According to the literature, and confirmed in our interviews, patients frequently report a clear-cut association between an infection, the development of some neurological, psychological and psychiatric symptoms, and effective response to antibiotics (Calaprice et al. 2018). In other cases, however, families seem to hit a wall with an unresponsive or partially responsive health-care system that delegitimises their suffering (Ware 1992) and forces them to search for answers and solutions inside and outside the established health-care networks and protocols.

Uncertainties, incompetence or a problem of medicine?

Renée C. Fox (1957) argues that medical students quickly realise that training in medicine is about learning how to deal with uncertainties. After medical school, physicians continue facing two basic types of uncertainty. One:

> derives from limitations in the current state of medical knowledge. There are many questions to which no physician, however well trained, can yet provide answers. The second type of uncertainty results from incomplete or imperfect mastery of available knowledge. No one can have at his command all the information, lore, and skills of modern medicine. (Fox 1998, 237–8)

When new conditions emerge, and medical knowledge is trying to make sense of them, the two types of uncertainty described by Fox (1998) seem to be particularly relevant, even more so when one of biomedicine's social roles is helping contain patient's anxieties as a result of uncertainty (West and West 2002). In our research, however, parents of children with PANS/PANDAS questioned whether we should think of lack of knowledge as uncertainty or as incompetence. Parents also experienced rigidity in the medical system, and a lack of humility and empathy from physicians when facing the unknown. This adds to a 'double burden' of living through a disease and having one's experience doubted by the institution that should offer answers (Dumes 2019; West and West 2002). In many narratives, families expressed anger at the sense of arrogance and dismissal of their pleas to consider their perspectives on their children's health, and they also engaged in larger reflections on the seeming impossibility of medicine to be open, acknowledge its own limitations and expand current understandings. 'What's wrong with these doctors?' was a rhetorical question that many families asked.

After speaking to the on-call neurologist, Ethan was started on an anti-hypertensive medication that reduces nerve impulses and controls tics. Things got better, according to Leah, but Ethan still was having '3 to 13 of these tic episodes a day'. When he started to bang his head against the wall, they switched to another 'nerve-calming' medication, which did not seem to help much. The next day, Leah took Ethan to their naturopath, who 'took one look at him' and told her, 'This is not a kid with a tic disorder … No. He's sick,' meaning that he had an untreated infection. She ordered labs, and advised Leah to keep Ethan at home and to keep on searching for the right diagnosis and the right clinician: 'She basically told me to find a physician who knew what the hell they were doing.' The next day, Leah brought Ethan back to the paediatrician's office to see another doctor in the practice to get 'another perspective'. But this doctor was also dismissive, and concluded that Ethan 'could be at school'. Adam, Leah's husband, responded incredulously: 'No, he can't be at school. He's sick!' Their narrative could be interpreted as a dynamic characterised by frustrated parents reckoning with an unmovable medical establishment. This failure to listen and show compassion resonates with long-term discussions about the crisis of the hegemonic medical model (Menéndez 1985), in which the technical aspects of disease diagnosis and therapeutics are trumping the intersubjective practices of care and caring (Ayres 2009; Kleinman 2009; Mol 2008).

The following day, Ethan developed very bad headaches. Leah called the paediatrician and neurologist, and both advised her to go to the emergency room (ER). Adam responded angrily to the people at the ER who were going to send them home: 'Listen to me. This is insane. We're now at day 19 [from the onset of his first symptoms].' Finally, Ethan got admitted, but to neurology, which Leah realised 'was not what he needed'. They did an EEG and magnetic resonance imaging (MRI) and found nothing, but they also 'gave him fluids, which gave him a bit of a bounce because *he was sick*'. Leah and Adam insisted on being seen by infectious disease specialists but, instead, they were thrown more unfitting differential diagnoses, such as 'stereotypic movement disorder', 'conversion disorder', or a return to the prednisone hypothesis. They decided to go home and just follow up with the gastroenterology (GI) out-patient clinic, because Ethan was also complaining of stomach pain. Leah elaborated on their decision: 'not that [going home] was against medical advice, they had nothing to offer … they had no idea what was going on with our kid'.

They visited family for the holiday weekend and, while there, they started to see something new: Ethan was passing out. Leah's parents came to their home to help, and they started to see more cycles of odd movements and passing out. Leah immediately began making phone calls. First, she followed up on an application she had submitted to a children's mental health clinic at a teaching hospital about an hour away. They told her, 'No we don't think it's PANS or PANDAS, based on the paperwork.' Then she spoke to their neurologist, and he asserted that 'This is a conversion disorder, because nothing else changes like this,' meaning the course of symptoms changing in such a progressive fashion. The next day, at the GI consultation, they faced what Leah describes as 'the first person with a brain'. The GI physician saw Ethan going through the cycles of odd movements and passing out, and immediately interrupted them and asked them if Ethan was a normal child. 'And we're like, yeah, and, by the way, I'm going to show you a video of him literally two days ago [participating in his soccer team's division championship],' and the GI responded, 'This is an infection, because nothing else moves like this.'

Ethan now got readmitted to the local children's hospital, but this time to see the medical management team that did investigations. The paediatricians on that team examined Ethan and still saw a bit of the rash. They brought in neurology again, even though Leah's mother, who had worked as an administrator at a top medical centre, 'was literally screaming in their face', saying 'we need infectious disease!' Leah's mother explained, 'That is the only way they hear you. I know how to talk to doctors, I have worked with doctors my whole life. You don't penetrate the ego unless you scream at their face.' Despite Leah's worries that her mother's aggressive approach to advocate for Ethan's needs was going to jeopardise his whole care, she did convince the neurologist, and infectious disease was finally called.

Even though one might think that doctors in some fields are unfamiliar with a new disease entity such as PANS/PANDAS, this narrative and our other data suggest that paediatricians, including both primary care and specialists, are either lagging behind or actively resisting incorporating the new disease into their way of thinking about children who, all of a sudden, develop neuropsychiatric symptoms. The infectious disease specialist who saw Ethan that day at the hospital did agree that an infection was probably behind Ethan's diagnostic puzzle, but that did not prompt a shift toward treating any underlying infections, and Leah explained, 'He didn't say PANS or PANDAS either, by the way. He just said yes, obviously there was some infection and it caused a tic, and then all the anxiety and all of this became a conversion disorder,' still suggesting that his current psychiatric symptoms were not related to an active infection. A paediatric psychiatrist was also brought in and concurred with the conversion disorder diagnosis. This psychiatrist had been identified as a practitioner who treated children with PANS; however, Leah concluded that the psychiatrist had a limited understanding, and only accepted a PANS/PANDAS diagnosis for children who presented with the classical manifestations and progression of symptoms, and had an active strep infection. Leah did not doubt that these physicians were well-intentioned, but, reflecting on her own growing knowledge of PANS, and the many failed interactions with a long list of doctors, she concluded: 'They are just incompetent. They just don't know enough.'

Bloodwork completed during Ethan's hospitalisation revealed active mycoplasma infection, but the doctors concluded that his body was already fighting the infection, and they did not prescribe antibiotics, which would have been the first line of treatment if Ethan was diagnosed with PANS. Instead, Ethan was referred to a partial hospitalisation programme for children with combined medical and psychiatric illness that provides therapeutic and behavioural interventions. In addition, Ethan was sent to the neurology department of a top-rated children's and teaching hospital two hours from their home. The experts from this hospital diagnosed Ethan with 'post-infectious neuropsychiatric syndrome'. They explained that they often see neuropsychiatric symptoms with mycoplasma and that they are not sure why, but that they think it is related to the pain response. They also recommended a partial hospitalisation rehabilitation programme, but one that was more pain oriented. Leah had entered this new neurology appointment armed with a well-developed and researched argument that Ethan had PANS, but she was told, 'We don't believe in PANS.'

Parents' frustrations and confrontations with an unmovable medical establishment are indicative of biomedicine's belief system (Good 1994) and the limits of an epistemology that falls short at explaining particular diseases (Dumes 2019). In the case of PANS, in spite of the clinical evidence, both in terms of symptoms and labs, and in terms of improvements after adequate treatment, physicians not only 'do not believe' that PANS exists, but also become adversarial if families bring up the diagnosis, and even turn them away from their clinics. This adamant resistance most likely indicates that by bridging neurological, psychiatric, immunological, nutritional, infectious and environmental processes in a single condition, PANS destabilises biomedical hegemony (Menéndez 1985) – that is, a kind of knowledge and practice structured around 'modern' divisions, such as acute infections versus chronic conditions, the mind and body dichotomy, and distinct body systems that correspond to medical specialties. It is not just that biomedicine has failed to catch up with diseases such as PANS, but also that, in order to acknowledge PANS, it needs a structural transformation. Perhaps not surprisingly, many of the specialty doctors who treat PANS are not mainstream, and practise integrative, osteopathic or naturopathic medicine. As one family said, they 'think outside the box'.

The same day as the neurology appointment, Leah received a call to say that the partial hospitalisation programme had a spot open up. They were desperate for help, so for two months, Leah stayed with Ethan in another state while he participated in this programme, and Adam stayed at home to take care of their daughter. The practitioners in this programme actually did not doubt that Ethan had PANS. However, insurance did not cover treatment for PANS, as it had not been recognised by the American Academy of Paediatrics and was not included in the reimbursement negotiations between insurers and providers, so they used the conversion disorder diagnosis code to get coverage for the partial hospitalisation. This also meant that they could provide only therapeutic and psychopharmacological interventions that corresponded to conversion disorder; they could not provide PANS treatments, such as those to fight infections or to support the immune system. 'There was progress', Leah acknowledged, but only because Ethan developed coping skills for managing his symptoms. After the two months, she recalled, 'It's just not enough progress … to function in the real world. He was not really better. So [we] went home.'

Adam then called the unit at the National Institute of Health that was financing PANS research. He was given a list of physicians who treated PANS in the states surrounding where they lived, but all of them had stopped taking new patients or had very long waiting lists. Leah called a friend of a friend who also had a son with PANS and had been active in the PANS advocacy community. She recommended their own doctor, one of the well-known physicians who treated children with PANS, but she warned that this doctor was expensive and did not take insurance. First-time appointments for these uncovered doctors are typically between US$1,200 and US$1,500, plus all the lab tests they order, some covered and some not, and the hundreds of dollars worth of supplements and herbal antimicrobials often prescribed, making this route prohibitive for many families. For this doctor, the waiting time was three to four months, but Leah 'got lucky' because of a cancellation, and she got an appointment in a month:

> So in April [six months after Ethan's first symptoms], we went to their office and they said, 'he is sick.' Number one, he needed antibiotic. They put him on 500 milligrams a day of azithromycin. They also put him on a bunch of herbal stuff because they [the medical team] are a combo of an MD [medical doctor] and an ND [naturopathic doctor]. And honestly within four days we saw Ethan back.

When we asked her to explain how 'Ethan was back', Leah said, 'He was feeling better. The episodes, as we came to call them, were gone. That was huge. Unbelievable.'

Nonetheless, Ethan was not cured. Like most of the families we interviewed, they still had to manage symptoms, ups and downs, and occasional flare-ups. Leah and Adam continued with their out-of-network 'medical team' and uncovered costs (such as supplements), but after meeting a US$300 deductible, they did get partial reimbursement. At the time of the interview, a year after the first episodes, they felt that Ethan was 'progressively getting better'. Still, Leah reflects on the experience: 'It's all negative. He's been through hell, as have I.' Although she recognised that finally finding their medical team was positive, she concluded: 'But beyond that, I don't have any faith in doctors anymore. I can't imagine that [Ethan] does [either].'

A collapsing model of medical care, inadequate social welfare and family destruction

Similar to Leah and Adam's story, Carla described a challenging journey to get proper care for her son Simon. However, the ways in which PANS and lack of support affected them economically were far more pronounced. Simon had many medical conditions, including autism, and even though caring for him was difficult, Carla, a successful professional, was managing. 'But the short story of our disaster is PANDAS, because Simon was doing really good, and I was so happy. I was working. Simon was happy at school and he did Christmas plays, and I'm like, oh my God, it's a dream, we can actually survive autism.' Simon's symptoms began with a weird rash. Over a couple of weeks, the rash got bigger and 'He started to get a little bit more of OCD and started developing weird fears.' As months went by, Simon became more fearful and anxious. His OCD was out of control, and he started to have psychotic episodes and eventually refused to go to school, an out-of-district placement for children with special needs where Simon was thriving. Seven months later, after many frustrating appointments, Simon got an appointment with a physician who treated PANS/PANDAS. Simon's bloodwork came back positive for streptococcus, babesia and mycoplasma. Fortunately, this doctor was covered by insurance. After antibiotics, Simon improved, but by this time he had lost much of the developmental progress he had made, and managing him was more difficult. His school did not understand the changes in his behaviour. Carla did her best to educate the school about

PANS/PANDAS, and worked with them on developing a behaviour intervention plan for Simon's aggressive episodes, which were triggered by severe anxiety and OCD. The plan mandated that at no point should they restrain him or put him in their isolation room, which would magnify his fears. However, soon after, Simon was restrained and put in isolation. The same day, Carla decided to pull Simon out of the school. She recalled, 'They just couldn't get it.' In her view, the school was used to treating all behaviours the same way, and even though they 'went over and over and over what the reasons were for' Simon's behavioural changes, the school was not able to adapt their approach. Even though she brought in test results and paperwork from Simon's doctor, the more Carla explained 'No, this is PANDAS … this isn't autism … this is PANDAS,' the more she felt that the school personnel disregarded her as a 'crazy' mother.

So Carla gave up on the school, and tried to home school and keep working. Even though her employer was extremely flexible, she reported:

> I just couldn't do it. I was getting sicker and sicker, and my cardiologist said, you're going to kill yourself and he's not going to have a mother. So in March of 2015, I resigned. My hope was, if I give him full time, we'll get this PANDAS thing straightened out, you know, like three months, maybe four or five months, and then I'll go back [to work]. And he just never got better [sighs]. And he just kept getting new problems after new problems after new problems. I blew through retirement, and then, I'd say by June 2017, we were like dead poor. So now we have food assistance, he has SSI [supplemental security income]. And we are poor. We just live off US$560 of child support [from his father] and Simon's SSI, which is a constant fight. I got to tell you, being poor is a full-time job.

Even though Simon's initial appointments for PANS were paid for by insurance, this case should not be thought of as 'covered' care. Since Carla is very good with numbers, she calculated for tax purposes that she had spent tens of thousands of dollars in medical care for Simon, which was the result of care being partially covered. Many of the diagnostic and therapeutic needs, such as special diagnostic procedures, herbal medications, homeopathy and supplements that many of the clinicians who treat children with PANS/PANDAS believe to be important for supporting children's immune system are not covered. Then, a combination of having to quit her job to be able to better care for Simon, and the amount of uncovered expenses, explains how Carla went from having a good salary and owning a house to going bankrupt and living in a family member's basement in such a short period of time. In this part of the narrative, we see how people experience the functioning or malfunctioning of the health-care system and the larger welfare system. On the one hand, it is clear that people's social, economic and cultural capitals are all important tools to navigate health-care systems successfully (Abadía-Barrero and Oviedo-Manrique 2008), but clearly, in complex care, social supports outside of the health-care system are of extreme importance for the family's wellbeing.

Yet, in Carla's case, poverty continued to be the most important factor that determined the kind of care she could afford for Simon. Although Carla was divorced from Simon's father and had custody, Simon still had private insurance through the health benefits provided through his father's employer. Carla was also able to get public insurance (subsidised government insurance that pays providers directly for the care of people who qualify based on limited income) as a secondary insurance to pick up whatever the private insurance did not cover. However, the doctor who they had been seeing for PANS treatment was suddenly dropped from the insurance company's coverage network, and he became 'out of pocket'. According to Carla, the insurance company dropped the physician for being an outlier, meaning that he acknowledged PANDAS and was ordering tests and prescribing treatments that were making him unprofitable for the network, a situation that has been described in other contexts (Ardila-Sierra and Abadía-Barrero 2020). Because of his removal from the network of covered providers, Carla explained, 'It's really difficult now. [We see him only] twice a year because we're poor.' Before, when he was part of the insurance network, Carla could schedule appointments based on medical need; now, she has to make the 'choice' of seeing him based on what she can afford, spacing out visits as much as possible, rather than scheduling appointments according to Simon's medical needs. 'We see him for 10 minutes for US$175, but if you go even a speck over 10 minutes, it's US$350.' When they told her this at the last visit, she said 'I don't have US$350.' The clinic agreed not to charge over US$175, but Carla agonised. 'I'm scared of next time. And I have to be super prepared when I go in. This time I wasn't, because I had a lot of questions for him, and I talked a little longer than I was supposed to, and I didn't know about [the increase in the fee].' The prospect of rising expenses and being stuck in poverty prompted Carla to acknowledge, 'I don't know how much longer we're going to be able to do it.'

In this narrative, affordability of medical care aligns with research that indicates that the market of insurance companies (Waitzkin and Working Group for Health Beyond Capitalism 2018) is the social force that shapes everyday moral debates about how much care people can afford (Abadía-Barrero 2015; Mulligan and Castañeda 2017). Families also reported the experience of providers needing to stick to codes and covered procedures that might not fit the medical needs of their patients, as in Ethan's case. Providers who are 'kicked out' of the insurance networks, or who decided from the very beginning not to bother with insurance in order to provide what they consider adequate care, also manage complex moral agendas in health-care delivery. Since these uncovered physicians are overbooked, and their waiting times are very long, they impose time limits so that they can be available to other patients. In addition, first appointments are often two to three hours long, which is considered necessary to gather a full history, progression of symptoms, and often a recounting of tests, misdiagnoses and complex treatment journeys. Insurance will not cover a three-hour first appointment, and families too are typically hesitant to pay US$1,500 for a first appointment, plus additional hundreds or thousands of dollars in uncovered specialty lab tests. However, they reach a point of desperation as they become tired of appointments with doctors who do not 'believe in' PANS, cannot find help covered by their insurance plan, and can no longer tolerate their child's suffering. Even though many families will not be able to afford these uncovered physicians, they are undoubtedly helping families in the context of a failed medical system that is denying adequate care for children with new and complex disorders. The failures of the larger social welfare infrastructure are also visible, as families do not receive adequate economic support, disability insurance, unemployment insurance or any home-based interventions. Importantly, when Carla quit her job to take over Simon's everyday care and school needs, he improved significantly. If an adequate welfare system were in place, perhaps Carla's life would not have been destroyed by PANS/PANDAS.

Carla felt strongly that money had been the biggest barrier to helping Simon: 'If I had the money, we would do the IVIG [intravenous immunoglobulin]', which, according to the existing protocols, is reserved for a handful of non-responsive and severe cases (Calaprice et al. 2018). In her mind, she would calculate how many treatments they could afford based on the price, 'you know, US$ 6,000, or whatever it is now'. Carla thought of IVIG as the next logical step in Simon's care, but 'we can't go any further until we can do that'. Carla, like other parents confronting PANS/PANDAS, is very aware that the children need a range of care practices that are not necessarily medical: calm environments, relaxing time, rest, supplements, and good-quality food without toxicants and with plenty of microbes – that is, 'organic', as MDs, NDs and osteopathic doctors at the forefront of these new epidemics are advising (Perro and Adams 2017). In Carla's case, if she had money, she would have Simon 'on a better diet, because when we got poor he couldn't have all organic, and the supplements that he needs more regularly'. The care demands of this generation of children affected by PANS/PANDAS and other complex medical conditions do seem to defy reductionist conceptualisations around health-care costs and risk assessments for cost-effective calculations of coverage (Waitzkin and Working Group for Health Beyond Capitalism 2018). When asked what she would like to see in the future, Carla mused, 'That it's more accepted by the mainstream medical community so … the kids can get treated and actually have lives … I don't think any of our lives are going to change until it's accepted, because right now, the only people who can get fixed are the rich.'

Both Ethan's and Simon's families suffered tremendously, witnessing the decompensation of their previously thriving child and confronting a medical system that inconsistently recognised and treated their child's disorder. However, Ethan and his family managed the economic impacts without going into poverty; Ethan's school was responsive and adapted to his needs; his mother missed 'just' six months of work; they had better out-of-network coverage and lower deductibles (US\$300, as compared to US\$6,000 under Simon's father's insurance plan); they did not lose their house; and they could afford the completely uncovered costs, such as supplements and healthy foods. Two families in our interview sample filed for bankruptcy, and several others could only afford treatment by incurring significant debt, or through family help, friends' support and donations (for example, through GoFundMe). These experiences highlight how an insurance-based medical system and inadequate welfare system, in combination, fail to protect families in the United States who are increasingly facing complex childhood illnesses that destabilise the hegemony of biomedical care and its market 'logics of care' (Mol 2008).

Conclusion: Diagnoses as uncertainty, chronicity and hope for the future

Carla thinks of PANS as a 'life sentence. That's what it is. It's destroyed any hope I had of my son having a life, and it's taken mine away from me. I never thought I'd be wanting just plain autism, but this is harder than plain autism.' Carla consistently presented her narrative through the lens of economic precarity, but she reflected on the different aspects that make PANS/PANDAS care even more challenging. In terms of what made it harder:

I'd say money, and then probably medical community support, because if the conventional community supported it, you wouldn't have to fight for it so much. It's like sometimes I wish Simon had cancer, you know, because then you'd have all the fundraisers [because other people] feel sorry for you. It's that [doctors] don't understand. It's like he's got something worse, you know, to me it's worse. It is insidious and it's a constant torture, but to have that support, that would be great. That would be really great. So money and physician support.

Such painful paradoxes in medical care, such as wanting 'just plain autism', or that Simon 'had cancer', refer to the moral assessments of deservingness that surround particular diagnoses (see the introduction to this book). In addition, for people living in poverty, certain diseases mean not only better medical care, but also access to economic resources that are made available to particular groups of patients out of moral assessments or histories of advocacy and activism (Abadía-Barrero 2011).

For most families in our study, the uncovered and exorbitant costs in a market-based health-care system, and the lack of a medical establishment that 'listens' and 'acknowledges', are prime determinants, not only of the child's care, but of the overall family's struggle to 'survive' PANS/PANDAS. The uncertainty around the child's future worsens when the medical establishment 'doesn't believe in PANS'. For other patients, it was extremely puzzling that clinicians might acknowledge and even track severe infections via the presence of antibodies, but refuse to prescribe any treatment or to call the children's condition PANS/PANDAS. Families could not make sense of this, given that PANS/PANDAS is recognised, and is included in official websites, such as that of the US National Institute of Health.

The aggressiveness with which some doctors interacted with the families, and the denial of PANS/PANDAS as a legitimate diagnosis, might be understood, following Veena Das (1995), as a reaction to a sort of 'poisonous knowledge' that could destabilise biomedicine's belief system – a certain 'code of silence' around a knowledge that must remain hidden in order to preserve the structuring order of medicine. With PANS/PANDAS, the idea of medical specialties with ultra-specialised knowledge seems very ineffective in dealing with a complex syndrome that not only cuts across specialty boundaries, but also asks for a remake of the understanding and treatment of diseases. Indeed, an infectious disease that leads to autoimmunity and a set of neurological and psychiatric manifestations challenges many of the diagnostic and therapeutic silos and pathophysiological explanations of diseases. For example, the pathophysiology of the gut–brain axis is changing how mental illness is understood (Kelly et al. 2015; Liu and Zhu 2018). Indeed, many children with PANS/PANDAS are prescribed pre- and probiotics to reconstitute a healthy microbiota and seal the blood–brain barrier, considered an important part of treatment by many PANS/PANDAS clinicians. While the infectious diseases specialty has been established based on the need to destroy pathogens, a healthy microbiota helps in processing the food we eat and signalling all the components of the neuro-immuno-endocrine axes or immune-neuroendocrine network (Kelly et al. 2015; Liu and Zhu 2018; Perro and Adams 2017).

Medicine is supposed to help families manage uncertainties (West and West 2002), and health care is supposed to be part of comprehensive welfare systems that avoid catastrophic expenses and help families navigate difficult and extraordinary times. However, both biomedicine and the insufficient US welfare system are failing families with children with PANS/PANDAS. Not only is the suffering of children and families not being acknowledged, but also families' life projects are being derailed as they need to search for answers and pay out of pocket for adequate care. In this process, many leave their jobs and undergo significant financial strain, even bankruptcy. Perhaps the increasing rates of new and chronic childhood diseases will force a structural transformation of biomedicine and the health-care system that supports it. Privileging a 'logic of care' over the 'logic of profits' seems a step in the right direction. While most families hope for a cure for PANS/PANDAS, and full insurance coverage, all do agree that the current medical system is failing them.

Notes

1. Both authors are considered first authors and both made equal contributions to the chapter.
2. Although there is no test for PANS/PANDAS, bloodwork can identify active infections or immune system alterations and clarify course of treatment.

References

Abadía-Barrero, César Ernesto. 2011. *I Have AIDS but I Am Happy: Children's subjectivities, AIDS, and social responses in Brazil*. Bogotá: Universidad Nacional de Colombia.

Abadía-Barrero, César Ernesto. 2015. 'Neoliberal justice and the transformation of the moral: The privatization of the right to health care in Colombia', *Medical Anthropology Quarterly* 30 (1): 62–79. https://doi.org/10.1111/maq.12161.

Abadía-Barrero, César Ernesto and Diana Goretty Oviedo-Manrique. 2008. 'Intersubjetividades estructuradas: la salud en Colombia como dilema epistemológico y político para las Ciencias Sociales', *Universitas Humanística* 66: 57–82. Accessed 29 May 2021. http://www.scielo.org.co/pdf/unih/n66/n66a06.pdf.

Abadía-Barrero, César Ernesto and Diana G. Oviedo. 2009. 'Bureaucratic itineraries in Colombia: A theoretical and methodological tool to assess managed-care health care systems', *Social Science & Medicine* 68: 1153–60. https://doi.org/10.1016/j.socscimed.2008.12.049.

Ardila-Sierra, Adiana and César Abadía-Barrero. 2020. 'Medical labour under neoliberalism: An ethnographic study in Colombia', *International Journal of Public Health* 65 (7): 1011–17. https://doi.org/10.1007/s00038-020-01420-4.

Ayres, José Ricardo C. M. 2009. *CUIDADO: trabalho e interação nas práticas de saúde*. CEPESC – IMS/ UERJ – ABRASCO. Accessed 29 May 2021. http://www.cepesc.org.br/wp-content/uploads/ 2013/08/miolo-livro-ricardo.pdf.

Bock, Kenneth, Cameron Stauth and Korri Fink. 2008. *Healing the New Childhood Epidemics: Autism, ADHD, asthma, and allergies: The groundbreaking program for the 4-A disorders*. New York: Ballantine.

Calaprice, Denise, Janice Tona, Ellisa Carla Parker-Athill and Tanya K. Murphy. 2017. 'A survey of pediatric acute-onset neuropsychiatric syndrome characteristics and course', *Journal of Child and Adolescent Psychopharmacology* 27 (7): 607–18. https://doi.org/10.1089/cap.2016.0105.

Calaprice, Denise, Janice Tona and Tanya K. Murphy. 2018. 'Treatment of pediatric acute-onset neuropsychiatric disorder in a large survey population', *Journal of Child and Adolescent Psychopharmacology* 28 (2): 92–103. https://doi.org/10.1089/cap.2017.0101.

Das, Veena. 1995. *Critical Events: An anthropological perspective on contemporary India*. Delhi: Oxford University Press.

Dolce, Jamie, Maria LaRusso and César Abadia-Barrero. Under review. 'Children with PANS/ PANDAS: Navigating a complex and severe condition and its impact on family functioning', *Journal of Child and Family Studies*.

Dumes, Abigail A. 2019. 'Lyme disease and the epistemic tensions of "medically unexplained illnesses"', *Medical Anthropology* 39 (6): 441–56. https://doi.org/10.1080/ 01459740.2019.1670175.

Dumes, Abigail A. 2020. *Divided Bodies: Lyme disease, contested illness, and evidence-based medicine*. Durham, NC: Duke University Press.

Fox, Renée C. 1957. 'Training for uncertainty'. In *The Student-Physician: Introductory studies in the sociology of medical education*, edited by Robert K. Merton, George G. Reader and Patricia L. Kendall, 207–41. Cambridge, MA: Harvard University Press.

Fox, Renée C. 1998. *Experiment Perilous: Physicians and patients facing the unknown*. New Brunswick, NJ: Transaction.

Good, Byron J. 1994. *Medicine, Rationality, and Experience: An anthropological perspective*. Cambridge: Cambridge University Press.

Juttel, Annemarie. 2018. 'Foreword'. In *Diagnostic Fluidity: Working with uncertainty and mutability*, edited by Nina Nissen and Mette Bech Risør, 7–10. Tarragona: Publicacions URV.

Kelly, John R., Paul J. Kennedy, John F. Cryan, Timothy G. Dinan, Gerard Clarke and Niall P. Hyland. 2015. 'Breaking down the barriers: The gut microbiome, intestinal permeability and stress-related psychiatric disorders', *Frontiers in Cellular Neuroscience* 9. https://doi.org/ 10.3389/fncel.2015.00392.

Kleinman, Arthur. 1988. *The Illness Narratives: Suffering, healing, and the human condition*. New York: Basic Books.

Kleinman, Arthur. 2009. 'Caregiving: The odyssey of becoming more human', *The Lancet* 373: 292–3. https://doi.org/10.1016/S0140-6736(09)60087-8.

Liu, Lu and Gang Zhu. 2018. 'Gut–brain axis and mood disorder', *Frontiers in Psychiatry* 9. https:// doi.org/10.3389/fpsyt.2018.00223.

Manderson, Lenore and Carolyn Smith-Morris, eds. 2010. *Chronic Conditions, Fluid States: Chronicity and the anthropology of illness*. New Brunswick, NJ: Rutgers University Press.

Menéndez, Eduardo L. 1985. 'El modelo médico dominante y las limitaciones y posibilidades de los modelos antropológicos', *Desarrollo Económico* 24 (96): 593–604. https://doi.org/10.2307/ 3466923.

Mol, Annemarie. 2002. *The Body Multiple: Ontology in medical practice*. Durham, NC: Duke University Press.

Mol, Annemarie. 2008. *The Logic of Care: Health and the problem of patient choice*. London: Routledge.

Mulligan, Jessica M. and Heide Castañeda, eds. 2017. *Unequal Coverage: The experience of health care reform in the United States*. New York: NYU Press.

NIH National Institute of Mental Health. n.d. *Information About PANS/PANDAS*. Accessed 5 December 2018. https://www.nimh.nih.gov/labs-at-nimh/research-areas/clinics-and-labs/ sbp/information-about-pans-pandas.shtml.

Nissen, Nina and Mette Bech Risør, eds. 2018. *Diagnostic Fluidity: Working with uncertainty and mutability*. Tarragona: Publicacions URV.

Perro, Michelle and Vincanne Adams. 2017. *What's Making Our Children Sick?: How industrial food is causing an epidemic of chronic illness, and what parents (and doctors) can do about it*. White River Junction, VT: Chelsea Green.

Risør, Mette Bech and Nina Nissen. 2018. 'Configurations of diagnostic processess and practices: An introduction'. In *Diagnostic Fluidity: Working with uncertainty and mutability*, edited by Nina Nissen and Mette Bech Risør, 11–32. Tarragona: Publicacions URV.

Smith-Morris, Carolyn, ed. 2016. *Diagnostic Controversy: Cultural perspectives on competing knowledge in healthcare*. New York: Routledge.

Swedo, Susan E. 1994. 'Sydenham's chorea: A model for childhood autoimmune neuropsychiatric disorders', *JAMA* 272 (22): 1788. https://doi.org/10.1001/jama.1994.03520220082035.

Swedo, Susan E. 2012. 'From research subgroup to clinical syndrome: Modifying the PANDAS criteria to describe PANS (pediatric acute-onset neuropsychiatric syndrome)', *Pediatrics & Therapeutics* 2 (2): 1–8. https://doi.org/10.4172/2161-0665.1000113.

Swedo, Susan E., Henrietta L. Leonard, Mark B. Schapiro, B.J. Casey, Glenn B. Mannheim, Marge Lenane and David C. Rettew. 1993. 'Sydenham's chorea: Physical and psychological symptoms of St Vitus dance', *Pediatrics* 91 (4): 706–13. https://pubmed.ncbi.nlm.nih.gov/8464654/.

Swedo, S.E., H.L. Leonard, M. Garvey, B. Mittleman, A.J. Allen, S. Perlmutter, L. Lougee, S. Dow, J. Zamkoff and B.K. Dubbert. 1998. 'Pediatric autoimmune neuropsychiatric disorders associated with streptococcal infections: Clinical description of the first 50 cases', *American Journal of Psychiatry* 155 (2): 264–71. https://doi.org/10.1176/ajp.155.2.264.

Swedo, Susan E., Jakob Seidlitz, Miro Kovacevic, M. Elizabeth Latimer, Rebecca Hommer, Lorraine Lougee and Paul Grant. 2015. 'Clinical presentation of pediatric autoimmune neuropsychiatric disorders associated with streptococcal infections in research and community settings', *Journal of Child and Adolescent Psychopharmacology* 25 (1): 26–30. https://doi.org/10.1089/ cap.2014.0073.

Waitzkin, Howard and Working Group for Health Beyond Capitalism, eds. 2018. *Health Care Under the Knife: Moving beyond capitalism for our health*. New York: Monthly Review Press.

Ware, Norma C. 1992. 'Suffering and the social construction of illness: The delegitimation of illness experience in chronic fatigue syndrome', *Medical Anthropology Quarterly* 6 (4): 347–61. https://doi.org/10.1525/maq.1992.6.4.02a00030.

West, A.F. and R.R. West. 2002. 'Clinical decision-making: Coping with uncertainty', *Postgraduate Medical Journal* 78: 319–21. http://dx.doi.org/10.1136/pmj.78.920.319.

10

Chronic living in zombieland: Care in between survival and death

Marcos Freire de Andrade Neves

Introduction

A former builder, Paul Lamb[1] lives in a house on the outskirts of Leeds, England. Ever since 1990, when he broke his spine in a car accident that left him almost completely paralysed from the neck down, Lamb has been living under constant care in his now adapted home. After the accident, as he recovered from multiple injuries, a medical specialist gave Lamb 12 years to live, suggesting he should use this time to put his affairs in order. While Lamb's tetraplegia embedded his new living in chronicity, the 12-year prognosis confined his life within a specific temporality. The accident was a turning point in his life: he would no longer be able to work in the same profession as before, or even to walk; his living would need to be rearranged, and his dreams, expectations and desires revisited. As he reorganised his everyday living in chronicity, reconciling his new routine with different habits and an unfamiliar way of being in the world, pain emerged to be a fundamental concern.

Lamb's chronicity meant experiencing pain as a constant and distressing feeling that permeated his new day-to-day life and informed his daily living. Pain was no longer occasional and peripheral, but constant and pervasive. It evolved to be a major aspect of his everyday living, creating a form of suffering that had to be responded to and cared for – and, as such, care had to be organised around this new reality. With the goal of improving his quality of life, care was provided through a configuration of health-oriented practices and technologies that pervaded almost every aspect of Lamb's living, from trivial tasks to medical and pharmaceutical assistance. Lamb's chronicity placed him inside a configuration of care devised to preserve his life and improve his wellbeing, particularly via the implementation of, and his adherence to, a specific drug regimen designed to alleviate his pain. But as his pain grew stronger and ever more intense, higher dosages of medications were needed.

Echoing the notion of care as tinkering (Mol et al. 2010), frequent adjustments in Lamb's caring routine were made necessary to better respond to his new living circumstances. A main focus of such adjustments was pain medication. In order for them to be effective, Lamb had to comply with strict medical and pharmaceutical instructions that would provide a clear blueprint to diminish his suffering and improve his quality of life. His adherence to this regimen was also necessary for his own survival, making him an active participant in a project of staying alive (Stevenson 2012, 601). Over the course of this project, however, drugs ended up playing an ambiguous role. As higher dosages were needed to diminish his pain, the side effects from continuous drug consumption started to become apparent. Over time, Lamb's short-term memory began to fade. He started to feel numb and confused, depersonalised and, in his own words, zombie-like. He soon came to realise that any drug-based response to his pain could only be effective if he was, for all intents and purposes, sedated.

The drug regimen designed to increase his quality of life also became the main source of a lost sense of self and personal dignity. By targeting the suffering produced by constant and intense pain, this configuration of care ended up creating the conditions for a different kind of suffering to emerge, one that made him question how far he would be willing to go to collaborate with this project – to collaborate in staying alive. Following Lamb's trajectory, this chapter discusses a situation in which the interplay of chronicity and care responded to a specific form of suffering by creating a different one, ultimately making a person's desire to stay alive – to survive – cease to be absolute and to become conditional. In this sense, Paul Lamb's trajectory is a prism of the circumstantial factors that shape a person's experience in chronicity and care, but one that raises a fundamental question: what follows when the desire to die a specific kind of death is articulated as a form of deservingness within political formations and configurations of care designed to be life-oriented?

Living in chronicity; living with affordances

The first I time I heard Paul Lamb's name was during a conversation with Dr Libby Wilson, a retired physician who, in 2000, founded the organisation Friends at the End (FATE), which advocates for end-of-life choices in Scotland.[2] Dr Wilson used to check on Lamb, who was then a member of FATE, regularly, either by phone or in person, visiting him in England. During one of our meetings in Glasgow, Dr Wilson seemed rather concerned about Lamb's situation: 'If he gets a urinary tract or a chest infection', she told me, 'he would have to go to the hospital, where he doesn't get a voice.' Besides, if this happened, he would require high doses of morphine: 'But if he takes too much of it, it confuses his brain, he says he can't take too much of it because he doesn't want to be a zombie.' At that time, I had been talking with several members of organisations that either provide or advocate for assisted suicide, so Lamb's story resonated with me. Thus, not long after this conversation with Dr Wilson, I went to visit him.

'I never thought I would walk again,' Lamb told me when we met in his home, a two-storey house in a quiet residential neighbourhood on the outskirts of Leeds. At that time, in 2016, he had lived 14 years past the original 12-year prognosis given to him in 1990 in the aftermath of the car accident that left him paralysed from the neck down – with the exception of his right hand, with which he controls his electric wheelchair. Similarly to Jain's (2007, 78–9) take on prognosis as something that appears to be a concrete scientific fact that can activate terror, Lamb remembered how he felt when July 2002, his *deadline*, arrived: 'I'm going this year,' he told me, 'I'm going because my 12 years are up. It was so implanted in my head. It was like me being on hot bricks. I haven't got done in life what I wanted to get done, so I don't feel like I'm ready to go yet.' The affects mobilised by his prognosis fostered an impression that he was living a life with a predefined expiration date. No matter what he did or felt, what he wished or desired, his life was bound by a straitjacket of time. But 12 years after the accident, Lamb was still alive. After outliving his prognosis – a prognosis he inhabited, experienced and feared for over a decade – Lamb was furious: 'I went flying back to the hospital, and I wanted to tell this specialist what I thought of this 12-years-to-live thing, how it affected me,' he shared, visibly outraged.

Lamb's prognosis embedded his living in a particular temporality, one that restricted his life to a deadline established on the basis of what he initially perceived to be a concrete scientific fact voiced by a medical specialist, but which turned out to be, above anything else, a main source of anxiety. As Jain (2007, 80) points out, living in prognosis 'is about living in the folds of various representations of time', and it was precisely in between different temporalities, juggling the reality of his daily routine with the affects and imaginaries elicited by inhabiting such a prognosis, that Lamb rearranged his living. Outliving his prognosis made him realise, despite his first impressions, that this straitjacket was actually loose. 'I've lived my life in a way, I took a lot more gambles with my body and things, but I must have done something right in a way', he concluded, 'because I'm over 26 years now, and I still don't feel like I'm going anywhere.'

Lamb's accident was severe, almost fatal, and had a profound impact on his life and everyday living. From that moment on, he started to inhabit a diagnostic category that disconnected his individual body from the environment around it, affecting his mobility and autonomy while, at the same time, emphasising aspects of dependence. Lamb and his family were living in the same house at the time of the accident, so continuing to live there was a vital step to preserve his wellbeing. However, because of his tetraplegia, both his living conditions and the environment around him needed to be reorganised. As critical disability theories of affordances have shown, disability is not something located within the individual body, something that can be defined in terms of individual 'lacks' and 'abnormalities', but rather is 'a problem of society' that emerges from discrimination, oppression and various other obstacles and barriers (Dokumaci 2019, 165). In this sense, disability emerges from the disconnection between the individual body and the environment around it (Stoffregen 2003) – or, in the words of Vivian Sobchack (2017, 62), from the realisation that the world is not your dance floor.

As Lamb's tetraplegia had an acute impact on his mobility, his house ceased to be a resourceful environment that facilitated his autonomy. Rather, his tetraplegia uncoupled his individual body from the material possibilities afforded by his house, a disconnect that ended up restricting his possibilities of action and reframing his disability in terms of dependence. Even with the assistance of a wheelchair, he could no longer move autonomously inside the house, thus exposing a problematic link between his individual body and the socio-material assemblage that composed the environment around him – the wheelchair that allowed him to move, the stairs that prevented him from using the wheelchair. As the material environment around him put in place barriers that hindered his mobility instead of facilitating it, his house was no longer an affordance (Dokumaci 2020); it was no longer his dance floor. In order to continue to live there with his family, Lamb had to realign his house to his mobility needs, which included the installation of a small lift.

Lamb's chronicity and disability made dependence a particularly severe condition, so to have his house back as an affordance that facilitated his mobility was a vital step in creating an environment that promoted his autonomy and wellbeing. Nonetheless, besides the material conditions of disability – such as Lamb's house – Dokumaci (2020) suggests that intimacy and care play important roles in the making of disability worlds, to the extent to which people can also be seen as affordances. If dis/ability is distributed according to heterogeneous socio-material configurations, rather than something located in the body alone, home-and-care become metonymic of the affordances that produce dis/ability in relation to individual bodies. To adapt his house was to fix the problematic link between Lamb's body and its environment, diminishing his dependence by realigning the material conditions to his mobility needs. By doing so, Lamb could once again move autonomously inside his own house, a situation similar to what Winance (2006) describes as an able person-in-the-wheelchair. In this sense, realigning the material affordances of his house with his individual body was vital in producing an environment where Lamb could ably move. But even though this re-alignment was a fundamental step towards his wellbeing, other forms of care were equally needed to preserve his health – in particular, to avoid the development of pressure sores on his skin and to diminish the risk of contracting infections.

After recovering from his multiple injuries and returning home from hospital, Lamb was eligible for the National Health Service's (NHS) continuing health-care package due to his chronic health needs, which would allow him access to social and medical care free of charge, including at home. To be eligible for this state-funded care, a person needs to be assessed by a team of health professionals, with a decision made according to the complexity and intensity of each individual case. This includes not only a person's current health situation, but also future risk factors. Although Lamb was eligible for this public-funded 'package of care', access to care can be challenging (Kennedy's chapter in this volume offers an interesting glimpse into some of these challenges in the context of patients with dementia), and the first care agency he went to did not have enough personnel to attend to his needs, making it necessary for him to go to hospitals on a regular basis. When Lamb protested that the agency was funded with public money to offer continuous care, and was responsible for his health and safe being, they suggested that he move to a nursing home instead. This was his red line, as Lamb recalled telling them: 'If it ever comes to that, if you come to my home to take me to a nursing home, you'll find that when you come, I won't be here.' They understood what 'not being here' implied. The message was loud and clear, so they interrupted him, warning that he should stop, otherwise they would have to report him. 'Well', Lamb remembered answering, 'do what you like, but you're not gonna put me in a nursing home. Ever. Nursing homes are just a waiting room before your final death.' Lamb's protest was fruitful and he was eventually able to find a different public-funded care agency, only this time with the necessary resources to provide him with full-time home care.

Home care was essential for Lamb's wellbeing, as it redistributed the pieces that produced his dis/ability in a different fashion, connecting them in a way that diminished his dependence and enhanced his autonomy. To this end, while his house played a primary role in this new redistribution, this assemblage could only be complete with medical care provided by professional caregivers and, fundamentally, pharmaceuticals. During our conversation, Lamb told me:

> I want to hang on to life as much as I can. And from the beginning I've always been the same. Always. And I've been on a bit of journey with all this that's been going on. But even if I come out of it, and I'm certainly a lot better off now, pain-wise, much more under control, although it's still bad. But what my biggest fear is ... I've got a pressure sore a few years ago, on my butt, and it lasted for five months. And it was only a small one. And I've seen people with huge ones, you know, they are not gonna heal. Not a chance. And this little one was concerning, very concerning, because I was on one side and then on the other for five months, in bed, and after that it took me a month or so to get used to getting up again and sitting in the chair and building my strength up. But I'm only too aware of what can happen with my body.

While Lamb's tetraplegia caused him to lose sensitivity and control of his body, it conversely made his body more visible to him. In this regard, Lamb's life and living in chronicity enabled a new relationship between him and his own body to surface, a relationship that relied on several affordances to diminish dependence and restore his autonomy. And in this new relationship, his individual body emerged as a crucial matter of concern that relied on pharmaceutical care in order to preserve its health and to manage its pain.

The pharmaceutical embrace

Anthropological discussions have shown various ways to empirically apprehend and conceptualise care, often emphasising its complex, unstable and ambiguous qualities. Stevenson (2014, 3), for instance, defines care 'as the way someone comes to matter and the correspond- ing ethics of attending to the other who matters'. It is, thus, not a matter of good intentions or necessarily a positive aspect, but rather a complex, messy and ambivalent set of relationships within which one comes to matter for various reasons. This ambivalence of care, its aversion to easy categorisations, was likewise stressed by de la Bellacasa (2011, 100), who suggested that 'a way of caring over here could kill over there' – mak- ing it necessary to ask 'how to care' in each specific situation. But at the heart of this ambivalence, however differently it may be articulated or manifested, lies what Ticktin (2011, 3) defines as the primary subject of care, the suffering body.

While losing control of his own body made Lamb more aware of it, losing sensitivity made pain more pervasive. 'Every hour I'm awake, every minute I'm awake, I'm in pain,' he told me. We were on the first floor of his house, in his study. He was sitting across from me, in his wheelchair, and a caregiver remained nearby in case he needed any assistance. They were both gentle and good-humoured, friendly and affectionate, but when Lamb started talking about pain, his voice switched to a different, rather intense tone. He went on:

> There isn't one doctor or pain specialist that's ever taken that away. And every tablet of whatever it is, I guarantee, the only thing they do is to start numbing the brain and make you go in what I call zom- bie side, and then you sleep, but then you're not you. I have been with a pain specialist for a lot of years now and he can't get it to that. When doctors argue the case against me, they say, we doctors can at least take away the pain. And then, if you're terminal, with cancer or something, then you go to this palliative care. To so many people, they don't take away the pain. The only time you're actu- ally away from it is when you're not awake. When you're asleep. So after 26 years ... all these medications are a form of suppressing your brain, calming you down, and making you almost zombie-like sometimes. My GPs have gone round the clock for 26 years trying to, and they have never been able to get through to my pain.

Ever since Lamb's accident, pain evolved to become a common experi- ence in his life: an experience that grew ever more intense, pervading every aspect of his everyday living and placing his body as a subject of caring interventions. If people can be affordances in the creation of dis/ability worlds, Lamb resorted to professional caregivers in order to prevent his family from experiencing his pain with him. Despite its intensity and ubiquity, he opted to shield his family from it: 'Nobody likes to see people in pain,' he told me, stressing that even after living under care for almost 30 years, his children – who were 11 and 9 years old at the time of the accident – never even saw a single catheter.

In its manifold ways of manifesting itself, pain is not only physical and individual, but also complex and social. It inhabits the individual body while also encompassing social and political lives, and the ways through which we acknowledge and attribute importance to pain and suffering, argue Harper et al. (2015, 10) based on Brown's (1995) work, can be a 'constitutive feature of modern political and social life'. For instance, it was precisely a multifaceted understanding of pain that inspired the hospice movement and enabled the emergence of palliative care as a discipline. Following an encounter with a patient in the late 1940s, Cecily Saunders, founder of the first modern hospice and catalyst of the movement, proposed the idea of 'total pain'. According to her proposal, total pain was based on the premise that pain should be understood in its full complexity, taking into consideration biographical and sociocultural contexts alike in order to organise and provide care (Clark 1999). To this end, Saunders (2001, 9) suggested four main dimensions to pain: physical, mental, social and spiritual.

However effective palliative care can be in certain circumstances, in others it may lack the tools to ameliorate someone's pain. As Rehmann-Sutter and Hagger (2013, 3) have shown, there are several factors of suffering that cannot be resolved by palliative care, such as continuous loss of function, dependency on caregivers, reliance on medication, severe pain and the loss of perceived dignity. According to them, in the US state of Oregon, where both palliative care and physician-assisted suicide are legally available options, between 1998 and 2009, 88.2 per cent of the terminally ill people who carried out assisted suicides had previously received high-quality palliative care, a figure that increased to 95.1 per cent from 2008 to 2009 (Rehmann-Sutter and Hagger 2013, 3). This holistic understanding of pain as something inherently complex that inhabits the individual body, but which cannot be limited to it, paved the way for new forms of care and medical disciplines (Seymour et al. 2005). However, it also promoted a common misconception that sees pain as something necessarily manageable, something that can be kept under control through the right medical and pharmaceutical means.

This perception of pain as something that can be managed via medical care and, more specifically, through the administration of pharmaceuticals, can be linked to a broader shift that saw public health strategies drifting away from prevention and clinical care and closer to drug-based, technical responses to disease and illness (Biehl and Eskerod 2007, 97–100). This pharmaceutical embrace suggests, as Biehl points out in the context of HIV medication, the consolidation of a discourse that sees a patient's adherence to a 'regimen of life-extending drugs' as a form of individual salvation that produces 'new and productive lives' (Biehl and Eskerod 2006, 459). When Lamb's pain became chronically severe – or severely chronic – it was responded to via the implementation of a specific drug regimen designed to alleviate his pain and diminish his suffering.

In order for this regimen to be effective, Lamb had to collaborate with it by following medical prescriptions and, by doing so, taking upon himself the responsibility for his wellbeing. This shift towards technical solutions, particularly based on pharmaceuticals, can produce situations where living with less chronic pain can only be achieved through overmedication – or, as Lamb puts it, when the person becomes 'zombie-like'. At one level, Lamb's adherence to a specifically designed drug regimen was displayed as the proper and most effective way to mitigate his pain. However, in his everyday life in chronicity, his adherence ended up producing unintended consequences. 'This is what annoys me with doctors, that can be on television and say, yes, we can reduce the pain,' Lamb protested. 'They can't. They can't.' This prominence of drug-based responses, however effective it can be in certain cases, often contrasts with the day-to-day realities of people living with pain, to whom effective pain mitigation can only come at a high personal cost. To Lamb, the price was his own sense of self and personal dignity:

> As well as all that I used to be on, I used to be on a medicated tablet called Gabapentin, and I was on 3,000 of that a day. And my pain specialist, he noticed my short-term memory has been getting worse, and he says to me, 'That's simply down to Gabapentin, that's the one, Paul,' 26 years always on the maximum, so the maximum goes up, my medication went up, and he says, that's what's taking your short-term memory. If you can get off a few of them … After a month, I got off a lot, and if you ask any medical people they'll tell you that is a lot. So I'm off now.

While seeking to diminish one form of suffering, this drug-based caring response culminated in the emergence of a different one. Thus, it is crucial to understand pharmaceuticals beyond their materiality, as moral technologies (Biehl 2005) that acquire meaning when embedded in specific contexts, both absorbing and entangling ideas, values and policies (Pordié 2014, 51–3). The focus on technical responses to pain and suffering produced medications that are effective, but that failed to consider the conditions and implications of their own efficacy.

Within this broader context of pharmaceuticalisation of care and public health, adherence to a drug regimen connects individual bodies and chemical actors under the guise of wellbeing, a link that holds the potential to produce healthy and productive bodies (Rose 2001, 16). To be a citizen thus becomes tantamount to assuming an active role in the pursuit of one's own health (Rose 2001, 6) – or, to put it in Stevenson's (2012, 2014) terms, to actively collaborate in the project of staying alive. However, this potential can only be achieved through a hierarchisation that favours physical over functional, cognitive and emotional health. As pharmaceuticals occupy an ever more prominent position in public health and care strategies, a person's pursuit of their own health and wellbeing becomes fundamentally entangled with their collaboration with drug regimens – and similar situations can be seen in contexts as varied and diverse as Brazil (Biehl 2004), India (Ecks 2014) and the United States (Dumit 2012).

In the context of Lamb's chronicity, to adhere to a drug regimen was to perceive himself, and to be perceived by others, as actively collaborating in staying alive by assuming responsibility for his own health and wellbeing. To be a good citizen was to experience this pharmaceutical embrace by adhering to a specific drug regimen that focused on his physical health, on his individual body, while neglecting other factors, such as his own sense of self and dignity. Nonetheless, to abandon this regimen could be tantamount to giving up on himself. Yet if Lamb's willingness to stay alive, to survive, was underlying his collaboration and adherence to this drug regimen, what happens if this will to survive gives way to something else? When Lamb realised that making his suffering legible to medicine ended up triggering a drug-based caring response that jeopardised his own sense of self and personal dignity, he questioned the terms of his collaboration and decided to articulate his pain away from medicine and into the law.

Judicialising the suffering body

In 1990 the second applicant was involved in a car accident as a result of which he sustained multiple injuries leaving him paralysed. He is completely immobile with the exception of his right hand which he can move to a limited extent. His condition is irreversible. He requires constant care and spends every day in a wheelchair. He experiences a significant amount of pain, as a consequence of which he has to take morphine. He feels that he is trapped in his body and that he cannot enjoy or endure a life that is so monotonous, painful and lacking in autonomy. (European Court of Human Rights, on Paul Lamb)[3]

In the aftermath of Lamb's accident, as he learned to live in chronicity, pain emerged to be a fundamental concern and distressing factor in his everyday living, as well as a main source of suffering. His pain needed to be cared for, to be managed, but in order to do so, his suffering had first to be recognised (Butler 2009). It was necessary to communicate his pain, to make it visible, in order to legitimise a form of suffering that could bring about an effective caring response. This process of recognition invests suffering with political, social and moral meaning, and it can often take place in diverse sites, such as medicine and law (Harper et al. 2015, 21–2) or the media (Richards 2014, 2017). When Dr Wilson first told me about Paul Lamb, she was rather upset about the outcome of a court case brought by him against the UK government. After 23 years living in chronicity with the assistance of full-time, public-funded caregivers, Lamb decided that compromising his own sense of self and personal dignity was too high a price to pay for mitigating his pain.

As Biehl (2013) argues, the judicialisation of the right to health is an important facet of the process of pharmaceuticalisation of care and public health, insofar as the prevalence of drugs as the preferred response to disease and illness coexists with a lack of access to them. Under these circumstances, the judiciary is often the site where access can be established – constituting a form of clinical court that can link the goal of improving health with the right technical tools to achieve it. Whereas the connection between pharmaceuticalisation and judicialisation is clear in a context where health is the ultimate goal, this connection produces a blindside in which suffering is similarly articulated away from medicine and into the law, but instead of claiming access to health, the goal is to bring about a certain kind of death. When Lamb joined an ongoing case in the UK's High Court, he did so to request judicial authorisation to receive assistance in dying with the use of lethal drugs.

In the UK, where Lamb lives, it is illegal under the Suicide Act 1961 to receive assistance in suicide – despite suicide itself being lawful. Because of his tetraplegia, Lamb stated in the court case that he was unable to take his own life without third-party assistance – thus preventing him from carrying out a lawful act for which assistance is criminally sanctioned. It was not his intention to die immediately. Rather, he wanted to be authorised to do so if and when the pain he constantly feels and, so far, has managed to endure becomes unbearable for him. He was still craving for life and wanted to remain alive for as long as he could. 'After 26 years now, going to the 27th year, the things that happened to my body ... I have all kinds of things,' he told me, 'so the day when I feel I can't do it anymore, and that day will come, I've been told it'll come, if I got at that stage, somebody better put me out of my misery.' His experience in chronicity, while collaborating with a drug regimen that imposed a compromise between pain and his own sense of self and personal dignity, produced a particular kind of suffering that made his willingness to collaborate no longer absolute. Now, fully aware of what could happen to his body and fearful that his pain, which remains constant and intense, could become unbearable, the circumstances he was willing to endure in order to stay alive became conditional. He would manage his pain for as long as he could, but was unwilling to return to the 'zombie-side'.

His initial involvement with the court case, however, was incidental. It was Tony Nicklinson, a British citizen with locked-in syndrome, who initiated the case at the High Court to challenge the law on assisted suicide and murder, which did not recognise the possibility of euthanasia (Richards 2014; Ward 2015). After Nicklinson's case failed, he refused nutrition and died six days after the High Court ruling. As Lamb recounted, 'Tony was legally allowed to take his case to the Supreme Court, but he didn't have the strength, he gave up.' After Nicklinson's death, his widow, Jane Nicklinson, and their solicitor contacted Dr Wilson to enquire whether she knew anyone who could help them taking the case back to court. Dr Wilson contacted Lamb, and the three of them went to visit him in Leeds. During this visit, Jane Nicklinson and her solicitor asked Lamb if he would be willing to help them in the case. He recalls them saying that they would name him 'L', so he would not have 'to come out in the open'. Following Lamb's consent, he became L for a few weeks, until the solicitor got back in touch with him to inform him that everyone was thinking that L was a fictitious character. She wanted him to 'come out in the open'. Lamb was not sure what coming out in the open entailed, so he asked her. 'Well, it means there might be a few people coming to see you,' she clarified. Once again, Lamb consented.

To his surprise, he started to receive phone calls every half hour from 11 a.m. to 7.30 p.m. He was on television and in newspapers. He started to fear people would go to his house and place signs on his front lawn stating what a bad person he was for 'going against God and all that'. But it was quite the opposite, he conveyed with a shy smile on his face. People were being mostly supportive. 'That's why I joined in,' Lamb concluded: 'to get it going again in the system. But they sent us to the High Court first and, lo and behold, it failed again.' During the court proceedings, he was taken by an overwhelming frustration: 'I barely nearly opened my mouth there,' he complained. He kept hearing judges saying that they had 'sympathy for the likes of Mr Lamb', without being able to react, despite being present while they expressed their sympathies. He remembered thinking to himself, 'No, he didn't say that,' until his frustration got the better of him and he no longer managed to hold back: 'Please don't say that word sympathy again. I don't want your sympathy, I don't want anybody's sympathy,' he said, this time out loud. 'It's just ridiculous if you can't say something,' he said to me, finally asking, 'I mean, do you want people to have sympathy for you?'

Similarly to Nicklinson's original case, their joint case was rejected at the High Court and, subsequently, at the Supreme Court in a seven to two decision. Around this time, Lamb's solicitor suggested the possibility of taking his case to the European Court of Human Rights (ECHR) – but to do so would be expensive. Lamb remembers their conversation:

> I've been on legal aid from the beginning and, on money terms, it's not the kind of money that ... Top solicitors earn a lot more on private cases. So when the legal aid ran out after the Supreme Court, they said they didn't want to take it to the ECHR now. And that was that. And my solicitor said to me, 'Is there any way you can earn a hundred to two hundred thousand pounds?' And I went, 'No, apart from selling my house, and that's going to my children and grandchildren.' And she said, 'Oh well, we can't go any further unless you can get that money together.'

The same house that played a fundamental role in preserving his wellbeing, that was adapted to his new living circumstances, was now at risk if he decided to take the case to the ECHR. Lamb already owned that house at the time of the accident, which made it easier for him to save the money necessary to eventually add the small lift. The financial resources necessary for a high-profile court case, however, would be beyond his means. 'How on earth can we raise two hundred thousand pounds?' Dr Wilson recalled thinking when she heard about this conversation: '[The solicitor] just sort of abandoned him at that stage, and said, you've got to get two hundred thousand pounds, it will take about two or three years, we are not interested any more. Once it failed, she wasn't interested in him.

She was completely callous, really, about the human side.' As he lived the day-to-day reality of his court case, Lamb's suffering and chronicity became embedded in a complex system that transformed his body into a site of dispute between his request to receive assistance in dying and political subjectivities, medical rationales and forms of care that see life as something that needs to be preserved regardless of individual circumstances.

While articulating his suffering to medicine, Lamb placed himself inside a configuration of care designed to protect his body and preserve his health. However, when the side effects of the proposed drug-based response became unbearable, he articulated his suffering away from medicine and into the law, but he did so by emphasising a deservingness to die under his own terms over an entitlement to health that made him feel zombie-like. As Huschke (2014) points out, the construction of deservingness can be performed, and courtrooms are sites where this often takes place. For instance, in the case of Christian Rossiter, an Australian citizen who requested the right to die, this was granted following his argument that he was unable to undertake 'any basic human function', such as, among others, 'wipe the tears from [his] eyes' (Menezes 2011). Court cases for the right to die negotiate deservingness and entitlement by performatively contrasting specific lives and trajectories with official law.

On the one hand, as many have argued (Docker 2015; Karsoho et al. 2016; Menezes 2011; Richards 2017; Verhofstadt et al. 2017), pain and suffering are common tropes in requests for assisted dying, and often help to justify the request (Andrade Neves 2020). On the other hand, there are other sites where pain and suffering can be articulated to attain legitimation – such as the media. Physicians 'may try to heal pain and suffering', write Harper et al. (2015, 9), 'but what counts as necessary or unnecessary suffering, suffering that should be prevented or allowed to continue, can be decided by law'. In Lamb's case, the court did not recognise his suffering as sufficiently legitimate to be granted access to the kind of death he requested – the court considered him undeserving of a voluntary death. Similarly to his, ten other cases[4] requesting assisted death, either by euthanasia or assisted suicide, reached the European Court of Human Rights – of which, two were initiated in the United Kingdom. In several other court cases concerning assisted dying, such as Pretty in the UK (Ward 2015), Rossiter in Australia and Chantal Sébire in France (Menezes 2011), the responsibility to legitimise suffering and translate this recognition into a decision over life and death fell on judges and not on doctors (Harper et al. 2015). Despite their different circumstances and specificities, all of these cases concerned a perception of suffering – psychological or physical – that was articulated away from medicine and into the law in order to find an alternative to health-oriented care, which dismissed the possibility, or legitimacy, of voluntary assisted death.

Final remarks

If initially Lamb's willingness to stay alive, to collaborate in improving his quality of life by adhering to a drug regimen designed to alleviate his pain and improve his wellbeing, was absolute, the consequences of overmedication made him question the conditions under which he would be willing to further cooperate – that is, the conditions he would be willing to endure in order to preserve his own survival. Harper et al. (2015, 21–2) suggest that both medicine and law are sites where pain and suffering can be made legible in order to attain social and moral meanings. By making his pain legible to medicine, Lamb was offered a caring response that could only be effective through overmedication. When he requested judicial authorisation to die, Lamb articulated his suffering away from medicine and into the law, walking down a different path to legitimise his suffering body not only as a subject of care, but also as deserving to die a specific kind of death, if he so wished.

According to Sarah Willen (2019, 17), personal sense of dignity is elusive, and the empirical challenge would be precisely to explore how this sense is lived as 'a powerful drive to make life bearable'. With his life caught up between chronicity and care, it was precisely Lamb's personal sense of dignity that was negatively affected. When the will to survive gives way to a wish to die a specific kind of death – making death emerge as a person's ultimate goal, instead of something to be avoided at all costs – the individual body can articulate its suffering away from an entitlement to health and into a deservingness to die. However, by living his life in chronicity and care, Lamb's personal sense of dignity was affected by, on the one hand, the pharmaceutical embrace that made him zombie-like and, on the other hand, the financial realities of the court case and the law's lack of recognition of him as someone who deserves access to assisted death. As Lamb protested during our conversation:

> It should be a fundamental right of somebody to say, I've been going on for years with this chronic pain, I've had enough, I had a life, and if you can justify yourself to the professionals as to why you can't do it anymore … I believe the law should be there to help people.

Paul Lamb's trajectory in chronicity and care chronicles how different discourses, from care to live to a deservingness to die, can be mobilised and rearranged in the name of suffering.

In this sense, Paul Lamb crystallises a situation where chronic living was closely linked with the use of pharmaceuticals – but instead of preventing suffering, they changed its form instead. Whereas a medical response to Lamb's pain highlighted an ambiguous role where pharmaceuticals were both the solution and source of suffering, when articulated to the judiciary, Lamb once again resorted to pharmaceuticals, only this time, instead of seeking to employ them as tools intended to give life, they were to be used to terminate one. As he attempted to articulate his suffering away from medicine, following a long judicial path that led him from the High Court to the ECHR, his life became enmeshed in a dispute where multiple social forces were at play, jeopardising his affordances – such as his house – and further compromising his own sense of personal dignity.

By living a life in chronicity under care and articulating his pain to both medicine and law, Lamb's body turned into a site where political subjectivities, entitlements and deservingness were negotiated and disputed. When articulating his suffering to law, it was made clear to him that the death he requested was not a death he could have. 'I wonder sometimes what do you have to do to shake something up,' Lamb told me during our conversation, which he ended with a final reflection:

> I mean, for all intents and purposes, would it make a difference if I was to say 'By the way, country, I'm going to Switzerland in these next 20 days unless you can do something proper to sort this out.' How far would they allow me to go? The whole way? Would anybody care?

Notes

1. Paul Lamb's case has been widely publicised in the United Kingdom, and he is a well-known figure in the right-to-die context. When we met, Paul Lamb signed an informed consent form in which he opted for the use of his real name, waiving anonymity. Because of this, and in order to preserve the specifics of his own trajectory that were made public over the course of several court cases and media appearances, his real name is used throughout the chapter.
2. From 2014 to 2017, in the context of my doctoral research, I conducted an ethnography of transnational assisted suicide. This research focused on the circulation of documents, people and technologies across national borders, particularly Switzerland, Germany and the United Kingdom. It was during this research, as I followed these flows against the background of organised assisted suicide, that I met and interviewed Paul Lamb at his house. This chapter is based on a series of interviews and on documentary analysis carried out during this period.

3. Application no. 1787/15, page 2.
4. *Pretty v. the United Kingdom* (2002); *Haas v. Switzerland* (2011); *Koch v. Germany* (2012); *Gross v. Switzerland* (2014); *Lambert and Others v. France* (2015); *Sanles Sanles v. Spain* (2000); *Ada Rossi and Others v. Italy* (2008); *Gard and Others v. the United Kingdom* (2017); *Afiri and Biddarri v. France* (2018); *Mortier v. Belgium* (2019).

References

Andrade Neves, Marcos Freire de. 2020. 'Protecting life, facilitating death: The bureaucratic experience of organized suicide assistance', *Medicine Anthropology Theory* 7 (1): 158–66. https://doi.org/10.17157/mat.7.1.654.

Biehl, João. 2004. 'The activist state: Global pharmaceuticals, AIDS, and citizenship in Brazil', *Social Text* 22 (3): 105–32. https://muse.jhu.edu/article/174056.

Biehl, João. 2005. *Vita: Life in a zone of social abandonment*. Berkeley: University of California Press.

Biehl, João. 2013. 'The judicialization of biopolitics: Claiming the right to pharmaceuticals in Brazilian courts', *American Ethnologist* 40 (3): 419–36. https://doi.org/10.1111/amet.12030.

Biehl, João and Torben Eskerod. 2006. 'Will to live: AIDS drugs and local economies of salvation', *Public Culture* 18 (3): 457–72. https://doi.org/10.1215/08992363-2006-015.

Biehl, João and Torben Eskerod. 2007. *Will to Live: AIDS therapies and the politics of survival*. Princeton, NJ: Princeton University Press.

Brown, Wendy. 1995. *States of Injury: Power and freedom in late modernity*. Princeton, NJ: Princeton University Press.

Butler, Judith. 2009. *Frames of War: When is life grievable?* London: Verso.

Clark, David. 1999. '"Total pain", disciplinary power and the body in the work of Cicely Saunders, 1958–1967', *Social Science & Medicine* 49 (6): 727–36. https://doi.org/10.1016/S0277-9536(99)00098-2.

de la Bellacasa, Maria Puig. 2011. 'Matters of care in technoscience: Assembling neglected things', *Social Studies of Science* 41 (1): 85–106. https://doi.org/10.1177/0306312710380301.

Docker, Chris. 2015. *Five Last Acts – The Exit Path: The arts and science of rational suicide in the face of unbearable, unrelievable suffering*. Edinburgh: Exit.

Dokumaci, Arseli. 2019. 'The "disabilitization" of medicine: The emergence of Quality of Life as a space to interrogate the concept of the medical model', *History of the Human Sciences* 32 (5): 164–90. https://doi.org/10.1177/0952695119850716.

Dokumaci, Arseli. 2020. 'People as affordances: Building disability worlds through care intimacy', *Current Anthropology* 61 (21). https://doi.org/10.1086/705783.

Dumit, Joseph. 2012. *Drugs for Life: How pharmaceutical companies define our health*. Durham, NC: Duke University Press.

Ecks, Stefan. 2014. *Eating Drugs: Psychopharmaceutical pluralism in India*. New York: NYU Press.

Harper, Ian, Tobias Kelly and Akshay Khanna. 2015. *The Clinic and the Court: Law, medicine and anthropology*. New York: Cambridge University Press.

Huschke, Susann. 2014. 'Performing deservingness: Humanitarian health care provision for migrants in Germany', *Social Science & Medicine* 120: 352–9. https://doi.org/10.1016/j.socscimed.2014.04.046.

Jain, Sarah Lochlann. 2007. 'Living in prognosis: Toward an elegiac politics', *Representations* 98 (1): 77–92. https://doi.org/10.1525/rep.2007.98.1.77.

Karsoho, Hadi, Jennifer R. Fishman, David Kenneth Wright and Mary Ellen Macdonald. 2016. 'Suffering and medicalization at the end of life: The case of physician-assisted dying', *Social Science & Medicine* 170: 188–96. https://doi.org/10.1016/j.socscimed.2016.10.010.

Menezes, Rachel Aisengart. 2011. 'Demanda por eutanásia e condição de pessoa: reflexões em torno do estatuto das lágrimas', *Sexualidad, Salud y Sociedad (Rio de Janeiro)* 9: 137–53. https://doi.org/10.1590/S1984-64872011000400007.

Mol, Annemarie, Ingunn Moser and Jeannette Pols, eds. 2010. *Care in Practice: On tinkering in clinics, homes and farms*. Bielefeld: Transcript.

Pordié, Laurent. 2014. 'Pervious drugs', *Asian Medicine* 9 (1–2): 49–76. https://doi.org/10.1163/15734218-12341292.

Rehmann-Sutter, Christoph and Lynn Hagger. 2013. 'Organised assistance to suicide in England?', *Health Care Analysis* 21 (2): 85–104. https://doi.org/10.1007/s10728-011-0191-y.

Richards, Naomi. 2014. 'The death of the right-to-die campaigners', *Anthropology Today* 30 (3): 14–17. https://doi.org/10.1111/1467-8322.12110.

Richards, Naomi. 2017. 'Assisted suicide as a remedy for suffering? The end-of-life preferences of British "suicide tourists"', *Medical Anthropology* 36 (4): 348–62. https://doi.org/10.1080/01459740.2016.1255610.

Rose, Nikolas. 2001. 'The politics of life itself', *Theory, Culture & Society* 18 (6): 1–30. https://doi.org/10.1177/02632760122052020.

Saunders, Cecily. 2001. 'The evolution of palliative care', *Journal of the Royal Society of Medicine* 94 (9): 430–2. https://doi.org/10.1177/014107680109400904.

Seymour, Jane, David Clark and Michelle Winslow. 2005. 'Pain and palliative care: The emergence of new specialties', *Journal of Pain and Symptom Management* 29 (1): 2–13. https://doi.org/10.1016/j.jpainsymman.2004.08.008.

Sobchack, Vivian. 2017. 'Choreography for one, two, and three legs (a phenomenological meditation in movements)', *International Journal of Performance Arts and Digital Media* 13 (2): 183–98. https://doi.org/10.1080/14794713.2017.1345583.

Stevenson, Lisa. 2012. 'The psychic life of biopolitics: Survival, cooperation, and Inuit community', *American Ethnologist* 39 (3): 592–613. https://doi.org/10.1111/j.1548-1425.2012.01383.x.

Stevenson, Lisa. 2014. *Life Beside Itself: Imagining care in the Canadian Arctic*. Oakland: University of California Press.

Stoffregen, Thomas A. 2003. 'Affordances as properties of the animal–environment system', *Ecological Psychology* 15 (2): 115–34. https://doi.org/10.1207/S15326969ECO1502_2.

Ticktin, Miriam. 2011. *Casualties of Care: Immigration and the politics of humanitarianism in France*. Berkeley: University of California Press.

Verhofstadt, Monica, Lieve Thienpont and Gjalt-Jorn Ygram Peters. 2017. 'When unbearable suffering incites psychiatric patients to request euthanasia: Qualitative study', *British Journal of Psychiatry* 211 (4): 238–45. https://doi.org/10.1192/bjp.bp.117.199331.

Ward, Amanda Jane. 2015. 'Who decides? Balancing competing interests in the assisted suicide debate'. LLM dissertation, University of Glasgow. Accessed 28 May 2021. http://theses.gla.ac.uk/6394/1/2015WardLLM.pdf.

Willen, Sarah S. 2019. *Fighting for Dignity: Migrant lives at Israel's margins*. Philadelphia: University of Pennsylvania Press.

Winance, Myriam. 2006. 'Trying out the wheelchair: The mutual shaping of people and devices through adjustment', *Science, Technology & Human Values* 31 (1): 52–72. https://doi.org/10.1177/0162243905280023.

Afterword

Ciara Kierans

> We are like sailors who on the open sea must reconstruct their
> ship but are never able to start afresh from the bottom. Where
> a beam is taken away a new one must at once be put there,
> and for this the rest of the ship is used as support. In this way,
> by using the old beams and driftwood the ship can be shaped
> entirely anew, but only by gradual reconstruction. (Neurath
> 1973, 198–9)

Neurath's ship is, forever, fixed at sea, mended from within its affordances; never to be repaired in a dry dock. This well-known analogy reminds us that questions of health, like questions of knowledge or identity, are encountered, confronted and (re)constructed in the midst of things – entangled in the indeterminacies of social relations, the contingencies of historical process and the potency of affect. Health – the sine qua non of 'a good life' – conditions our embodied capacities to live well, to be in and have different bodies and, as a consequence, to be in and have different worlds (Merleau-Ponty 2012). When things go wrong – as they invariably do – we must take our moorings from where we are – in the thick of living. For those who have to manage chronicity – live and suffer with and care for it – these truths are, as Jain (2007) reminds us, intimately and enduringly, a feature of living in prognosis.

Neurath's ship is particularly poignant in the context of the rise, spread and efforts to manage COVID-19. Local and global responses have been constructed and reconstructed in an ocean of uncertainty, without a coherent blueprint for guidance, and with effects which are either mitigated or intensified by variable infrastructures of care, support and welfare. Indeed, as our editors, Montesi and Calestani, remind us, COVID-19 has thrown the frailty of health-care and welfare infrastructures into stark relief. In many parts of the world, it has made visible the very processes which have given rise to this fragility in the first place: the privatisation of public goods, the failures to provide safe, secure work, and the erosion of the social contract between society and the state. A global pandemic is indeed a salutary reminder that we have no view from nowhere, no dry dock to land. COVID-19 provides a sobering context within which this volume comes to fruition. It is one that further sharpens our perspectives on matters of health as simultaneously matters of society, culture, political economy and history; matters that the contributors to this volume never lose sight of. The trials of chronic living are, thus, painfully and profoundly part of the present moment (Manderson and Smith-Morris 2010; Manderson and Wahlberg 2020). Opportunities to live well in chronicity are increasingly compromised at the fault lines of care, as well as by the limits of techno-medical promises. However, it is also at these fault lines that vulnerability to harm, systematic neglect and exclusion are emerging to foster new solidarities of interest within and across nations. *Managing Chronicity in Unequal States* thus attends to chronic health as a cross-national concern. It can be read as a composite of journeys, all equipped with navigational points to illuminate the lived-with and emergent tensions between political economy and the social relations of health care.

Cartographies of chronicity

I will start these journeys in the US, with the problem of paediatric acute-onset neuropsychiatric syndrome (PANS). PANS is a diagnostic conundrum which unsettles the epistemic authority of biomedicine. Without categorical certainties, as LaRusso and Abadía-Barrero show, a diagnosis of PANS fails to unlock the institutional or social pathways to care. PANS thus reveals the particular ways that regimes of care, and the institutional bridges on which they depend, are contingent on the definitional properties of chronic conditions, pulling problem-definition and problem-response into direct alignment. In the absence of an aetiological narrative, families shoulder the responsibilities of care as well as its costs – financial and moral. This engenders desire for the kind of chronicity one can trust: a cancer or, in the case of this particular neuropsychiatric syndrome, 'just plain autism'.

Moving to the UK, chronic pain and its pharmaceutical regimes of care constitute sites from which other desires – the desire to live or die – become profoundly intertwined, and where efforts to alleviate suffering through medication remake the ground of suffering, and, by extension, the ground of care. In doing so, this does not constitute an imperative for better care, but for a better death. Andrade Neves explores the moves the patient must make beyond medical and national infrastructures to make pain legible as a judicial concern, positioning the law as final arbitrator for the deserving subject.

Staying in the UK, and with the navigational labours of care, Kennedy attends to dementia care as families manage complex bureaucratic and administrative processes to assume the autonomy, right and capacity to decide for others. Bureaucracy produces ambivalent affects, urging a rethink of how the requirements and distributions of care and support can best be recognised and enacted. Bureaucracy is an important seen-but-unseen care infrastructure. It is one brought into the foreground by many of the volume's contributors. It provides a significant lens for Flaherty's work on health-care access and liminality in the US Virgin Islands (USVI). Here, citizens live at the margins of US health-care provision, and at the mercy of ambiguous logistical and governmental arrangements. In the USVI, the provision of a functioning health-care system is decoupled from statutory commitments to care, giving rise to a haphazard logic of access to life-sustaining medical equipment, drug therapies and welfare coverage. For those in the USVI who are 'poor, black and culturally other', living with multiple chronic conditions has meant substituting hospice care for other forms of therapeutic care, denying even the possibilities and potentialities for chronic living.

Proceeding to Tanzania, and staying with problems of marginality, Brocco describes how those with albinism are vulnerable to attack, commodification and stigmatisation. Albinism exists on the thresholds of moral order, the occult and social norms. It is at these thresholds that questions of responsibility for caring and inclusion are turned back on to the suffering subject, not only to establish new relations of care but, in doing so, to mitigate the lived-with effects of austerity, economic and political instability, impoverished health-care coverage, encroaching marketisation and limited human rights. This raises the critical question of deservingness – a motif central to all chapters – which shapes the logics of exclusion and abandonment. Kottai and Ranganathan employ deservingness to explicate the entangled relations of homelessness, addiction, and mental and chronic health, all bound to problems of poverty, violence and neglect in India. They do so via the effects of psychiatric interventions, their persistent failure to engage the structural conditions of chronic health, and their complicity in reinforcing and reproducing health inequalities. In Montreal, Motta-Ochoa and Arruda are similarly concerned with issues of street-level addiction and homelessness, and the individualising project of public health responses. Interrogating the pharmaceuticalisation of public health, they position the human pharmakon (Biehl 2011) as site of experimentation, self-care and the reciprocal relations of addiction, but also as the site of critique on harm reduction in the context of marginal living in Canada.

As the specificities of 'place' matter to the ways in which chronicity is differentially drawn, experienced and managed, so too does the intersecting work of 'time'. In Mexico, Bresciani is concerned with the social and cultural complexities of alcoholism, as part of a historical ethos of suffering. For Mexico's dispossessed populations, alcoholism is a colonial and cultural legacy, a distinct interweaving of ritual, social obligation and deviance, as well as the contradictions this produces. However, in the absence of welfare state supports, alcoholism opens up new spaces for mobilising public health. Evangelical churches, in particular, have stepped in to ensure new forms of intervention are tied to new forms of conditionality, reconfiguring the historical and cultural narrative of alcoholism in the process.

Just as chronic conditions are end points of historical processes, so too are the regimes of health and welfare on which they depend, themselves products of the shifting balance between labour, capital and the state over time (Esping-Anderson 1990). Nordic countries have long been the exemplar of welfare state provision. Recent years have seen them increasingly vulnerable to private interests via market-driven reforms. Focusing on eldercare in a marginal town in Finland, Takahashi challenges the normative dichotomies of private versus public health, and home versus institutional care, so bound to contemporary discourses of state–market relations. Instead, she advances new hybridised carescapes, to unsettle the differential moral and economic obligations tied to family, community, friendship and the salaried worker. She shows how carescapes are continually redrawn to offer new possibilities for managing inequalities to care, within which state and market interests cannot so easily be pulled apart or naively critiqued. These are issues which resonate loudly within the UK in particular, showing stronger alignments between state and private market interests in health care, expressed as new forms of 'corporate' welfare (Shaoul 2011). Public–private interests are a backdrop to Ballesteros's chapter. Living in London, she offers a testimony of caring for a chronically ill child, and reflects on the changing support needs of parents, and their encounters with the precarious circumstances of those on whom they depend. Left to the vagaries of unstable privatisations, infrastructures of care and support are always primed to fall apart. Advocating for a hybridised model of regulated care,

Ballesteros provides new ways of thinking about family in the context of chronicity and what it means to live a good life.

Waymarking entanglements

Taken together, the chapters in this volume show the entangled territories of chronic living to be inherently political-economic as they focus on the variable reconfigurations of welfare states: the effects of neoliberal health-care reforms; the precarity of labour; the consequences of austerity; infrastructural and logistical breakdowns; the outsourcing of care and the effects *of* and *on* migration, displacement, marginalisation and dispossession *for* and *of* equitable health-care access. These entangled territories are vexed and troubled spaces. They constitute what Biehl and Locke (2017, xi) describe as leaky social fields, worlds which are 'at once material, social and symbolic, simultaneously precarious and in motion', and where 'individuals and collectives are constituted as much by affects and intensities as by structural forces'. The quest for wellbeing, for the good life, the desire for death – for things to be otherwise – the urgencies to care for others and oneself, are affective states examined in different ways and in different places by the contributors to this volume.

Such sensitivity to the complex, political and enmeshed character of health has long been the concern for the critical medical anthropologist. This is exemplified via the tensions which arise between 'upstream' forces and 'downstream' effects, but also importantly by attending to what mediates and intervenes their interrelations (Yates-Doerr 2020). Attending so necessitates critical diligence to the ways in which lifeworlds are differentially threaded and composed. From the perspective of those whose lifeworlds matter to us, how precisely is such complexity encountered? Or, as Elizabeth Roberts (2017, 596) puts it, 'what does an entangled prescription for being in the world do for those who have always had to stay with the trouble?' What this volume shows is that for those who stay with the trouble – the migrant, the parent of a sick child, the person dependent on alcohol or drugs, the person who self-medicates, the welfare recipient, the paid or unpaid carer – chronicity is not endlessly entangled in the myriad features and connections of everyday life, but empirically and materially grounded, mediated through sited and identifiable waymarks – encounters with specific personnel in specific institutions, in specific times and in specific places. It is via these waymarks that the contours of chronic living are traced, and the unequal and stratified effects of health and its care are documented. *Managing*

Chronicity in Unequal States provides us with such waymarks: empirical starting points from which to take our bearings.

What I have appreciated most about the contributions to this volume is precisely their capacity to stay with the troubles of others; to station themselves in alignment with their interlocutors, to show how life's demands and possibilities yield, as Haraway (2016) suggests, unexpected collaborations and combinations. Although troubles may be existential, moral or practical matters to be resisted or resolved, for the ethnographic participant, for the ethnographer, they provide methodological affordance. Troubles disclose the tacit, taken-for-granted orders of everyday living (Garfinkel 1967); they also provide the means to work through their hazards (Greiffenhagen et al. 2015). Throughout this volume, chronic troubles reveal not only what it has meant to live well, but also what it might mean to live well again as *the* project of becoming through chronic living (see Ballesteros). At the same time, they direct our attention to what it means to die well, to desire final endings (see Andrade Neves). The troubles of chronicity remind us that the problems we face today are end points of cultural histories – colonial and post-colonial – thus, the cumulative problems of others (see Bresciani). We are shown that critique is not born from the dogmas of abstract theorising, but that it is always and already in the world, emerging from the standpoints of alienation, stigma and precarity, through which an understanding of neglect, disregard and deservingness fasten their hold (see Brocco; Flaherty; Kottai and Ranganathan). Chronic troubles reveal the social, ambivalent and productive relations of care, as public and private interests collapse, converge and hybridise (see Takahashi), or when bureaucratic and administrative imperatives reframe human agency and decision making (see Kennedy), or indeed when self-medication as self-care subverts normative perspectives on harm reduction and addiction (see Motta-Ochoa and Arruda). Chronic troubles are epistemic troubles. They underlie diagnostic and therapeutic uncertainty, and as a consequence construct all manner of barriers to recognition, care, welfare and support (see LaRusso and Abadía-Barrero). Taken together, the preceding chapters advance and extend our appreciation of chronicity, not merely as an affective personal state, but as a social practice, a set of ongoing and enduring labours for all those bound to its demands (Kierans 2019).

Managing Chronicity in Unequal States thus engages what Biehl and Locke (2017, x) describe as a 'conscientious empiricism wedded to a radical analytical openness'. Critique is organised from the vantage of the ethnographic subject, thus modulating the interpretive impulses of the ethnographer (Love 2010). From here, new ways of thinking about the relationship between sickness and the state, aetiology and therapeutics, power and human agency, emerge through a peopling of critical theory (Biehl and Locke 2017). Empathising as our contributors do with the predicaments and trials of their participants, this volume retains ethnographic rigour in its sensitivity to the diverse lives of others, and their efforts to live otherwise.

Making and unmaking of worlds: 'Becoming' with chronicity

Managing chronicity is, with little doubt, an everyday reality for more and more people. What this means in practice, and how best to do it, is less a concern *of* and *for* biology than *of* and *for* political economy (Manderson and Wahlberg 2020). It is, therefore, towards questions of political economy that we are urged to reorient our perspective. In reorienting so, chronicity is shown to be lived out and managed in the midst of things – to return briefly to Neurath – in the unknown and uncertain spaces between bodies and worlds. It is from inside these uncertain spaces that the variegations of state–market–society relations are made visible; that new connections are made, and new relations are formed (Strathern 1992); that new ways of caring are established, and new agendas forged (Tsing 2013). This volume shows that one can grasp both the scale and complexity of chronic living, while attending to its lived ground. It helps to break the deadlocks in thinking that accompany the persistence of inequalities, their capacity to overwhelm and unmake the world. *Managing Chronicity in Unequal States* provides us with critique, but also with optimism, rarely found in examinations of sickness and suffering – this is its achievement. It provides us with the conditions for becoming, for remaking worlds (Goodman 1978), through solidarities of concern.

References

Biehl, João G. 2011. 'Human pharmakon: The anthropology of technological lives'. In *In Search of Self: Interdisciplinary perspectives on personhood*, edited by J. Wentzel Van Huyssteen and Erik P. Wiebe, 213–31. Grand Rapids, MI: William B. Eerdmans Publications.

Biehl, João and Peter Locke. 2017. *Unfinished: The anthropology of becoming*. Durham, NC: Duke University Press.

Esping-Andersen, Gosta. 1990. *The Three Worlds of Welfare Capitalism*. Cambridge: Polity Press.

Garfinkel, Harold. 1967. *Studies in Ethnomethodology*. Englewood Cliffs, NJ: Prentice-Hall.

Goodman, Nelson. 1978. *Ways of Worldmaking*. Indianapolis, IN: Hackett.

Greiffenhagen, Christian, Michael Mair and Wes Sharrock. 2015. 'Methodological troubles as problems and phenomena: Ethnomethodology and the question of method in the social sciences', *British Journal of Sociology* 66 (3): 460–85. https://doi.org/10.1111/1468-4446.12136.

Haraway, Donna J. 2016. *Staying with the Trouble: Making kin in the Chthulucene*. Durham, NC: Duke University Press.

Jain, Sarah Lochlann. 2007. 'Living in prognosis: Toward an elegiac politics', *Representations* 98 (1): 77–92. https://doi.org/10.1525/rep.2007.98.1.77.

Kierans, Ciara. 2019. *Chronic Failures: Kidneys, regimes of care and the Mexican state*. New Brunswick, NJ: Rutgers University Press.

Love, Heather. 2010. 'Close but not deep: Literary ethics and the descriptive turn', *New Literary History* 41 (2): 371–91. https://doi.org/10.1353/nlh.2010.0007.

Manderson, Lenore and Carolyn Smith-Morris, eds. 2010. *Chronic Conditions, Fluid States: Chronicity and the anthropology of illness*. New Brunswick, NJ: Rutgers University Press.

Manderson, Lenore and Ayo Wahlberg. 2020. 'Chronic living in a communicable world', *Cross-Cultural Studies in Health and Illness* 39 (5): 428–39. https://doi.org/10.1080/01459740.2020.1761352.

Merleau-Ponty, Maurice. 2012. *Phenomenology of Perception*, translated by Donald Landes. London: Routledge.

Neurath, Otto. 1973. 'Anti-Spengler'. In *Empiricism and Sociology* (Vienna Circle Collection, vol. 1), edited by Marie Neurath and Robert S. Cohen, 158–213. Dordrecht: D. Reidel.

Roberts, Elizabeth. F.S. 2017. 'What gets inside: Violent entanglements and toxic boundaries in Mexico City', *Cultural Anthropology* 32 (4): 592–19. https://doi.org/10.14506/ca32.4.07.

Shaoul, Jean. 2011. '"Sharing" political authority with finance capital: The case of Britain's Public Private Partnerships', *Policy and Society* 30 (3): 209–20. https://doi.org/10.1016/j.polsoc.2011.07.005.

Strathern, Marilyn. 1992. *Reproducing the Future: Anthropology, kinship and the new reproductive technologies*. New York: Routledge, Chapman and Hall.

Tsing, Anna. 2013. 'More-than-human sociality: A call for critical description'. In *Anthropology and Nature*, edited by Kirsten Hastrup, 27–42. New York: Routledge.

Yates-Doerr, Emily. 2020. 'Reworking the social determinants of health: Responding to material-semiotic indeterminacy in public health interventions', *Medical Anthropology Quarterly* 34 (3): 378–97. https://doi.org/10.1111/maq.12586.

Index

CPSIA information can be obtained
at www.ICGtesting.com
Printed in the USA
BVHW092124130222
628761BV00015B/161